Maternity Leave

Policy and Practice

Maternity Leave

Policy and Practice

Victoria Gordon

CRC Press
Taylor & Francis Group
Boca Raton   London   New York

CRC Press is an imprint of the
Taylor & Francis Group, an **Informa** business

CRC Press
Taylor & Francis Group
6000 Broken Sound Parkway NW, Suite 300
Boca Raton, FL 33487-2742

© 2013 by Taylor & Francis Group, LLC
CRC Press is an imprint of Taylor & Francis Group, an Informa business

No claim to original U.S. Government works

Printed on acid-free paper
Version Date: 20130514

International Standard Book Number-13: 978-1-4665-7358-1 (Hardback)

This book contains information obtained from authentic and highly regarded sources. Reasonable efforts have been made to publish reliable data and information, but the author and publisher cannot assume responsibility for the validity of all materials or the consequences of their use. The authors and publishers have attempted to trace the copyright holders of all material reproduced in this publication and apologize to copyright holders if permission to publish in this form has not been obtained. If any copyright material has not been acknowledged please write and let us know so we may rectify in any future reprint.

Except as permitted under U.S. Copyright Law, no part of this book may be reprinted, reproduced, transmitted, or utilized in any form by any electronic, mechanical, or other means, now known or hereafter invented, including photocopying, microfilming, and recording, or in any information storage or retrieval system, without written permission from the publishers.

For permission to photocopy or use material electronically from this work, please access www.copyright.com (http://www.copyright.com/) or contact the Copyright Clearance Center, Inc. (CCC), 222 Rosewood Drive, Danvers, MA 01923, 978-750-8400. CCC is a not-for-profit organization that provides licenses and registration for a variety of users. For organizations that have been granted a photocopy license by the CCC, a separate system of payment has been arranged.

Trademark Notice: Product or corporate names may be trademarks or registered trademarks, and are used only for identification and explanation without intent to infringe.

Library of Congress Cataloging-in-Publication Data

Gordon, Victoria (Associate professor)
  Maternity leave : policy and practice / author, Victoria Gordon.
   p. ; cm.
  Includes bibliographical references and index.
  ISBN 978-1-4665-7358-1 (hardcover : alk. paper)
   1. Maternity leave--United States. 2. Parental leave--United States. I. Title.
   [DNLM: 1. Parental Leave--United States. 2. Public Policy--United States. 3. Women, Working--United States. 4. Workplace--organization & administration--United States. HD 6065.5.U6]

HD6065.5.U6G67 2013
331.4'4--dc23   2013013440

Visit the Taylor & Francis Web site at
http://www.taylorandfrancis.com

and the CRC Press Web site at
http://www.crcpress.com

For Wilma, my mother

Because of Maggie, my first granddaughter

In tribute to Natascha, Travis, and Valaria, my children

and

Dedicated to the twins

Contents

List of Figures xi
List of Tables xiii
Preface xv
Acknowledgments xvii
The Author xix

Chapter 1 Introduction: What Have We Done to
Our Daughters? 1

Maternity Leave—An Unresolved Conversation? 1
Are Maternity Leave Expectations and Realities
Mismatched? 2
References 4

Chapter 2 Background: Understanding the Legislative Intent
and Symbolism of Public Policies 5

In the Beginning: The Pregnancy Discrimination Act 5
The Tax Code and Child Care and Child Tax Credits 11
The Promises and Problems of the Family and Medical
Leave Act 14
The Patient Protection and Affordable Care Act 21
The Economic, Social, and Symbolic Implications of
Maternity Leave Policies 24
Appendix 28
References 81

Chapter 3 The Evolution and Devolution of Maternity Leave
as an Employee Benefit 85

Trends in Birthrates, Fertility Rates, Employment
Patterns, and Use of Maternity Leave Benefits 85
Types of Maternity Leave Taken—Paid and Unpaid 93

vii

viii • Contents

Types of Paternity and Parental Leave Policies.................... 96
Examples of Maternity Leave Policies 98
Antenatal Leave and Short-Term Disability Leave 104
No Leave and Permanent Exit from the Workplace...........105
References..108

Chapter 4 Women's Health Care and the Workplace......................111
Health Insurance for Women of Childbearing Age........... 111
Fertility Issues...113
Intended and Unintended Pregnancies............................... 114
Pregnancy and Work 116
Pregnancy and Factors Impacting Infant Mortality 118
Delivery..119
Maternity Leave and Infant Mortality 121
Mother's Return to Work and Breast-Feeding 122
Well-Baby Doctor Visits... 123
Postpartum Issues 124
Optimal Length of Maternity Leave....................................127
The Baby's Perspective 128
The Need for a Holistic Approach to Women's Health......132
References..136

Chapter 5 Research Approach 139
The Methodology: Why Qualitative Research?..................139
Analysis of the Interviews.. 141
Study Limitations 143
The Participants: Who Are These Women?......................144
Description of the In-Depth Interview Questions 146
References..147

Chapter 6 The Interviews: Profiles of Women and Their
Perceptions and Experiences... 149
Employees of Public Universities 150
Employees of Private Universities.......................................183
Employees of the Pharmaceutical Industry.......................199
References..218

Chapter 7 The Themes: How Women Cope with the Myths and Realities of Maternity Leave.................................. 219

Inconsistencies in Administration of Maternity Leave Policies 219
It Is All in the Timing 221
Transition Back to Work 224
Child Care 228
Breast-Feeding, Pumping, and the Workplace 230
Unmet Needs and Professional Concerns 234

Chapter 8 The Other Voices 243

Students Who Are Mothers: Is It Better to Have Children at a Younger Age? 243
Fathers Who Utilized Paternity Leave 247
Challenges Faced by Same-Sex Couples Who Decide to Become Parents 251
Women Who Decided Not to Have Children 255
Unsupportive versus Supportive Colleagues—The Stereotypes and Biases 258
Administrative Views—Rules versus Discretion 262
Appendix 265
References 266

Chapter 9 An International Comparison—The Other Kingdoms 269

What Maternity Leave, Paternity Leave, and Parental Leave Benefits Are Offered in Other Countries? 269
Why Is the United States Lagging behind Other Countries in Providing Maternity Leave Benefits? 282
References 284

Chapter 10 Conclusion: Can the Fairy Tale Be Realized or Should It Be Rewritten? 287

What Are the Obstacles to a Happy Ending for Our Daughters? 287
What Can We Reasonably Expect to Change within Our Organizations? 289

What Is Best for Society?...293
Restoring the Fairy Tale 294
References...295

Index.. 297

List of Figures

Figure 3.1 Childbearing in the United States 1920–2011. ... 86
Figure 6.1 Pregnancy tests. ... 217
Figure 7.1 Baby in hospital. ... 220
Figure 7.2 Premature baby. ... 221
Figure 7.3 Baby at door. ... 222
Figure 7.4 Mom with baby in stroller and dog. ... 223
Figure 7.5 Baby eating. ... 224
Figure 7.6 Baby playing with books. ... 225
Figure 7.7 Baby and dog at window. ... 226
Figure 7.8 Dad and baby. ... 227
Figure 7.9 Dad with guitar and baby. ... 229
Figure 7.10 Mom with breast milk for baby in hospital. ... 231
Figure 7.11 Mom and baby with bubbles. ... 236
Figure 7.12 Mom and baby at orchard. ... 237
Figure 7.13 Mom and baby smiling. ... 239
Figure 9.1 Maternity leave. ... 283

List of Tables

Table 2.1 Pregnancy Discrimination Charges Received by the EEOC and Resolution Type, Selected Years 9

Table 2.2 Family Characteristics, Need for Child Care, Child-Care Patterns and Supply 13

Table 3.1 Births, Birthrate, and Total Fertility Rate, United States and by State, 2011 87

Table 3.2 Employment Status of the Civilian Noninstitutional Population, Women 16 Years of Age and Over, for Selected Years 1970–2009, Annual Averages (Numbers in Thousands) 90

Table 3.3 Employment Status of Women in Civilian Labor Force by Presence and Age of Youngest Child, for Selected Years 1975–2009 (Numbers in Thousands) 91

Table 3.4 Contribution of Wives' Earnings to Family Income, Selected Years 1970–2008 92

Table 3.5 Employment History of Women before First Birth, 1961 to 2008 (Numbers in Thousands) 93

Table 3.6 Selected Leave Arrangements Used by Women Who Worked during Pregnancy Preceding First Birth, 1981–2008 (Numbers in Thousands) 95

Table 3.7 Detailed Leave Arrangement Used by Women Who Worked during Pregnancy Preceding First Birth, 2006–2008 (Percentages Based on 3,363,000 Women) 96

Table 4.1 Outcomes of Assisted Reproductive Technology (ART) by Procedures, 2000–2006 115

Table 4.2 Mean Value "Happy to Be Pregnant" (on Scale of 1 to 10, with 1 Being Very Unhappy to Be Pregnant and 10 Being Very Happy to Be Pregnant) 116

Table 4.3 Infant Mortality Rates for 2008 by Selected Characteristics for 22 States Reporting as of January 1, 2007 119

xiii

List of Tables

Table 5.1	Demographic Information on Interviewees	145
Table 9.1	Maternity Leave in Selected Countries	271
Table 9.2	Paternity Leave in Selected Countries	275
Table 9.3	Parental Leave in Selected Countries	277

Preface

This book traces the journey I undertook to understand maternity leave as it exists today. I had no predetermined agenda, only a sincere interest. I had no idea where this exploration might take me or the reader. While I hope that both experienced practitioners and scholars in a multitude of academic fields will find value in reading this book, my intended audience was always anyone—male, female, employer, employee—who wanted to gain a better understanding of maternity leave, both in policy and in practice. To accomplish this, I approached maternity leave from a variety of perspectives: legal, political, social, institutional, organizational, and most importantly from the personal perspectives of the women interviewed. While this book is strengthened by relevant research, the importance of this book is found in the individual stories of ordinary working women who have recently utilized maternity leave.

This book is especially timely. Since I started this project three years ago, there has been an increasing discussion worldwide of what it means to be a successful, working mother. In the national media, the debate rages on about whether women can or should "have it all," and there is even debate as to what "having it all" actually means. Maternity leave is a very relevant part of this timely conversation. I hope all readers of this book will gain from it a more comprehensive understanding of maternity leave as it exists today and will actively join in the work that still needs to be undertaken. This book will equip the reader to participate even more in much-needed conversation on the topic. Please read on.

Acknowledgments

I would like to thank Taylor and Francis and editor Lara Zoble for ensuring the timely publication of my research. Thank you also to Jessica Vakili for assisting me through the details of the publication process. Special thanks go to Matt Beck, Natascha Beck, Valaria Lovell, and Dennis Kouba for providing technical support. Thank you also to the health-care professionals, including Dr. Dawn Charles-Heizman, for providing invaluable expertise to this project.

Special appreciation goes to Western Kentucky University and Potter College of Arts and Letters for providing financial support under PCAL Faculty Scholarship Award 12-003; the Department of Political Science for providing help through the efforts of excellent MPA graduate assistants Austin Klaine, Luhan Wang, and Matt Westbrook; and my department head, Dr. Saundra Ardrey, for giving me time and support to complete this project.

Most importantly, this project would not have been possible without the willingness of one young man and so many women to generously share their time and stories. Thank you!

And last, but never least, my most heartfelt thank-you is due to Gary Gordon, my husband, for providing moral support, encouragement, and never-ending patience.

Victoria Gordon

The Author

Victoria Gordon is an associate professor in the Department of Political Science, MPA program, and she serves as director of the Center for Local Governments at Western Kentucky University, Bowling Green. She earned her Doctor of Public Administration degree from the University of Illinois–Springfield. Her areas of research interest include municipal finance, regional economic development, and human resources management.

1

Introduction: What Have We Done to Our Daughters?

MATERNITY LEAVE—AN UNRESOLVED CONVERSATION?

Sometimes the research journey begins because you read an article or a book and something just does not ring true—or the topic simply attracts your interest when a conversation or event contradicts conventional wisdom. My research journey into maternity leave policy and practice began when my interest was piqued on two separate occasions in two different parts of the country. Two women from two very different academic disciplines confided to me two very similar stories. The first young woman was considering not having a baby because it might be "frowned upon" by her colleagues who would be voting on her promotion status. The second woman—also a nontenured female assistant professor—confided that she had not taken any maternity leave after the birth of her child because she did not want to be "judged harshly" by her colleagues. My first thought after hearing both stories was, "what have we done to our daughters?"

In my worldview, maternity leave was to be expected by mothers (and fathers) and supported by enlightened institutions, wasn't it? Although I had never taken maternity leave myself—because I was not working at the time of the births of my first two children and I was a student when my third child was born—I assumed maternity leave was offered by all organizations of most any size, and utilized by women in all fields and professions. I suppose I had some idea that maybe a very small company might not offer paid maternity leave, but in a smaller organization, there might be more flexibility and room for negotiating time off. Surely, this issue had been resolved long ago by employers and their employees.

At the time of the second conversation, I had become a grandmother for the first time. My daughter worked for a pharmaceutical company, and she told me very early in her pregnancy what the maternity leave benefits would be for her. She was eligible for 12 weeks' paid leave, followed by an option to return to work part time for an additional 8 weeks of flextime. All told, she would potentially have up to 20 weeks to be home with her new baby. For my daughter, this was an employer-supported leave period—a time to recover physically and to bond with her baby—with the promise she could return to her job at the end of the leave.

While I recognized that my daughter was in a very fortunate position to have so much time available, I started to wonder about what was going on in higher education that these two other young women were having such a different experience. Was this purely an anecdotal anomaly? Or was the private sector doing such a better job of providing benefits for employees? More importantly in my mind was the nagging question: Were all the sacrifices made by women of my age, generation, or era—all done in the name of having it all in terms of career and family—for naught? Had the last fairy tale for young women evaporated? And more to the point, why had no one noticed? Why was no one talking about this?

In the interest of full disclosure, I entered this research project feeling a little indignant, partly because aside from my daughter's experience in the private sector, I had witnessed in my own academic department at a public institution of higher learning, my female department head supporting our young male faculty as they became first-time fathers. She offered them time off, through the option to teach online courses or bi-term courses, a reduced teaching load, and the like so that they could enjoy being new dads and bond with their infants. Were most other institutions unenlightened when it came to maternity leave? Thus, I started on my quest for understanding maternity leave in the 21st century. My goal was to unravel the mystery of maternity leave—what are the myths, what are the realities?

ARE MATERNITY LEAVE EXPECTATIONS AND REALITIES MISMATCHED?

The overarching research question that guided this project was: "What are the perceptions and experiences of participants about their utilization of maternity leave benefits?" Secondarily, I wanted to understand if organizational policies and employee perceptions match. If not, what is contributing to this disconnect? In effect, I wanted to understand if informal cultural beliefs and norms are more influential in employee decision making regarding the use of maternity leave benefits than are the formal policies available to them (Barnett 1999, 147). What obstacles get in the way of developing sound and consistent policies across universities? Finally, I wanted to understand if there are truly differences in perceptions and experiences of women across private universities, public universities, and within the private sector—specifically, in the pharmaceutical industry.

This book is organized into ten chapters.

- Following this introduction, the second chapter provides an overview of legislation related to pregnancy and maternity leave.
- The third chapter explores trends in birthrates, fertility rates, employment patterns, and the relationship to the types of maternity leave offered and taken.
- The fourth chapter explores the topic of women's health issues and policies in the workplace.
- Chapter five describes the research approach used to conduct this study and offers a summary description of the participants.
- Chapters six and seven present profiles of the women studied and focus on the individual interviews presented in the women's voices. Included in the seventh chapter are the themes and patterns that developed from the interviews—inconsistencies in administration of maternity leave policies; timing; transition back to work; child care; breast-feeding and pumping; and unmet needs and professional concerns.
- The eighth chapter focuses on the voices and perspectives of those who are absent from the core interviews—women who have children at a young age, men who did utilize paternity leave, women in same-sex relationships who started families, women who did not choose to have children, and administrative views, and stories about why some colleagues may be unsupportive of maternity leave.
- Chapter nine provides a brief comparison regarding maternity and paternity leave policies in other countries as compared to the United States.
- Finally, chapter ten offers some conclusions and practical recommendations for policy and organizational change.

It is hoped this book not only will shed some light on the mystery of maternity leave—both policy and practice—but also will encourage others to join this important and timely conversation.

REFERENCES

Barnett, R. 1999. A new work-life model for the twenty-first century. *Annals of the American Academy of Political and Social Science* 562: 143–158.

2

Background: Understanding the Legislative Intent and Symbolism of Public Policies

As with all stories, we sometimes have to return to the beginning to understand where the journey has taken us thus far. This chapter provides a brief overview of national legislation that impacts the narrower issues of pregnancy and maternity leave, and the broader issues of women in the workplace. Relevant legislation is presented and discussed in somewhat chronological order. Most of the legislation discussed has been amended, some several times, since the original enactment. This chapter concludes with a discussion of the symbolism of maternity leave and its connection to these policies. We suggest that perhaps we will need to reframe maternity leave, both in how it is perceived by women, their coworkers, and supervisors, and in how it is viewed by employers and society if we are to be successful in enacting substantive policy changes.

IN THE BEGINNING: THE PREGNANCY DISCRIMINATION ACT

The Pregnancy Discrimination Act of 1978 was enacted for several reasons. First, there was a long, documented history of discrimination in hiring—both covertly and overtly—against pregnant women and in forcing women out of the workforce if they did become pregnant. Some pregnant women were forced to take unpaid leave, while others were simply and permanently out of a job. Second, it was time to recognize that women were needed in the workplace, and this need helped to open the door for equal access for women in obtaining and keeping jobs. Third, there were two court cases in the mid-1970s that in essence made calling for the enactment a logical next step to stop discrimination (Grossman 2008).

In 1974, in the case of *Geduldig v. Aiello*, the U.S. Supreme Court ruled that pregnancy discrimination was not sex or gender discrimination. This case involved California's refusal and financial inability to pay for pregnancy-related disability benefits, and the court ruled to support this exclusion of benefits (Grossman 2008; McGlen and O'Connor 1998). In the 1976 case of *General Electric v. Gilbert*, the court ruled on the same basis (Grossman 2008). In this case, pregnancy was excluded by a private employer's disability plan, and the court upheld this exclusion, saying the employer's plan was not discriminatory (McGlen and O'Connor 1998).

Clearly, these cases did not directly advance the state of maternity leave, and they certainly did not solve the problems the plaintiffs sought to address. However, they did illuminate the ongoing problem of pregnancy discrimination. Thus, these cases opened the way and served as a catalyst for the passage of the Pregnancy Discrimination Act, signed into law by President Jimmy Carter on October 31, 1978. Carter addressed these recent cases in part on the day he signed this legislation when he wrote:

> It does not bestow favored treatment on America's 42 million working women. Nor does it diminish in any way the rights and benefits of their male coworkers. It simply requires employers who have medical disability plans to provide for disability due to pregnancy and related conditions on an equal basis with other medical conditions.

The full content of the Act, PL 95-555, is presented in the Appendix, along with the legislative history. An excerpt that amends Title VII of the Civil Rights Act of 1964 to prohibit sex discrimination on the basis of pregnancy reads as follows:

> That section 701 of the Civil Rights Act of 1964 is amended by adding at the end thereof the following new subsection:
>
> > "(k) The terms 'because of sex' or 'on the basis of sex' include, but are not limited to, because of or on the basis of pregnancy, childbirth, or related medical conditions; and women affected by pregnancy, childbirth, or related medical conditions shall be treated the same for all employment-related purposes, including receipt of benefits under fringe benefit programs, as other persons not so affected but similar in their ability or inability to work...."

More than 30 years after this legislation was adopted, commentators and researchers are still pointing out the flaws in the law and its deficiencies. General deficiencies include the following: (1) pregnant women may only be protected to the extent they can work at full capacity, uninterrupted by pregnancy, childbirth, or related conditions; and (2) accommodations or modified duties that an employer could offer that would allow a pregnant woman to continue to work are not mandated (Grossman 2008). Again, these long-standing deficiencies may impact women who work in very physical or labor-intensive jobs more so than someone working in an office environment, but this absence of accommodations or modified job duties continues to present very real problems for many women.

To address these long-standing deficiencies, the Pregnant Workers Fairness Act was introduced to the House of Representatives in May 2012 as HR 5647 by Representatives Jerrold Nadler (D-NY), Carolyn Maloney (D-NY), Jackie Speier (D-CA), and Susan Davis (D-CA). This act, if passed, would make it unlawful not to provide for necessary accommodations in covered workplaces. The bill has 105 sponsors, and was referred to the House Subcommittee on the Constitution. The text of the bill is presented in the Appendix.

In his introductory remarks to the House on May 8, 2012, Representative Nadler recounted the following story to illustrate the need for the Act:

> Some months ago, I heard an account of a woman, Victoria Serednyj, who worked as an activity director at a nursing home in Valparaiso, Indiana, when she became pregnant in 2007. When she started experiencing some complications, Victoria's doctor advised her to avoid strenuous activities. Victoria told her boss about her doctor's advice, noting that she "would just need a little bit of help" with tasks such as rearranging tables and pushing heavy wheelchairs—tasks that took up about 20 minutes of her workday. Despite the fact that Victoria's coworkers already pitched in to help with these tasks, her boss fired her. Shockingly, when Victoria turned to the courts for protection, the court denied her even a trial by granting the employer's summary judgment motion. Addressing the patent unfairness in the ruling, the court noted that, due to the courts' near universal understanding of the laws dealing with pregnant workers, Victoria had the misfortune of "fall[ing] in the blind spot in the statutory scheme created by Congress" and that she was "lost in the gaps in the law for pregnant women." Victoria is not alone. We're hearing about thousands of such cases around the country. And this is outrageous.

In support of this act, a letter of endorsement was sent to Congress by organizations supporting the bill and which outlines specific examples of why this act is necessary. The letter of support is also presented in the Appendix.

As further testament that this issue remains unresolved, the U.S. Equal Employment Opportunity Commission (EEOC), which enforces employment-related law and provides guidance to employers and employees on the administration of the law, is still issuing "discussion letters" to guide the public to a better understanding of the Pregnancy Discrimination Act. This seems to be an indication that the issue is not as clear-cut as it should be in terms of interpretation or administration. For example, in February 2007 the EEOC Office of General Counsel issued this discussion letter in response to a general inquiry from a member of the public about the law, the hiring process, and the appropriateness of certain questions asked during job interviews. The questions asked by this person seeking clarification were

1. Is it illegal under federal law to ask a woman during a job interview if and when she plans to become pregnant in the future?
2. Is it illegal under federal law for an employer to ask a man during a job interview if and when he and his partner plan to have children in the future?
3. Is it illegal under federal law to ask a job candidate during a job interview if they are married or single?
4. Is it illegal under federal law to ask a job candidate during a job interview if they have children? (U.S. EEOC February 2, 2007)

An excerpt from the discussion letter responding to these questions reads as follows:

As you are aware, the Equal Employment Opportunity Commission (EEOC) enforces, among other laws, Title VII of the Civil Rights Act of 1964, 42 U.S.C. § 2000e et seq. (Title VII), which bars discrimination in employment on the bases of race, color, sex, national origin, and religion. Title VII was amended in 1978 to include the Pregnancy Discrimination Act, which prohibits an employer from refusing to hire a pregnant woman because of her pregnancy, childbirth, or related medical condition.

There is no language in Title VII which expressly prohibits employers from making any of the above inquiries. Title VII does, however, prohibit covered employers from basing hiring decisions on pregnancy or sex. Thus, an employer may not refuse to hire a woman because she is or expects to become pregnant. In addition, although Title VII does not prohibit discrimination based on marital or parental status, its does prohibit employers from treating men and women differently with regard to such status. Accordingly, employers may not refuse to hire married women or women with children if it hires married men or men with children.

Although asking applicants about pregnancy or their marital or parental status does not violate Title VII, a fact finder is likely to presume that the answers to such questions formed the basis for a selection decision. As a result, if the selection decision is challenged, the fact that the employer made such inquiries will be evidence that the employer unlawfully used sex or pregnancy as a factor in the selection decision (U.S. EEOC February 2, 2007).

The EEOC has tracked the number of pregnancy-related discrimination cases that have been filed with the agency for resolution over the past 20 years. Table 2.1 presents data on these cases for selected years. The data in the table reflect charges filed with EEOC and with the state and local fair employment practices agencies that have a work-sharing agreement with the commission. As defined by the EEOC, reasonable cause means the EEOC believes that discrimination occurred based on evidence obtained in investigation, and merit resolutions are charges with outcomes favorable to charging parties and/or charges found to have meritorious allegations. These outcomes include negotiated settlements, withdrawals with benefits, successful conciliations, and unsuccessful conciliations (U.S. EEOC 2012a; 2012b).

While the number of complaints in total, and those deemed as having a reasonable basis for cause are not overwhelming, the fact that each year there are any claims filed shows that this issue of discrimination has not been eliminated. A greater need for employer education is evident. It

TABLE 2.1

Pregnancy Discrimination Charges Received by the EEOC and Resolution Type, Selected Years

	FY 1992	FY 1997	FY 2002	FY 2007	FY 2011
Receipts	3,385	3,977	4,714	5,587	5,797
Resolutions[a]	3,045	4,595	4,778	4,979	6,482
Reasonable cause	87	279	283	186	266
Merit resolutions	781	1,053	1,298	1,529	1,646

Source: Data from U.S. EEOC 2012a; 2012b website. http://www.eeoc.gov/eeoc/statistics/enforcement/pregnancy.cfm and http://www.eeoc.gov/eeoc/statistics/enforcement/pregnancy-a.cfm (accessed August 24, 2012).

[a] Numbers may include complaints received in previous years.

should be noted that about one-half of the complaints filed each year are dismissed by the EEOC as having no reasonable basis for cause that discrimination occurred. However, the number of claims filed each year over time has increased.

More troubling perhaps is that women perceive that there is still blatant discrimination in the interview process and in hiring decisions made both in the public and private sectors. Two examples from higher education serve to illustrate this point. Connelly and Ghodsee (2011, 1) open their book, *Professor Mommy: Finding Work-Family Balance in Academia*, with a recounting of Ghodsee's interview with a university for a faculty position a month after giving birth in 2001. They write: "Kristen had been warned that certain departments would look unfavorably on her status as a new mother, fearing that her family obligations would compromise her ability to publish high-quality scholarship and thereby weaken her chances of getting tenure." As a result of this warning, Dr. Ghodsee hid from the interview panel the fact that she needed a break during the day-long interview process to pump her breast milk. When she finally made it to a bathroom to pump without anyone knowing it, she recalled thinking, "There is no way I can do this.... How am I going to start a new job with a new baby?... It's just too hard" (Connelly and Ghodsee 2011, 2, 3).

In a second example, a young woman who was interviewed for this research project and who was eight months pregnant at the time of her job interview with a university said:

> I made it a point to hide that I was pregnant as best as I could. I wasn't sure what the climate around here would be like for pregnancy and maternity. Once it came time to discuss job offer negotiations I was still in the mindset that I didn't really want to tell them that I was pregnant, as I wasn't sure what the reaction would be. Later after I was hired and settled in at my new school, a couple of people told me they were a little suspicious that maybe I was pregnant.

Both of these young women were hired by the institutions at which they interviewed, but they both agonized through the interviews and even the job offer process about whether revealing that they were starting families would negatively affect their careers. No matter how long a law has been in place or how closely it is adhered to by an institution or organization, laws do not change perceptions, especially if any discrimination is still practiced. Somewhere, along the way, these young women were sent the message that their professional worth was diminished by the fact that they chose to be mothers. While legislators may have the best intentions, they cannot change the messages sent by ill-informed or unsupportive colleagues and supervisors.

THE TAX CODE AND CHILD CARE AND CHILD TAX CREDITS

For women or men with young children to be able to apply for jobs and enter the workforce, child care has to be a consideration. In an effort to offset the cost of raising families, the U.S. Congress has enacted tax laws to aid families. A child-care credit is a nonrefundable credit based on employment-related expenses of household-type services for the care of children under age 13, a disabled spouse, or other dependent. However, none of these credits or allowances truly meets or fully offsets the costs of child care or of raising a family. In terms of child care, since the mid-1970s child-care credits, deductions, or exclusions have been part of the tax code. Numerous changes have been made to the laws and regulations governing these provisions of the tax code in an effort to make this a more progressive, rather than regressive, credit or deduction. Generally speaking, these laws do lead to more women with young children entering the labor force and remaining in it (Dunbar 2012).

Since the late 1990s, some income-eligible families have been allowed a tax credit for having a qualifying child or children under the age of 17 in the household. For some, this credit could be refundable. Changes were made to this policy under the 2001 Economic Growth and Tax Relief Reconciliation Act, and further changes were made in 2003 (Esenwein 2012).

The cost of child care is another problematic aspect of women entering the labor force. Many two-earner families say that one of them is working just to pay for day care. While this may be an exaggeration, one young woman interviewed for this research project had three children in day care at one time—ages 4 and 3, and an infant. The weekly cost was $900. She said:

> But what do you do? Stop working? You know you just kind of ... have to think it's just six more months of this, and then one child is going to graduate from there and go to school. But it is expensive!

Cost for day care in the United States differs by region, type of care setting (center or home based), length of time the child spends in care each day, and age of the child. There may be some governmental or employer subsidy to offset the cost, but most costs are paid for by the family. The National Association of Child Care Resources and Referral Agencies (NACCRRA) tracks and reports on an annual basis both the cost of day care and the number of children in day care in each state. The average ranges of annual child-care costs in the United States based on age of child and type of care setting according to the state data reported by the NACCRRA (2012) are

- $4,600–$20,200 full-time care for an infant in a center
- $4,000–$12,350 full-time care for an infant in a family child-care home
- $3,900–$15,450 full-time care for a 4-year-old child in a center
- $3,850–$9,600 full-time care for a 4-year-old child in a family child-care home.

These ranges are estimates rounded to the nearest $50 increment based on data collected by the NACCRRA. The cost of care for newborns is substantially higher than the cost of caring for toddlers and older children (National Association of Child Care Resources and Referral Agencies July 2011 and July 2012). These ranges do not reflect the percentage of the amount of the family's income that is spent on child care, which is much greater for lower-income families.

As is shown in Table 2.2, there are more than 23 million children in the United States under age 6, and 15 million of those children have parents who work, thus creating a significant demand for quality and affordable child care. The table also includes information about when new mothers return to work after childbirth, and information on types of child-care arrangements used by families.

Of course, the cost of child care has nothing to do with the availability of care that meets the particular needs of the family's schedule, nor does it reflect the quality of the care facility or staff. Most preschool-aged children spend an average of 35 hours per week in child care (National Association of Child Care Resources and Referral Agencies July 2011 and July 2012). About one-third of families who use day care have to use more than one provider to cover all their needs, which further drives up the cost of day care for the family. The licensing requirements for day-care centers and home-based care centers vary from state to state.

Of utmost concern to parents as they consider day-care arrangements are the findings from studies that point to a link in positive cognitive outcomes for children who are in a quality day-care setting at a young age.

TABLE 2.2

Family Characteristics, Need for Child Care, Child-Care Patterns and Supply

Family Characteristics and Need for Child Care

Number of children under age 6 in the United States[a]	23,363,909
Percentage of children under age 6 living with both parents[a]	65%
Percentage of children under age 6, living with two parents, whose parents are both working[a]	58%
Number of children under age 6 living with a single parent[a]	8,126,541
Percentage of children under age 6, living with a single parent, whose parent is working[a]	76%
Number of children under age 6 requiring child care, as both parents are working[a]	15,060,140
Number of women in the labor force who gave birth in last 12 months[a]	2,654,396
Percentage of children under age 5 who are in multiple child-care arrangements while their mothers work[b]	29%
Percentage of children under age 5 who live in poverty and have working mothers[b]	16%
Percentage of new mothers returning to work within the first three months of giving birth[c]	44%
Percentage of new mothers returning to work within the first six months of giving birth[c]	57%
Percentage of new mothers returning to work within the first year of giving birth[c]	64%

Child Care Patterns and Supply

Number of children under age 5 who are in some type of child care while their mother works[b]	10.9 million
Percentage of children under age 5 in child-care arrangements while their mother works by primary caregiver[b] (percentages will not total 100% due to children in multiple child-care arrangements and some children with other parent)	
Center-based care (centers, nurseries, preschools, Head Start)	26%
Grandparent	21%
Other relative (not including fathers)	6%
Family child-care homes	6%
Other nonrelative	8%
Number of children under age 5 with no regular child-care arrangement whose mothers are in the workforce[b]	1.2 million
Number of children under age 5 with multiple child-care arrangements whose mothers are in the workforce[b]	3.1 million

Continued

TABLE 2.2 (Continued)
Family Characteristics, Need for Child-Care, Child Care Patterns and Supply

Number of hours per week, on average, preschool-aged children of working mothers spend in child care or nonparental care[d]	35 hours

Source: Child Care Aware' of America formerly the National Association of Child Care Resources and Referral Agencies, July 2011 and July 2012. As reported by the NACCRRA, their data sources are:

[a] U.S. Census Bureau. 2011. American Community Survey, 2008–2010 three-year estimates. http://www.census.gov (accessed May 30, 2012).
[b] U.S. Census Bureau. August 2011. Who's minding the kids? Child care arrangements: Spring 2010: Detailed tables. http://www.census.gov/hhes/childcare/data/sipp/2010/tables.html (accessed April 18, 2012).
[c] U.S. Census Bureau. October 2011. Maternity leave and employment patterns of first time mothers: 1961–2008. http://www.census.gov/prod/2011pubs/p70-128.pdf (accessed April 18, 2012).
[d] U.S. Census Bureau. November 2005. Who's minding the kids? Child care arrangements: Winter 2002. http://www.census.gov/prod/2005pubs/p70-101.pdf (accessed June 20, 2011).

In 2010, the National Institute of Child Health and Human Development (NICHD) reported that children who received high-quality care in the first few years of life scored higher in measures of academic and cognitive achievement when they were 15 years of age, and were less likely to misbehave than those who were enrolled in lower-quality child care (Vandell, Belsky, Burchinal, Steinberg, Vandergrift, and NICHD Early Child Care Research Network 2010). A state of Kentucky research report on child care (Childress 1999) quoted a 1998 RAND report that found that "for individual states and communities, early (childhood) intervention programs may be a means of reducing the escalating costs of corrections, welfare, and special education" (Karoly, Greenwood, Everingham, Houbé, Kilburn, Rydell, Sanders, and Chiesa 1998, 108). They suggested that "early intervention programs can improve childhood development and maternal well-being and may generate future savings that more than offset their costs" (Karoly et al. 1998, 105). Clearly, there are long-term societal benefits in providing quality day-care options for all children. There are societal benefits, too, in supporting the parents' efforts to place their children in quality settings by including provisions in the tax code as well as direct subsidies.

THE PROMISES AND PROBLEMS OF THE FAMILY AND MEDICAL LEAVE ACT

After a decade of trying to pass a law with provisions similar to those found in the current Family and Medical Leave Act, one was finally passed in 1993. Over the years, many business interests opposed FMLA based on the premise that it was another unfunded mandate that would drive up the cost of doing business. Other groups opposed FMLA simply on the archaic idea that perhaps women should not work outside the home (Lenhoff 2004). Despite this opposition, FMLA was the first piece of legislation signed into law by President Clinton on February 5, 1993. In President Clinton's statement issued on the day he signed this legislation, he wrote:

> The need for this legislation is clear. The American work force has changed dramatically.... These changes have created a substantial and growing need for family and medical leave.... The rising cost-of-living has also made two incomes a necessity.... There is a direct correlation between health and job security in the family home and productivity in the workplace.... When businesses do not give workers leave for family needs, they fail to establish a working environment that can promote heightened productivity, lessened job turnover, and reduced absenteeism.

The full content of the Family and Medical Leave Act of 1993 is presented in the Appendix. An excerpt of PL 103-3, below, succinctly summarizes the attitude of Congress toward this issue and presents the findings and purposes of the act as defined by Congress. The act was amended in part in 2008 and again in 2009 to address the needs of military families caring for wounded or recuperating military members and for those military families preparing for deployment. In 2009, the act was amended to address particular issues with regard to airline flight crews, specifically the number of hours of service requirement that would make these workers eligible for FMLA benefits (U.S. Department of Labor February 2010).

Twenty years after the initial passage of FMLA, the rationale for this law and the promise of the legislation still makes sense and rings true. FMLA applies generally to workers in organizations that employ at least 50 employees within 75 miles of the work site; who have worked for the employer for at least 12 months; and who have worked at least 1,250 hours during the previous year. An excerpt reads as follows:

SEC. 2. FINDINGS AND PURPOSES.

FINDINGS.—Congress finds that—

1. the number of single-parent households and two-parent households in which the single parent or both parents work is increasing significantly;

2. it is important for the development of children and the family unit that fathers and mothers be able to participate in early childrearing and the care of family members who have serious health conditions;
3. the lack of employment policies to accommodate working parents can force individuals to choose between job security and parenting;
4. there is inadequate job security for employees who have serious health conditions that prevent them from working for temporary periods;
5. due to the nature of the roles of men and women in our society, the primary responsibility for family caretaking often falls on women, and such responsibility affects the working lives of women more than it affects the working lives of men; and
6. employment standards that apply to one gender only have serious potential for encouraging employers to discriminate against employees and applicants for employment who are of that gender.

PURPOSES.—It is the purpose of this Act—

- to balance the demands of the workplace with the needs of families, to promote the stability and economic security of families, and to promote national interests in preserving family integrity;
- to entitle employees to take reasonable leave for medical reasons, for the birth or adoption of a child, and for the care of a child, spouse, or parent who has a serious health condition;
- to accomplish the purposes described in paragraphs (1) and (2) in a manner that accommodates the legitimate interests of employers;
- to accomplish the purposes described in paragraphs (1) and (2) in a manner that, consistent with the Equal Protection Clause of the Fourteenth Amendment, minimizes the potential for employment discrimination on the basis of sex by ensuring generally that leave is available for eligible medical reasons (including maternity-related disability) and for compelling family reasons, on a gender-neutral basis; and
- to promote the goal of equal employment opportunity for women and men, pursuant to such clause.

As with the Pregnancy Discrimination Act, the FMLA has had its share of critics and commentators. Extensive research has been conducted that attempts to measure the effectiveness of the policy and to measure the satisfaction level of both employees who utilize FMLA as a benefit and employers who administer the policy.

The U.S. Department of Labor (DOL) published an extensive background and summary of the responses received as a result of its Request for Information on the FMLA issued in 2006. While this report was not limited to the problematic issues faced by persons taking leave for the birth or adoption of a child, it allowed for public comment from both employees and employers and identified many problems faced by all persons using FMLA. In general, people agreed that the policy was good for workers, was in the public's interest, and was a good policy, but concerns from the 15,000 comments submitted to the DOL also indicated that it was questionable as to whether the law was being administered in accordance with the act and within the intent of Congress (U.S. Department of Labor 2007).

The report states that "in those sections of the FMLA dealing with leave for the birth of a child, for the adoption of a child, and associated with health conditions that require blocks of leave and are undeniably 'serious' … the law appears to be working as anticipated and intended, and working very successfully. When addressing these areas, there is near unanimity in the comments—FMLA leave is a valuable benefit to the employee, improves employee morale, improves the lives of America's families, and, as a result, benefits employers" (U.S. Department of Labor 2007, 35,555).

At the same time, several problematic issues were uncovered. One of the most universal problems reported involved a lack of education both on the part of the employee and the employer. Part of the problem stemmed from inadequate notice from both parties, which was no surprise to the DOL, as some of these problems had worked their way through the court system. One case, *Ragsdale v. Wolverine World Wide, Inc.*, received a lot of public comment regarding the categorical penalty provision for failure to appropriately designate FMLA leave. In its Final Rule on Family and Medical Leave fact sheet (2008, 2), the DOL stated: "The final rule therefore removes these categorical penalty provisions and clarifies that where an employee suffers individualized harm because the employer failed to follow the notification rules, the employer may be liable."

Another problematic issue that arose from the comments was the medical certification process for utilizing FMLA and the potential invasion of privacy that might result from such certification. To assist organizations with this process, the DOL has developed two forms. Although an employer may create its own form, the DOL cautions that the employer may not ask for information that goes beyond what is allowed by FMLA. These two forms, identified by the DOL as WH-380-E and WH-380-F, are presented in the Appendix; the first form is used to certify an employee's serious health condition, and the second is used to certify a family member's serious health condition.

Still another issue is that an employee has to take time away from work to go to the doctor to get the certification forms signed. Doctors are reluctant to commit on paper exactly how long the employee will need to be absent from work or what day the employee will return to work, which then means more trips to the doctor for updated forms and signatures (U.S. Department of Labor 2007, 35,552). In one example from the interviews for this research project, the new mother did not realize that she needed to have new medical certification forms signed every 30 days per her organization's policy for use of FMLA benefits. She was contacted by the human resources department, and then had to contact her doctor to ask for another form to be signed. In another example, a male employee who worked for an organization that provided for paternity leave ran into problems with the medical certification process. The baby's doctor did not want to sign the father's medical certification form, nor did the mother's doctor want to do so. Both doctors pointed to the fact that the father was not their patient.

Another problem involves the fact that conditions related to pregnancy, such as severe morning sickness, may not be serious, long term, or permanent. Thus, in some cases, a condition might or might not qualify under FMLA but certainly would not qualify under the Americans with Disabilities Act (ADA) or under provisions of employer-provided short-term disability coverage. This may create a variety of administrative problems when no one is certain under which law the employee is qualified to have leave or accommodations (U.S. Department of Labor 2007, 35,599).

The U.S. Chamber of Commerce called for changes to FMLA in 2005 based on complaints from businesses that say FMLA is (1) abused by those taking intermittent leave; (2) bad for employee morale for those employees who must work extra shifts for absent employees; (3) unclear with regard to medical documentation reporting; and (4) costing businesses money because they cannot discipline employees for attendance problems (U.S. Chamber of Commerce 2005). The use of intermittent leave is problematic, especially when there is no time to notify the employer of the absence. For many companies involved in service businesses, such as a hospital serving patients, or that deal with time-sensitive materials, such as a delivery service, intermittent leave can produce its own set of administrative and managerial problems. This type of problem usually arises when an employee has a chronic, recurring condition (U.S. Department of Labor 2007, 35,551–35,552). However, an employee's need for intermittent leave can also arise when a new mother returns to work. She may find that on occasion her newborn cannot go to day care or the child may experience health issues requiring her to be at home or to take the baby to the doctor.

Another problem identified in the DOL report (2007) was the issue of substituting paid leave. Employers do not have to pay for time that employees are using FMLA, but an employee can use paid time he or she has earned, and the employer can require that this paid time be used. Further, the employer can mandate that the employee use the paid leave only if he or she also meets the organization's terms of using the paid time that is accrued. So, if sick time earned can be used with no notice, but vacation time requires a two-week notice, for example, then it would be difficult for someone to utilize accrued vacation time or there might be a delay before that time could be utilized. The DOL's Final Rule on Family and Medical Leave fact sheet (2008, 3) reads as follows:

> The current regulations apply different procedural requirements to the use of vacation or personal leave than to medical or sick leave. Complicating matters even further, the Department has treated family leave differently than vacation and personal leave. Accordingly, under the final rule, all forms of paid leave offered by an employer will be treated the same, regardless of the type of leave substituted (including generic "paid time off"). An employee electing to use any type of paid leave concurrently with FMLA leave must follow the same terms and conditions of the employer's policy that apply to other employees for the use of such leave. The employee is always entitled to unpaid FMLA leave if he or she does not meet the employer's conditions for taking paid leave and the employer may waive any procedural requirements for the taking of any type of paid leave.

In short, if an employee can be paid for time off based on time already accrued, it is more likely that the person will use the FMLA benefit when needed. However, because the employer can require the employee to use this paid time concurrently with the FMLA time available for leave, employees who utilize FMLA are typically persons who are accruing sick and vacation time already. Employees who earn or accrue lower levels of benefits or fewer days of paid leave benefits may not be in a position to use FMLA because they cannot financially afford to take time off.

This issue of paid versus unpaid leave is particularly problematic for persons working in institutions of higher learning and has application for some of the women interviewed for this project. Many faculty members work on a nine-month contract basis and consequently do not earn sick, vacation, or personal paid time off. For faculty, time off for maternity leave is often a negotiated process. However, at the same academic institutions, staff members who work year-round do accrue such leave. This often creates a two-tiered system for utilization of FMLA within the same organization.

Similarly, there are often differences in the actual and potential use of FMLA between the Fair Labor Standards Act (FLSA)-designated exempt and nonexempt employees. Exempt employees, who do not track their hours or have to turn in a time sheet, may not choose to utilize FMLA for intermittent medical leave absences—because they do not report those short-term or intermittent absences to their employer. For example, these employees may leave early or come in late in order to go to a doctor's appointment. This may mean that actual costs to the organization are underrepresented for these types of absences or, at the very least, the use of intermittent absences are underreported. However, at the other end of the spectrum, exempt employees may actually work more than 40 hours per week, or may work from home outside of the normal business hours of the organization, which means the intermittent leave taken by these employees is not a cost incurred by the organization (U.S. Department of Labor 2007, 35,620, 35,624).

A comprehensive study of the FMLA was undertaken by Anthony (2008) to look at the unintended negative consequences of FMLA. In her study, Anthony provides an extensive history of laws pertaining to women in the workplace and the passage of the FMLA. She suggests that women with low to moderate incomes may be disproportionately harmed despite the good intentions of the law (461). She attributes this first to women not qualifying for FMLA when they need it, even if they work in an organization covered by FMLA, due to length of time on the job, or because they work part time rather than full time. Second, because of a short work history with a company, or less than full-time status, even if women work in an organization covered by FMLA, they may not be able to afford to take it because it is unpaid, and they may not have paid leave benefits accrued that would allow them to be paid for their time off. Third, collectively women still earn less than men, and if they head a single-parent household they have no one to help with the ongoing financial obligations during the unpaid time off. Fourth, women may work in organizations simply not covered by FMLA, but that does not mean they are not in need of this type of leave (475–476). Anthony contends that gender-neutral laws such as the FMLA often serve to perpetuate inequality by drawing attention to the differences between male and female workers, reinforcing the stereotypes of women as primary caregivers, and thus perpetuating the idea that women must be less committed than their male counterparts to their work (473). Anthony's final argument that FMLA falls short of its intended promises, is that there is still a "stigma" or bias against female employees who utilize FMLA. This bias, whether spoken or implied, is part of some organizational cultures, and it impacts whether a woman takes leave. This occurs even when organizations have policies in place that go above the minimum requirements of leave allowed under FMLA (480).

This statement is borne out in the interviews conducted for this study and presented in the detailed examples in forthcoming chapters. As with the women who hid their pregnancies in the interview process, discussed previously with regard to the Pregnancy Discrimination Act, women are reluctant to ask for leave under FMLA and unfortunately even more women are reluctant to take it when it is available.

FMLA provides for protection of the individual's job while taking unpaid time off, but many faculty members, just like low-wage earners across many employment sectors, cannot afford to take unpaid time off even if they are working in organizations covered under FMLA. So, while the job security assurance of FMLA is attractive, the use of FMLA may be cost-prohibitive for a family. As a consequence, FMLA is underutilized by those who are qualified to use it and who could use it for the benefit of their families.

Finally, FMLA is still just a first step toward a needed comprehensive leave policy because it "guarantees only unpaid leave, excludes employees in most workplaces having fewer than 50 employees, excludes employees who do not have sufficient tenure, and covers only a few of the many reasons an employee might need leave" (Lenhoff 2004, 2). FMLA does not provide for paid leave, and organizations fail to recognize that an employee who utilizes FMLA for maternity leave may have other family leave needs arise during the course of the same year. Many organizations over the past 20 years have actually decreased the paid maternity leave benefits offered to female employees, choosing instead to let unpaid leave under FMLA serve in its place. This is perhaps the greatest unintended consequence of FMLA and surely was not the intent of Congress.

THE PATIENT PROTECTION AND AFFORDABLE CARE ACT

The Patient Protection and Affordable Care Act (PPACA) was enacted on March 23, 2010, when signed into law by President Barack Obama. It is also known as PL 111-148. This act covers a myriad of women's health-related issues. For the purposes of this chapter on legislation related to maternity leave, only a brief excerpt is presented below. Section 4207 of the PPACA covers reasonable break time for nursing mothers in the workplace. This provision does not cover all employers or employees, but it is an example of meaningful legislation that supports breast-feeding. (The health benefits of breast-feeding for mother and child are covered in Chapter 4, and examples of breast-feeding difficulties faced by women interviewed for this project are provided in Chapters 6, 7, and 8.) This section of the law reads as follows:

> Section 7 of the Fair Labor Standards Act of 1938 (29 U.S.C. 207) is amended by adding at the end the following:
> "(r)(1) An employer shall provide—
>
> (A) a reasonable break time for an employee to express breast milk for her nursing child for 1 year after the child's birth each time such employee has need to express the milk; and
> (B) a place, other than a bathroom, that is shielded from view and free from intrusion from coworkers and the public, which may be used by an employee to express breast milk.
> (2) An employer shall not be required to compensate an employee receiving reasonable break time under paragraph (1) for any work time spent for such purpose.
> (3) An employer that employs less than 50 employees shall not be subject to the requirements of this subsection, if such requirements would impose an undue hardship by causing the employer significant difficulty or expense when considered in relation to the size, financial resources, nature, or structure of the employer's business.
> (4) Nothing in this subsection shall preempt a State law that provides greater protections to employees than the protections provided for under this subsection."

Prior to the passage of this law, about half of the states provided for some type of law that encouraged breast-feeding and supported those efforts to breast-feed or pump in the workplace. These laws generally served one or more of the following purposes: required accommodations for employees, provided incentives to employers who provided accommodations, provided protections for breast-feeding women, or recognized the benefits and importance of breast-feeding (Sloan Work and Family Research Network 2007).

The Wage and Hour Division of the U.S. DOL (December 2010) has issued several employer and employee informational fact sheets to aid in educating all parties involved to make sure employers are in compliance with this provision of the PPACA. As noted above, not all employees are covered. Generally, only persons entitled to overtime pay are covered. There are several groups of employees not eligible for "reasonable break time" and who are not covered under this law for various reasons. However, if a state law is in place, then that employee might qualify for this benefit under requirements of the state law.

Some of the considerations brought forward about meeting the reasonable length of break time requirements under this law are (1) how long it takes to physically get to and from the provided break area; (2) where the storage area is for the pumping equipment and the milk after it is pumped; (3) how long it takes to set up and pack up the equipment; (4) whether there is a water source appropriate for cleaning the pump and equipment after its use; and (5) the time it takes to pump (Kleba and Batchis 2011, 2).

The actual facility provided by the employer may be temporary, but must meet the privacy requirement and must provide (1) a place for the mother to sit, (2) a flat surface, other than the floor, for the pump, (3) adequate space for more than one mother, and (4) a storage area (not refrigerated) for the mother's insulated container that will be free of disturbance or contamination (Kleba and Batchis 2011, 2, 3).

One of the major reasons cited by women for stopping breast-feeding is the return to the workplace. The typical workplace is just not conducive to pumping or storing milk, and even when women try to continue breast-feeding, they often face difficulties. The longer the maternity leave taken, the longer women have the opportunity to breast-feed without facing as many obstacles. Skafida (2012) found evidence of a positive association between maternity leave and breast-feeding duration for women she studied in Scotland (524), "Delaying the return to work may facilitate prolonged breastfeeding" (525). Skafida acknowledges that many factors could play a part in how long a woman breast-feeds. She suggests that older mothers may breast-feed longer because they have more life experience, are more confident, are better educated and better paid, and may work for organizations that provide for longer paid leaves (525). However, the change in law through the adoption of the PPACA does not address what women are to do if they feel they are discriminated in the workplace for choosing to continue to breast-feed and pump (Murtagh and Moulton 2011, 219, 222).

THE ECONOMIC, SOCIAL, AND SYMBOLIC IMPLICATIONS OF MATERNITY LEAVE POLICIES

In this chapter, we have presented summaries and excerpts of legislation that are in some direct or indirect manner related to maternity leave policies. In Chapter 3, maternity leave as an employee benefit will be discussed in great detail, but before moving into the specifics, it is important to consider the economic, social, and symbolic implications of maternity leave policies. Each one of the preceding pieces of legislation or policies discussed had critics who first wanted to quantify the costs to business, government, or society of enacting the associated policies, laws, or regulations. The social and emotional cost to women and their families without the presence of a particular benefit or law never seems to factor into the economic analysis. The benefit of increased loyalty and commitment to organizations that the employer might receive from its employees if it provided a satisfactory maternity leave policy does not enter the analysis either. Financial costs for the employer are calculated, but never the benefits or the consequences for the families involved. Trying to address or understand this issue in strictly quantifiable measures or strictly from the perspective of the employer is not the answer for something so personal, so emotional, and so significant.

Why is it so difficult to make positive and meaningful organizational changes for women and their families when it comes to maternity leave policies? As a policy issue, it would seem that no one could be against maternity leave—even as ambiguous as that term is. Against babies, motherhood, the sanctity of home and family? Why does the market approach (Stone 2002) to solving this public policy issue not work for maternity leave?

The answer is manifold.

First, there is no "mother's club" to help rally the cause. Women do not pool their resources to work for substantive changes in this area (Stone 2002). Generally, we expect that lack of formal organization to mean there is a lack of interest or no one is dissatisfied with the status quo (Edelman 1985). The reality is that when something is as unclear as maternity leave policies, people are hesitant to work for change because they see it as unchangeable.

Second, maternity leave policies include rules, and those rules "include and exclude, unite and divide." Rules work when there is equal treatment and predictability, and rules work when they are perceived as legitimate and acceptable (Stone 2002, 287), but as forthcoming chapters will demonstrate, there is no such thing as predictability in pregnancy, delivery, or in some cases how much time off a person will be afforded. With regard to maternity leave policies specifically, new mothers may not know or realize ahead of time how much time they may really want and need with their infant. After the baby is here, the time-off clock starts ticking, and it is too late to make changes to an agreement made earlier or to go back to negotiate for more leave. When policies are inconsistent or unclear, negotiated leave is sometimes a woman's best chance at getting the time off she needs, but when that is left to the discretion of her supervisor, it can present problems as each supervisor may interpret the rules differently. Also, negotiated leave does nothing to initiate organizational change (Edelman 1985). So, yes, women need to work to improve their individual, personal employee benefits, but they need to do it in a way that will encourage collective societal and organizational change (Stone 2002).

Third, there is fear of retaliation if women speak up about their dissatisfaction with maternity leave benefits. Over the long term, the employer has economic power over the employee. The fact that women need to work, to have a livelihood, to earn a living, contributes to no action being taken. Women do not think they have the power to make a change, and so they do not try. In the context of maternity leave policies, the employer also has the symbolic power to define the situation and to determine the outcome. This outcome, solution, or policy is defined and given legitimacy by the party holding that symbolic power—the employer. Even when these policies produce negative outcomes for a woman and her family, and even when the negative outcome may be unintentional on the part of the employer, it is still difficult for women to take a stand against their employer (Hallett 2003). And so women remain silent, and this silence reinforces the validity and legitimacy of their employer's policies.

At the very same time, women do not want to be seen as victims who cannot handle the demands of work and motherhood (Stone 2002). If the decision to have a child is a woman's choice, then some believe managing family and career demands are solely a woman's responsibility (Hallstein 2008, 148). If a woman asks for a benefit or expresses the need, she may perceive that it is an indication that she is "less than" her male counterpart. Further, when women segregate or isolate themselves from men in policy and benefit discussions, in meetings, in decision making, they are missing what is going on in their absence. When what they want is full inclusion and participation, there is often exclusion and a sense of not belonging (Grossman 2008).

There is also foregone opportunity—an opportunity cost when one exits the boys' club, even for a short time, and a fear of what will happen if women bring attention to their own needs (Stone 2002). These arguments are reminiscent of discussions that women have historically been oppressed and demoted to "second-class citizenship," which was used in calls for women's suffrage and the right to own property (Grossman 2008). This is not something women want to return to, admit to, or be a part of, and so some prefer to remain invisible and suffer in silence, rather than open up and demand change.

Fourth, to achieve equality in the workplace, there may need to be some inequality in this particular employee benefit, and this is difficult for women to accept (Stone 2002). Even with the passage of the FMLA, the consideration of maternity leave was only a part of the broader issue of helping all employees meet family needs and responsibilities. Similarly, there is some indication that if parental leave covered both males and females, and as such was gender neutral, then this comprehensive employee leave benefit might improve in terms of organizational acceptance and in terms of duration, and this leave might actually include partial or full pay. At a minimum, a discussion of parental leave might open the door for further dialogue about maternity leave policies. Mother and father both need to bond with the new baby, but the reality is that women have a physical need to recover from childbirth during maternity leave. So, allocating the resources evenly between men and women may not be the best solution and may not lead to the greatest value being obtained for the employee, for the family, or for the organization, but it is an option.

Alternatively, calling for both paternity and maternity leave might be a better solution as this dual approach recognizes that "having a family is a shared responsibility" (Brill 2007) but also acknowledges that women have different physical needs than the father when a baby is born. And yet, women are reluctant to say that their needs should count as more important in this policy issue. "The way we think about problems is extremely sensitive to the language used to describe them" (Stone 2002, 249). If we talk about the maternity leave issue and place women and newborns in the context of being in vulnerable roles, we change the tone of the policy conversation to something far different than if we talk about parental leave strictly as an employee leave benefit irrespective of gender (Stone 2002).

Finally, who is to decide what an adequate policy is, or for that matter, a better maternity leave policy? If we approach this utilizing Rawls' theory of justice (1971), then we need to think about how we achieve the greatest benefit for the least advantaged. "Rawls argues that social structures and social policies should be so constructed that whatever inequalities they allow favor the most disadvantaged group.... Rawls' argument uses our own rational self-interest to encourage us to take the position of disadvantaged groups and sympathize with them" (Frederickson 1997, 108). Can we collectively, male and female—but all acting as rational, self-interested persons—put on the veil of ignorance? Without knowing our place in society, or anyone else's place, or how we compare to each other, can we think about those who are not eligible for any maternity leave and come up with an approach to providing a reasonable paid maternity leave for all? What would each of us want? Who is it that really counts in this discussion? Who are the stakeholders? Could we collectively agree that who we really need to think about are the babies—what is best for them? If we answer this question, we may just also find what is best for society (Stone 2002).

Whatever the answer is, it does not lie in listening only to women who have the financial resources to decide to "opt out" of the workplace, forego maternity leave entirely, and stay home with their young children (O'Leary 2007). Nor does it lie in listening only to politicians who believe the answer can be mandated or legislated—and that somehow legislation will reassure us that everything is okay because we have a national law that addresses the issue, even if the law calls for no tangible or economic benefit to women in terms of actually guaranteeing a paid maternity leave (Edelman 1985). Nor does the answer lie in listening to women who choose to return to work almost immediately after childbirth, not out of desperate financial necessity, but as a choice. The answer lies maybe somewhere in between. We may just learn the most about how to reframe this discussion of maternity leave and how to create substantive changes by listening to those voices that have been silent—those underrepresented, hardworking, and committed women who are looking for more than platitudes and symbolic reassurance. In the next chapter, we explore the demographic trends of birth and fertility rates as they relate to the employment patterns of women. We also examine the evolution and devolution of maternity leave as an employee benefit in the workplace by looking at the specific types of maternity leave offered by organizations.

APPENDIX

PUBLIC LAW 95-555—OCT. 31, 1978

Public Law 95-555
95th Congress

An Act

Oct. 31, 1978
[S. 995]

To amend title VII of the Civil Rights Act of 1964 to prohibit sex discrimination on the basis of pregnancy.

Pregnancy, sex discrimination, prohibition.
42 USC 2000e.
Definitions

Be it enacted by the Senate and House of Representatives of the United States of America in Congress assembled, That section 701 of the Civil Rights Act of 1964 is amended by adding at the end thereof the following new subsection:

42 USC 2000e-2.

"(k) The terms 'because of sex' or 'on the basis of sex' include, but are not limited to, because of or on the basis of pregnancy, childbirth, or related medical conditions; and women affected by pregnancy, childbirth, or related medical conditions shall be treated the same for all employment-related purposes, including receipt of benefits under fringe benefit programs, as other persons not so affected but similar in their ability or inability to work, and nothing in section 703(h) of this title shall be interpreted to permit otherwise. This subsection shall not require an employer to pay for health insurance benefits for abortion, except where the life of the mother would be endangered if the fetus were carried to term, or except where medical complications have arisen from an abortion: *Provided,* That nothing herein shall preclude an employer from providing abortion benefits or otherwise affect bargaining agreements in regard to abortion.".

Effective date.
42 USC 2000e note.

SEC. 2. (a) Except as provided in subsection (b), the amendment made by this Act shall be effective on the date of enactment.

(b) The provisions of the amendment made by the first section of this Act shall not apply to any fringe benefit program or fund, or insurance program which is in effect on the date of enactment of this Act until 180 days after enactment of this Act.

42 USC 2000e note.

SEC. 3. Until the expiration of a period of one year from the date of enactment of this Act or, if there is an applicable collective-bargaining agreement in effect on the date of enactment of this Act, until the termination of that agreement, no person who, on the date of enactment of this Act is providing either by direct payment or by

PUBLIC LAW 95-555—OCT. 31, 1978   92 STAT. 2077

making contributions to a fringe benefit fund or insurance program, benefits in violation with this Act shall, in order to come into compliance with this Act, reduce the benefits or the compensation provided any employee on the date of enactment of this Act, either directly or by failing to provide sufficient contributions to a fringe benefit fund or insurance program: *Provided*, That where the costs of such benefits on the date of enactment of this Act are apportioned between employers and employees, the payments or contributions required to comply with this Act may be made by employers and employees in the same proportion: *And provided further*, That nothing in this section shall prevent the readjustment of benefits or compensation for reasons unrelated to compliance with this Act.

Approved October 31, 1978.

LEGISLATIVE HISTORY:

HOUSE REPORTS: No. 95-948 accompanying H.R. 6075 (Comm. on Education and Labor) and No. 95-1786 (Comm. of Conference).
SENATE REPORT No. 95-331 (Comm. on Human Resources).
CONGRESSIONAL RECORD:
    Vol. 123 (1977): Sept. 15, 16, considered and passed Senate.
    Vol. 124 (1978): July 18, H.R. 6075 considered and passed House; proceedings vacated and S. 995, amended, passed in lieu.
    Oct. 13, Senate agreed to conference report.
    Oct. 15, House agreed to conference report.
WEEKLY COMPILATION OF PRESIDENTIAL DOCUMENTS:
    Vol. 14, No. 44 (1978): Oct. 31, Presidential statement.

112TH CONGRESS
2D SESSION **H. R. 5647**

To eliminate discrimination and promote women's health and economic security by ensuring reasonable workplace accommodations for workers whose ability to perform the functions of a job are limited by pregnancy, childbirth, or a related medical condition.

IN THE HOUSE OF REPRESENTATIVES

MAY 8, 2012

Mr. NADLER (for himself, Mrs. MALONEY, Ms. SPEIER, Mrs. DAVIS of California, Ms. FUDGE, Mr. GEORGE MILLER of California, Mr. HIGGINS, Mr. RANGEL, Mr. JACKSON of Illinois, Mr. GRIJALVA, Mr. ROTHMAN of New Jersey, Ms. LEE of California, Mr. McDERMOTT, Mrs. CAPPS, Ms. DELAURO, Ms. NORTON, Mr. ENGEL, Ms. SCHAKOWSKY, Ms. HAHN, Mr. CONYERS, Mrs. LOWEY, Mrs. CHRISTENSEN, Ms. MOORE, Mr. FARR, Ms. CHU, Ms. RICHARDSON, Ms. McCOLLUM, Mr. CROWLEY, Mr. PASCRELL, Mr. HINCHEY, Ms. BROWN of Florida, Mr. MORAN, Mr. ACKERMAN, Mr. BOSWELL, Mr. OLVER, Mr. BRADY of Pennsylvania, Mr. CLARKE of Michigan, Ms. WOOLSEY, Mr. LEWIS of Georgia, Ms. LINDA T. SÁNCHEZ of California, Mr. HONDA, Mr. TOWNS, Mr. DAVIS of Illinois, Mr. CARSON of Indiana, Mr. BERMAN, Ms. WATERS, Mr. JOHNSON of Georgia, Mr. KILDEE, Mr. MARKEY, Ms. MATSUI, Ms. TSONGAS, Ms. CLARKE of New York, Mr. HINOJOSA, Mr. CARNAHAN, Mr. SHERMAN, Ms. DEGETTE, Ms. SUTTON, Mr. LANGEVIN, Mr. BACA, Ms. PINGREE of Maine, Mr. SERRANO, Mr. ELLISON, Mr. KUCINICH, Ms. ESHOO, Mr. LARSEN of Washington, and Ms. SLAUGHTER) introduced the following bill; which was referred to the Committee on Education and the Workforce, and in addition to the Committees on House Administration, Oversight and Government Reform, and the Judiciary, for a period to be subsequently determined by the Speaker, in each case for consideration of such provisions as fall within the jurisdiction of the committee concerned

---

A BILL

To eliminate discrimination and promote women's health and

economic security by ensuring reasonable workplace accommodations for workers whose ability to perform the functions of a job are limited by pregnancy, childbirth, or a related medical condition.

Be it enacted by the Senate and House of Representatives of the United States of America in Congress assembled,

SECTION 1. SHORT TITLE.

This Act may be cited as the "Pregnant Workers Fairness Act".

SEC. 2. NONDISCRIMINATION WITH REGARD TO REASONABLE ACCOMMODATIONS RELATED TO PREGNANCY.

It shall be an unlawful employment practice for a covered entity to—

(1) not make reasonable accommodations to the known limitations related to the pregnancy, childbirth, or related medical conditions of a job applicant or employee, unless such covered entity can demonstrate that the accommodation would impose an undue hardship on the operation of the business of such covered entity;

(2) deny employment opportunities to a job applicant or employee, if such denial is based on the need of the covered entity to make reasonable accommodations to the known limitations related to

3

the pregnancy, childbirth, or related medical conditions of an employee or applicant;

(3) require a job applicant or employee affected by pregnancy, childbirth, or related medical conditions to accept an accommodation that such applicant or employee chooses not to accept; or

(4) require an employee to take leave under any leave law or policy of the covered entity if another reasonable accommodation can be provided to the known limitations related to the pregnancy, childbirth, or related medical conditions of an employee.

SEC. 3. REMEDIES AND ENFORCEMENT.

(a) EMPLOYEES COVERED BY TITLE VII OF THE CIVIL RIGHTS ACT OF 1964.—

(1) IN GENERAL.—The powers, procedures, and remedies provided in sections 705, 706, 707, 709, 710, and 711 of the Civil Rights Act of 1964 (42 U.S.C. 2000e–4 et seq.) to the Commission, the Attorney General, or any person, alleging a violation of title VII of that Act (42 U.S.C. 2000e et seq.) shall be the powers, procedures, and remedies this title provides to the Commission, the Attorney General, or any person, respectively, alleging an unlawful employment practice in violation of this title against an

4

1 employee described in section 5(2)(A), except as pro-
2 vided in paragraphs (2) and (3).
3 (2) COSTS AND FEES.—The powers, remedies,
4 and procedures provided in subsections (b) and (c)
5 of section 722 of the Revised Statutes of the United
6 States (42 U.S.C. 1988), shall be the powers, rem-
7 edies, and procedures this title provides to the Com-
8 mission, the Attorney General, or any person, alleg-
9 ing such a practice.
10 (3) DAMAGES.—The powers, remedies, and pro-
11 cedures provided in section 1977A of the Revised
12 Statutes of the United States (42 U.S.C. 1981a), in-
13 cluding the limitations contained in subsection (b)(3)
14 of such section 1977A, shall be the powers, rem-
15 edies, and procedures this title provides to the Com-
16 mission, the Attorney General, or any person, alleg-
17 ing such a practice (not an employment practice spe-
18 cifically excluded from coverage under section
19 1977A(a)(1) of the Revised Statutes of the United
20 States).
21 (b) EMPLOYEES COVERED BY CONGRESSIONAL AC-
22 COUNTABILITY ACT OF 1995.—
23 (1) IN GENERAL.—The powers, remedies, and
24 procedures provided in the Congressional Account-
25 ability Act of 1995 (2 U.S.C. 1301 et seq.) to the

•HR 5647 IH

Board (as defined in section 101 of that Act (2 U.S.C. 1301)), or any person, alleging a violation of section 201(a)(1) of that Act (2 U.S.C. 1311(a)(1)) shall be the powers, remedies, and procedures this title provides to that Board, or any person, alleging an unlawful employment practice in violation of this title against an employee described in section 5(2)(B), except as provided in paragraphs (2) and (3).

(2) COSTS AND FEES.—The powers, remedies, and procedures provided in subsections (b) and (c) of section 722 of the Revised Statutes of the United States (42 U.S.C. 1988), shall be the powers, remedies, and procedures this title provides to that Board, or any person, alleging such a practice.

(3) DAMAGES.—The powers, remedies, and procedures provided in section 1977A of the Revised Statutes of the United States (42 U.S.C. 1981a), including the limitations contained in subsection (b)(3) of such section 1977A, shall be the powers, remedies, and procedures this title provides to that Board, or any person, alleging such a practice (not an employment practice specifically excluded from coverage under section 1977A(a)(1) of the Revised Statutes of the United States).

6

(4) OTHER APPLICABLE PROVISIONS.—With respect to a claim alleging a practice described in paragraph (1), title III of the Congressional Accountability Act of 1995 (2 U.S.C. 1381 et seq.) shall apply in the same manner as such title applies with respect to a claim alleging a violation of section 201(a)(1) of such Act (2 U.S.C. 1311(a)(1)).

(c) EMPLOYEES COVERED BY CHAPTER 5 OF TITLE 3, UNITED STATES CODE.—

(1) IN GENERAL.—The powers, remedies, and procedures provided in chapter 5 of title 3, United States Code, to the President, the Commission, the Merit Systems Protection Board, or any person, alleging a violation of section 411(a)(1) of that title, shall be the powers, remedies, and procedures this title provides to the President, the Commission, such Board, or any person, respectively, alleging an unlawful employment practice in violation of this title against an employee described in section 5(2)(C), except as provided in paragraphs (2) and (3).

(2) COSTS AND FEES.—The powers, remedies, and procedures provided in subsections (b) and (c) of section 722 of the Revised Statutes of the United States (42 U.S.C. 1988), shall be the powers, remedies, and procedures this title provides to the Presi-

dent, the Commission, such Board, or any person, alleging such a practice.

(3) DAMAGES.—The powers, remedies, and procedures provided in section 1977A of the Revised Statutes of the United States (42 U.S.C. 1981a), including the limitations contained in subsection (b)(3) of such section 1977A, shall be the powers, remedies, and procedures this title provides to the President, the Commission, such Board, or any person, alleging such a practice (not an employment practice specifically excluded from coverage under section 1977A(a)(1) of the Revised Statutes of the United States).

(d) EMPLOYEES COVERED BY GOVERNMENT EMPLOYEE RIGHTS ACT OF 1991.—

(1) IN GENERAL.—The powers, remedies, and procedures provided in sections 302 and 304 of the Government Employee Rights Act of 1991 (42 U.S.C. 2000e–16b, 2000e–16c) to the Commission, or any person, alleging a violation of section 302(a)(1) of that Act (42 U.S.C. 2000e–16b(a)(1)) shall be the powers, remedies, and procedures this title provides to the Commission, or any person, respectively, alleging an unlawful employment practice in violation of this title against an employee de-

7

dent, the Commission, such Board, or any person, alleging such a practice.

(3) DAMAGES.—The powers, remedies, and procedures provided in section 1977A of the Revised Statutes of the United States (42 U.S.C. 1981a), including the limitations contained in subsection (b)(3) of such section 1977A, shall be the powers, remedies, and procedures this title provides to the President, the Commission, such Board, or any person, alleging such a practice (not an employment practice specifically excluded from coverage under section 1977A(a)(1) of the Revised Statutes of the United States).

(d) EMPLOYEES COVERED BY GOVERNMENT EMPLOYEE RIGHTS ACT OF 1991.—

(1) IN GENERAL.—The powers, remedies, and procedures provided in sections 302 and 304 of the Government Employee Rights Act of 1991 (42 U.S.C. 2000e–16b, 2000e–16c) to the Commission, or any person, alleging a violation of section 302(a)(1) of that Act (42 U.S.C. 2000e–16b(a)(1)) shall be the powers, remedies, and procedures this title provides to the Commission, or any person, respectively, alleging an unlawful employment practice in violation of this title against an employee de-

scribed in section 5(2)(D), except as provided in paragraphs (2) and (3).

(2) COSTS AND FEES.—The powers, remedies, and procedures provided in subsections (b) and (c) of section 722 of the Revised Statutes of the United States (42 U.S.C. 1988), shall be the powers, remedies, and procedures this title provides to the Commission, or any person, alleging such a practice.

(3) DAMAGES.—The powers, remedies, and procedures provided in section 1977A of the Revised Statutes of the United States (42 U.S.C. 1981a), including the limitations contained in subsection (b)(3) of such section 1977A, shall be the powers, remedies, and procedures this title provides to the Commission, or any person, alleging such a practice (not an employment practice specifically excluded from coverage under section 1977A(a)(1) of the Revised Statutes of the United States).

(e) EMPLOYEES COVERED BY SECTION 717 OF THE CIVIL RIGHTS ACT OF 1964.—

(1) IN GENERAL.—The powers, remedies, and procedures provided in section 717 of the Civil Rights Act of 1964 (42 U.S.C. 2000e–16) to the Commission, the Attorney General, the Librarian of Congress, or any person, alleging a violation of that

10

(f) PROHIBITION AGAINST RETALIATION.—No person shall discriminate against any individual because such individual has opposed any act or practice made unlawful by this title or because such individual made a charge, testified, assisted, or participated in any manner in an investigation, proceeding, or hearing under this title. The remedies and procedures otherwise provided for under this section shall be available to aggrieved individuals with respect to violations of this subsection.

SEC. 4. RULEMAKING.

Not later than 2 years after the date of enactment of this Act, the Commission shall issue regulations in an accessible format in accordance with subchapter II of chapter 5 of title 5, United States Code, to carry out this Act. Such regulations shall identify some reasonable accommodations addressing known limitations related to pregnancy, childbirth, or related medical conditions that shall be provided to a job applicant or employee affected by such known limitations unless the covered entity can demonstrate that doing so would impose an undue hardship.

SEC. 5. DEFINITIONS.

As used in this Act—

    (1) the term "Commission" means the Equal Employment Opportunity Commission;

(2) the term "covered entity"—

    (A) has the meaning given the term "respondent" in section 701(n) of the Civil Rights Act of 1964 (42 U.S.C. 2000e(n)); and

    (B) includes—

        (i) an employing office, as defined in section 101 of the Congressional Accountability Act of 1995 (2 U.S.C. 1301) and section 411(c) of title 3, United States Code;

        (ii) an entity employing a State employee described in section 304(a) of the Government Employee Rights Act of 1991 (12 U.S.C. 1220(a)); and

        (iii) an entity to which section 717(a) of the Civil Rights Act of 1964 (42 U.S.C. 2000e–16(a)) applies;

(3) the term "employee" means—

    (A) an employee (including an applicant), as defined in section 701(f) of the Civil Rights Act of 1964 (42 U.S.C. 2000e(f));

    (B) a covered employee (including an applicant), as defined in section 101 of the Congressional Accountability Act of 1995 (2 U.S.C. 1301);

(C) a covered employee (including an applicant), as defined in section 411(c) of title 3, United States Code;

(D) a State employee (including an applicant) described in section 304(a) of the Government Employee Rights Act of 1991 (12 U.S.C. 1220(a)); or

(E) an employee (including an applicant) to which section 717(a) of the Civil Rights Act of 1964 (42 U.S.C. 2000e–16(a)) applies;

(4) the term "person" has the meaning given such term in section 701(a) of the Civil Rights Act of 1964 (42 U.S.C. 2000e(a)); and

(5) the terms "reasonable accommodation" and "undue hardship" have the meanings given such terms in section 101 of the Americans with Disabilities Act of 1990 (42 U.S.C. 12111) and shall be construed as such terms have been construed under such Act and as set forth in the regulations required by this Act.

SEC. 6. RELATIONSHIP TO OTHER LAWS.

Nothing in this Act shall be construed to invalidate or limit the remedies, rights, and procedures of any Federal law or law of any State or political subdivision of any State or jurisdiction that provides greater or equal protection for workers affected by pregnancy, childbirth, or related medical conditions.

May 7, 2012

Re: Pregnant Workers Fairness Act

Dear Member of Congress:

As organizations dedicated to combating sex discrimination and promoting the health and economic security of our nation's families, we write to urge you to support the Pregnant Workers Fairness Act, a bill that would promote nondiscrimination by ensuring that pregnant workers are not forced out of their jobs unnecessarily or denied reasonable job modifications that would allow them to continue working and supporting their families. This bill promotes the health and economic security of pregnant women, their babies, and their families without harming the economy.

Three-quarters of women entering the workforce will be pregnant and employed at some point. Since the Pregnancy Discrimination Act (PDA) became law in 1978, there has been a dramatic demographic shift in the workforce. Not only do women now make up almost half of the workforce, but there are more pregnant workers than ever before and they are working later into their pregnancies. At some point in their pregnancies, some of these women—especially those in physically strenuous jobs—will face a conflict between their duties at work and the demands of pregnancy.

Under current pregnancy law, the PDA, employers cannot discriminate based on pregnancy, childbirth, or related medical conditions. This means that employers cannot fire, refuse to hire, or otherwise treat an employee adversely because of pregnancy and must treat pregnant workers at least as well as those similar in their ability or inability to work. Despite these existing protections, pregnant workers are all too often forced out of their jobs unnecessarily and denied the minor modifications to job duties, job rules or job policies that would enable them to continue working. For example, a retail worker in Salina, Kansas was fired because she needed to carry a water bottle to stay hydrated and prevent bladder infections.[i] An activity director at a nursing home in Valparaiso, Indiana was terminated because she required help with some physically strenuous aspects of her job to prevent having another miscarriage.[ii] In Landover, Maryland, a delivery truck driver was forced out on unpaid leave because she had a lifting restriction and was denied light duty.[iii] These women lost in court, even though workers covered by the Americans with Disabilities Act Amendments Act would be entitled to carry water or receive help on the job. Despite the protections of the PDA, pregnant women are still often treated *worse* than other workers who may be limited in their ability to perform certain aspects of a job.

The Pregnant Workers Fairness Act, modeled after the Americans with Disabilities Act, addresses this problem through an existing and familiar reasonable accommodations framework. Specifically, this legislation prevents employers from forcing pregnant women out of the workplace (either by placing them on leave or firing them altogether) and ensures that, where a minor job modification would allow a woman to continue working, an employer must provide it unless doing so would pose an undue hardship. California enacted similar legislation in 2000, where it has been used countless times to help pregnant women stay healthy and keep their jobs. Connecticut, Hawaii, Louisiana, Alaska, Texas, and Illinois also explicitly require certain employers to provide reasonable accommodation to pregnant employees. While plenty of women are able to work through their pregnancies without any job modifications, those who cannot desperately need a clear right to do so. This bill would empower women while benefitting employers by providing certainty about their responsibilities.

Minor job modifications for pregnant women are a public health necessity. A choice between working under unhealthy conditions and potentially losing income is no choice at all. Women who cannot perform some aspects of their usual duties without risking their own health or the health of their pregnancy, but are in need of income, may have to continue working under dangerous conditions. There are health consequences to pushing women out of the workforce as well. Stress from job loss can increase the risk of having a premature baby and/or a baby with low birth weight. In addition, women who can continue to work during pregnancy may be able to take a longer period of leave following childbirth, which in turn facilitates breastfeeding, bonding with and caring for a new child, and recovering from childbirth. Breastfeeding has extensive health benefits for mothers and infants, which may reduce future illness related absences.

Pregnancy-related adjustments at work also promote family economic security. In this difficult economy, workers cannot afford to be pushed out or terminated from their jobs because of pregnancy and childbirth. By continuing to work, pregnant women can maintain income and seniority at work, while forced leave sets new mothers back with lost wages and missed advancement opportunities. When pregnant women are fired, not only do they and their families lose critical income, but they must fight extra hard to re-enter a job market that is especially brutal on the unemployed and on pregnant women. Similarly, new mothers often confront mounting hiring bias. On the other hand, providing reasonable accommodations carries benefits for employers, including reduced turnover and increased productivity.

Ensuring equal opportunity for working women is vital to the health and economic security of our nation's families. We urge you to co-sponsor the Pregnant Workers Fairness Act and would welcome the opportunity to provide you with detailed information on these recommendations and to speak with you further about the critical needs of pregnant women and new mothers.

Sincerely,

A Better Balance: The Work & Family Legal Center
American Civil Liberties Union (ACLU)
California Women's Law Center
Equal Rights Advocates
The Legal Aid Society—Employment Law Center
Legal Momentum
National Partnership for Women and Families
National Women's Law Center
9to5, National Association of Working Women
9to5 Atlanta Working Women
9to5 Bay Area (CA)
9to5 Colorado
9to5 Los Angeles
9to5 Milwaukee
AIDS Foundation of Chicago
Alliance for Early Care and Education

44 • *Maternity Leave: Policy and Practice*

American Academy of Nursing
American Association of University Women (AAUW)
American Federation of Labor and Congress of Industrial Organizations (AFL-CIO)
American Federation of State, County and Municipal Employees (AFSCME)
American Federation of Teachers
American Nurses Association
Association Employees Union (AEU)
Association of Reproductive Health Professionals (ARHP)
Association of Women's Health, Obstetric and Neonatal Nurses
Black Women's Health Imperative
Business and Professional Women's Foundation
Center for Law and Social Policy (CLASP)
Childbirth Connection
Coalition of Labor Union Women
Communications Workers of America
Community Service Society
Department for Professional Employees, AFL-CIO
Direct Care Alliance
Disciples Justice Action Network
Disciples Women, Christian Church (Disciples of Christ)
Economic Opportunity Institute
Employment Justice Center
The Every Child Matters Education Fund
Family and Children's Ministries, Disciples Home Missions, Christian Church (Disciples of Christ)
Family Equality Council
Family Forward Oregon
Family Values @ Work Consortium
Feminist Majority
Florida Federation of Business and Professional Women's Club, Inc.
Hadassah, The Women's Zionist Organization of America, Inc.
Healthy Teen Network
HIV Prevention Justice Alliance (HIV PJA)
Human Rights Project for Girls
The Indiana Toxics Action Project
International Union, United Automobile, Aerospace & Agricultural Implement Workers of America (UAW)
Jewish Women International
Job Opportunities Task Force
Labor Project for Working Families
Leadership Conference on Civil and Human Rights
Legal Voice
Maryland Women's Coalition for Health Care Reform
Main Street Alliance
Mexican American Legal Defense and Educational Fund
MomsRising
Mothering Justice

National Association for the Advancement of Colored People (NAACP)
National Association of Commissions for Women (NACW)
National Association of Mothers' Centers
National Asian Pacific American Women's Forum
National Center for Transgender Equality
National Council of Jewish Women
National Council of La Raza (NCLR)
National Council of Negro Women
National Council of Women's Organizations
The National Crittenton Foundation
National Domestic Workers Alliance
National Education Association
National Employment Law Project
National Employment Lawyers Association NY
National Fair Housing Alliance
National Gay and Lesbian Task Force Action Fund
National Military Family Association
National Organization for Women
National Women's Conference Committee
Neighborhood Funders Group
NETWORK, A National Catholic Social Justice Lobby
New Jersey Citizen Action
North Carolina Justice Center
Occupational and Environmental Health Center of Eastern NY
Partnership for Working Families
Pediatric AIDS Chicago Prevention Initiative
Physicians for Reproductive Choice and Health
Planned Parenthood of Western New York
The Praxis Project
Pride at Work
Progressive Maryland
Public Health Institute of Metropolitan Chicago
Public Justice Center
Religious Coalition for Reproductive Choice
RESOLVE: The National Infertility Association
Restaurant Opportunities Centers United
Restaurant Opportunities Center – Miami
Retail Action Project
Ritz Clark & Ben-Asher LLP
Service Employees International Union (SEIU)
Sexuality Information and Education Council of the U.S. (SIECUS)
Society for Women's Health Research
Sugar Law Center for Economic and Social Justice
UN Women - Greater L.A. Chapter (of USNC)
Unitarian Universalist Association of Congregations
Unitarian Universalist Women's Federation

United Food and Commercial Workers International Union
United Food and Commercial Workers – Local 5
Washington Area Women's Foundation
Washington Work and Family Coalition
The What To Expect Foundation
Wider Opportunities for Women
Women Employed
Women Donors Network
Women's Employment Rights Clinic, Golden Gate University School of Law
The Women's Fund of Long Island
Women's Law Project
Young Workers United

---

[i] *Wiseman v. Wal-Mart Stores, Inc.*, No. 08-1244-EFM, 2009 WL 1617669 (D. Kan. June 9, 2009).
[ii] *Serednyj v. Beverly Healthcare*, 656 F.3d 540 (7th Cir. 2011).
[iii] *Young v. United Parcel Service, Inc.*, No. DKC 08-2586, 2011 WL 665321 (D. Md. Feb. 14, 2011).

107 STAT. 6   **PUBLIC LAW 103-3—FEB. 5, 1993**

Public Law 103-3
103d Congress

An Act

Feb. 5, 1993
[H.R. 1]

To grant family and temporary medical leave under certain circumstances.

Family and
Medical Leave
Act of 1993.
29 USC 2601
note.

Be it enacted by the Senate and House of Representatives of the United States of America in Congress assembled,

SECTION 1. SHORT TITLE; TABLE OF CONTENTS.

(a) SHORT TITLE.—This Act may be cited as the "Family and Medical Leave Act of 1993".

(b) TABLE OF CONTENTS.—The table of contents is as follows:

Sec. 1. Short title; table of contents.
Sec. 2. Findings and purposes.

TITLE I—GENERAL REQUIREMENTS FOR LEAVE

Sec. 101. Definitions.
Sec. 102. Leave requirement.
Sec. 103. Certification.
Sec. 104. Employment and benefits protection.
Sec. 105. Prohibited acts.
Sec. 106. Investigative authority.
Sec. 107. Enforcement.
Sec. 108. Special rules concerning employees of local educational agencies.
Sec. 109. Notice.

TITLE II—LEAVE FOR CIVIL SERVICE EMPLOYEES

Sec. 201. Leave requirement.

TITLE III—COMMISSION ON LEAVE

Sec. 301. Establishment.
Sec. 302. Duties.
Sec. 303. Membership.
Sec. 304. Compensation.
Sec. 305. Powers.
Sec. 306. Termination.

TITLE IV—MISCELLANEOUS PROVISIONS

Sec. 401. Effect on other laws.
Sec. 402. Effect on existing employment benefits.
Sec. 403. Encouragement of more generous leave policies.
Sec. 404. Regulations.
Sec. 405. Effective dates.

TITLE V—COVERAGE OF CONGRESSIONAL EMPLOYEES

Sec. 501. Leave for certain Senate employees.
Sec. 502. Leave for certain House employees.

TITLE VI—SENSE OF CONGRESS

Sec. 601. Sense of Congress.

29 USC 2601.

SEC. 2. FINDINGS AND PURPOSES.

(a) FINDINGS.—Congress finds that—

(1) the number of single-parent households and two parent households in which the single parent or both parents work is increasing significantly;

(2) it is important for the development of children and the family unit that fathers and mothers be able to participate in early childrearing and the care of family members who have serious health conditions;

(3) the lack of employment policies to accommodate working parents can force individuals to choose between job security and parenting;

(4) there is inadequate job security for employees who have serious health conditions that prevent them from working for temporary periods;

(5) due to the nature of the roles of men and women in our society, the primary responsibility for family caretaking often falls on women, and such responsibility affects the working lives of women more than it affects the working lives of men; and

(6) employment standards that apply to one gender only have serious potential for encouraging employers to discriminate against employees and applicants for employment who are of that gender.

(b) PURPOSES.—It is the purpose of this Act—

(1) to balance the demands of the workplace with the needs of families, to promote the stability and economic security of families, and to promote national interests in preserving family integrity;

(2) to entitle employees to take reasonable leave for medical reasons, for the birth or adoption of a child, and for the care of a child, spouse, or parent who has a serious health condition;

(3) to accomplish the purposes described in paragraphs (1) and (2) in a manner that accommodates the legitimate interests of employers;

(4) to accomplish the purposes described in paragraphs (1) and (2) in a manner that, consistent with the Equal Protection Clause of the Fourteenth Amendment, minimizes the potential for employment discrimination on the basis of sex by ensuring generally that leave is available for eligible medical reasons (including maternity-related disability) and for compelling family reasons, on a gender-neutral basis; and

(5) to promote the goal of equal employment opportunity for women and men, pursuant to such clause.

TITLE I—GENERAL REQUIREMENTS FOR LEAVE

SEC. 101. DEFINITIONS.

As used in this title:

(1) COMMERCE.—The terms "commerce" and "industry or activity affecting commerce" mean any activity, business, or industry in commerce or in which a labor dispute would hinder or obstruct commerce or the free flow of commerce, and include "commerce" and any "industry affecting commerce", as defined in paragraphs (1) and (3) of section 501 of the Labor Management Relations Act, 1947 (29 U.S.C. 142 (1) and (3)).

(2) ELIGIBLE EMPLOYEE.—

(A) IN GENERAL.—The term "eligible employee" means an employee who has been employed—

(i) for at least 12 months by the employer with respect to whom leave is requested under section 102; and

(ii) for at least 1,250 hours of service with such employer during the previous 12-month period.

(B) EXCLUSIONS.—The term "eligible employee" does not include—

(i) any Federal officer or employee covered under subchapter V of chapter 63 of title 5, United States Code (as added by title II of this Act); or

(ii) any employee of an employer who is employed at a worksite at which such employer employs less than 50 employees if the total number of employees employed by that employer within 75 miles of that worksite is less than 50.

(C) DETERMINATION.—For purposes of determining whether an employee meets the hours of service requirement specified in subparagraph (A)(ii), the legal standards established under section 7 of the Fair Labor Standards Act of 1938 (29 U.S.C. 207) shall apply.

(3) EMPLOY; EMPLOYEE; STATE.—The terms "employ", "employee", and "State" have the same meanings given such terms in subsections (c), (e), and (g) of section 3 of the Fair Labor Standards Act of 1938 (29 U.S.C. 203 (c), (e), and (g)).

(4) EMPLOYER.—

(A) IN GENERAL.—The term "employer"—

(i) means any person engaged in commerce or in any industry or activity affecting commerce who employs 50 or more employees for each working day during each of 20 or more calendar workweeks in the current or preceding calendar year;

(ii) includes—

(I) any person who acts, directly or indirectly, in the interest of an employer to any of the employees of such employer; and

(II) any successor in interest of an employer; and

(iii) includes any "public agency", as defined in section 3(x) of the Fair Labor Standards Act of 1938 (29 U.S.C. 203(x)).

(B) PUBLIC AGENCY.—For purposes of subparagraph (A)(iii), a public agency shall be considered to be a person engaged in commerce or in an industry or activity affecting commerce.

(5) EMPLOYMENT BENEFITS.—The term "employment benefits" means all benefits provided or made available to employees by an employer, including group life insurance, health insurance, disability insurance, sick leave, annual leave, educational benefits, and pensions, regardless of whether such benefits are provided by a practice or written policy of an employer or through an "employee benefit plan", as defined in section 3(3) of the Employee Retirement Income Security Act of 1974 (29 U.S.C. 1002(3)).

(6) HEALTH CARE PROVIDER.—The term "health care provider" means—

PUBLIC LAW 103-3—FEB. 5, 1993   107 STAT. 9

(A) a doctor of medicine or osteopathy who is authorized to practice medicine or surgery (as appropriate) by the State in which the doctor practices; or
(B) any other person determined by the Secretary to be capable of providing health care services.
(7) PARENT.—The term "parent" means the biological parent of an employee or an individual who stood in loco parentis to an employee when the employee was a son or daughter.
(8) PERSON.—The term "person" has the same meaning given such term in section 3(a) of the Fair Labor Standards Act of 1938 (29 U.S.C. 203(a)).
(9) REDUCED LEAVE SCHEDULE.—The term "reduced leave schedule" means a leave schedule that reduces the usual number of hours per workweek, or hours per workday, of an employee.
(10) SECRETARY.—The term "Secretary" means the Secretary of Labor.
(11) SERIOUS HEALTH CONDITION.—The term "serious health condition" means an illness, injury, impairment, or physical or mental condition that involves—
(A) inpatient care in a hospital, hospice, or residential medical care facility; or
(B) continuing treatment by a health care provider.
(12) SON OR DAUGHTER.—The term "son or daughter" means a biological, adopted, or foster child, a stepchild, a legal ward, or a child of a person standing in loco parentis, who is—
(A) under 18 years of age; or
(B) 18 years of age or older and incapable of self-care because of a mental or physical disability.
(13) SPOUSE.—The term "spouse" means a husband or wife, as the case may be.

SEC. 102. LEAVE REQUIREMENT.   29 USC 2612.

(a) IN GENERAL.—
(1) ENTITLEMENT TO LEAVE.—Subject to section 103, an eligible employee shall be entitled to a total of 12 workweeks of leave during any 12-month period for one or more of the following:
(A) Because of the birth of a son or daughter of the employee and in order to care for such son or daughter.
(B) Because of the placement of a son or daughter with the employee for adoption or foster care.
(C) In order to care for the spouse, or a son, daughter, or parent, of the employee, if such spouse, son, daughter, or parent has a serious health condition.
(D) Because of a serious health condition that makes the employee unable to perform the functions of the position of such employee.
(2) EXPIRATION OF ENTITLEMENT.—The entitlement to leave under subparagraphs (A) and (B) of paragraph (1) for a birth or placement of a son or daughter shall expire at the end of the 12-month period beginning on the date of such birth or placement.
(b) LEAVE TAKEN INTERMITTENTLY OR ON A REDUCED LEAVE SCHEDULE.—
(1) IN GENERAL.—Leave under subparagraph (A) or (B) of subsection (a)(1) shall not be taken by an employee intermit-

107 STAT. 10   PUBLIC LAW 103-3—FEB. 5, 1993

tently or on a reduced leave schedule unless the employee and the employer of the employee agree otherwise. Subject to paragraph (2), subsection (e)(2), and section 103(b)(5), leave under subparagraph (C) or (D) of subsection (a)(1) may be taken intermittently or on a reduced leave schedule when medically necessary. The taking of leave intermittently or on a reduced leave schedule pursuant to this paragraph shall not result in a reduction in the total amount of leave to which the employee is entitled under subsection (a) beyond the amount of leave actually taken.

(2) ALTERNATIVE POSITION.—If an employee requests intermittent leave, or leave on a reduced leave schedule, under subparagraph (C) or (D) of subsection (a)(1), that is foreseeable based on planned medical treatment, the employer may require such employee to transfer temporarily to an available alternative position offered by the employer for which the employee is qualified and that—

(A) has equivalent pay and benefits; and
(B) better accommodates recurring periods of leave than the regular employment position of the employee.

(c) UNPAID LEAVE PERMITTED.—Except as provided in subsection (d), leave granted under subsection (a) may consist of unpaid leave. Where an employee is otherwise exempt under regulations issued by the Secretary pursuant to section 13(a)(1) of the Fair Labor Standards Act of 1938 (29 U.S.C. 213(a)(1)), the compliance of an employer with this title by providing unpaid leave shall not affect the exempt status of the employee under such section.

(d) RELATIONSHIP TO PAID LEAVE.—
(1) UNPAID LEAVE.—If an employer provides paid leave for fewer than 12 workweeks, the additional weeks of leave necessary to attain the 12 workweeks of leave required under this title may be provided without compensation.
(2) SUBSTITUTION OF PAID LEAVE.—
(A) IN GENERAL.—An eligible employee may elect, or an employer may require the employee, to substitute any of the accrued paid vacation leave, personal leave, or family leave of the employee for leave provided under subparagraph (A), (B), or (C) of subsection (a)(1) for any part of the 12-week period of such leave under such subsection.
(B) SERIOUS HEALTH CONDITION.—An eligible employee may elect, or an employer may require the employee, to substitute any of the accrued paid vacation leave, personal leave, or medical or sick leave of the employee for leave provided under subparagraph (C) or (D) of subsection (a)(1) for any part of the 12-week period of such leave under such subsection, except that nothing in this title shall require an employer to provide paid sick leave or paid medical leave in any situation in which such employer would not normally provide any such paid leave.

(e) FORESEEABLE LEAVE.—
(1) REQUIREMENT OF NOTICE.—In any case in which the necessity for leave under subparagraph (A) or (B) of subsection (a)(1) is foreseeable based on an expected birth or placement, the employee shall provide the employer with not less than 30 days' notice, before the date the leave is to begin, of the employee's intention to take leave under such subparagraph, except that if the date of the birth or placement requires

leave to begin in less than 30 days, the employee shall provide such notice as is practicable.

(2) DUTIES OF EMPLOYEE.—In any case in which the necessity for leave under subparagraph (C) or (D) of subsection (a)(1) is foreseeable based on planned medical treatment, the employee—

(A) shall make a reasonable effort to schedule the treatment so as not to disrupt unduly the operations of the employer, subject to the approval of the health care provider of the employee or the health care provider of the son, daughter, spouse, or parent of the employee, as appropriate; and

(B) shall provide the employer with not less than 30 days' notice, before the date the leave is to begin, of the employee's intention to take leave under such subparagraph, except that if the date of the treatment requires leave to begin in less than 30 days, the employee shall provide such notice as is practicable.

(f) SPOUSES EMPLOYED BY THE SAME EMPLOYER.—In any case in which a husband and wife entitled to leave under subsection (a) are employed by the same employer, the aggregate number of workweeks of leave to which both may be entitled may be limited to 12 workweeks during any 12-month period, if such leave is taken—

(1) under subparagraph (A) or (B) of subsection (a)(1); or

(2) to care for a sick parent under subparagraph (C) of such subsection.

SEC. 103. CERTIFICATION.

29 USC 2613.

(a) IN GENERAL.—An employer may require that a request for leave under subparagraph (C) or (D) of section 102(a)(1) be supported by a certification issued by the health care provider of the eligible employee or of the son, daughter, spouse, or parent of the employee, as appropriate. The employee shall provide, in a timely manner, a copy of such certification to the employer.

(b) SUFFICIENT CERTIFICATION.—Certification provided under subsection (a) shall be sufficient if it states—

(1) the date on which the serious health condition commenced;

(2) the probable duration of the condition;

(3) the appropriate medical facts within the knowledge of the health care provider regarding the condition;

(4)(A) for purposes of leave under section 102(a)(1)(C), a statement that the eligible employee is needed to care for the son, daughter, spouse, or parent and an estimate of the amount of time that such employee is needed to care for the son, daughter, spouse, or parent; and

(B) for purposes of leave under section 102(a)(1)(D), a statement that the employee is unable to perform the functions of the position of the employee;

(5) in the case of certification for intermittent leave, or leave on a reduced leave schedule, for planned medical treatment, the dates on which such treatment is expected to be given and the duration of such treatment;

(6) in the case of certification for intermittent leave, or leave on a reduced leave schedule, under section 102(a)(1)(D),

a statement of the medical necessity for the intermittent leave or leave on a reduced leave schedule, and the expected duration of the intermittent leave or reduced leave schedule; and

(7) in the case of certification for intermittent leave, or leave on a reduced leave schedule, under section 102(a)(1)(C), a statement that the employee's intermittent leave or leave on a reduced leave schedule is necessary for the care of the son, daughter, parent, or spouse who has a serious health condition, or will assist in their recovery, and the expected duration and schedule of the intermittent leave or reduced leave schedule.

(c) SECOND OPINION.—

(1) IN GENERAL.—In any case in which the employer has reason to doubt the validity of the certification provided under subsection (a) for leave under subparagraph (C) or (D) of section 102(a)(1), the employer may require, at the expense of the employer, that the eligible employee obtain the opinion of a second health care provider designated or approved by the employer concerning any information certified under subsection (b) for such leave.

(2) LIMITATION.—A health care provider designated or approved under paragraph (1) shall not be employed on a regular basis by the employer.

(d) RESOLUTION OF CONFLICTING OPINIONS.—

(1) IN GENERAL.—In any case in which the second opinion described in subsection (c) differs from the opinion in the original certification provided under subsection (a), the employer may require, at the expense of the employer, that the employee obtain the opinion of a third health care provider designated or approved jointly by the employer and the employee concerning the information certified under subsection (b).

(2) FINALITY.—The opinion of the third health care provider concerning the information certified under subsection (b) shall be considered to be final and shall be binding on the employer and the employee.

(e) SUBSEQUENT RECERTIFICATION.—The employer may require that the eligible employee obtain subsequent recertifications on a reasonable basis.

SEC. 104. EMPLOYMENT AND BENEFITS PROTECTION.

(a) RESTORATION TO POSITION.—

(1) IN GENERAL.—Except as provided in subsection (b), any eligible employee who takes leave under section 102 for the intended purpose of the leave shall be entitled, on return from such leave—

(A) to be restored by the employer to the position of employment held by the employee when the leave commenced; or

(B) to be restored to an equivalent position with equivalent employment benefits, pay, and other terms and conditions of employment.

(2) LOSS OF BENEFITS.—The taking of leave under section 102 shall not result in the loss of any employment benefit accrued prior to the date on which the leave commenced.

(3) LIMITATIONS.—Nothing in this section shall be construed to entitle any restored employee to—

(A) the accrual of any seniority or employment benefits during any period of leave; or

(B) any right, benefit, or position of employment other than any right, benefit, or position to which the employee would have been entitled had the employee not taken the leave.

(4) CERTIFICATION.—As a condition of restoration under paragraph (1) for an employee who has taken leave under section 102(a)(1)(D), the employer may have a uniformly applied practice or policy that requires each such employee to receive certification from the health care provider of the employee that the employee is able to resume work, except that nothing in this paragraph shall supersede a valid State or local law or a collective bargaining agreement that governs the return to work of such employees.

(5) CONSTRUCTION.—Nothing in this subsection shall be construed to prohibit an employer from requiring an employee on leave under section 102 to report periodically to the employer on the status and intention of the employee to return to work.

(b) EXEMPTION CONCERNING CERTAIN HIGHLY COMPENSATED EMPLOYEES.—

(1) DENIAL OF RESTORATION.—An employer may deny restoration under subsection (a) to any eligible employee described in paragraph (2) if—

(A) such denial is necessary to prevent substantial and grievous economic injury to the operations of the employer;

(B) the employer notifies the employee of the intent of the employer to deny restoration on such basis at the time the employer determines that such injury would occur; and

(C) in any case in which the leave has commenced, the employee elects not to return to employment after receiving such notice.

(2) AFFECTED EMPLOYEES.—An eligible employee described in paragraph (1) is a salaried eligible employee who is among the highest paid 10 percent of the employees employed by the employer within 75 miles of the facility at which the employee is employed.

(c) MAINTENANCE OF HEALTH BENEFITS.—

(1) COVERAGE.—Except as provided in paragraph (2), during any period that an eligible employee takes leave under section 102, the employer shall maintain coverage under any "group health plan" (as defined in section 5000(b)(1) of the Internal Revenue Code of 1986) for the duration of such leave at the level and under the conditions coverage would have been provided if the employee had continued in employment continuously for the duration of such leave.

(2) FAILURE TO RETURN FROM LEAVE.—The employer may recover the premium that the employer paid for maintaining coverage for the employee under such group health plan during any period of unpaid leave under section 102 if—

(A) the employee fails to return from leave under section 102 after the period of leave to which the employee is entitled has expired; and

(B) the employee fails to return to work for a reason other than—

(i) the continuation, recurrence, or onset of a serious health condition that entitles the employee to leave under subparagraph (C) or (D) of section 102(a)(1); or

(ii) other circumstances beyond the control of the employee.

(3) CERTIFICATION.—

(A) ISSUANCE.—An employer may require that a claim that an employee is unable to return to work because of the continuation, recurrence, or onset of the serious health condition described in paragraph (2)(B)(i) be supported by—

(i) a certification issued by the health care provider of the son, daughter, spouse, or parent of the employee, as appropriate, in the case of an employee unable to return to work because of a condition specified in section 102(a)(1)(C); or

(ii) a certification issued by the health care provider of the eligible employee, in the case of an employee unable to return to work because of a condition specified in section 102(a)(1)(D).

(B) COPY.—The employee shall provide, in a timely manner, a copy of such certification to the employer.

(C) SUFFICIENCY OF CERTIFICATION.—

(i) LEAVE DUE TO SERIOUS HEALTH CONDITION OF EMPLOYEE.—The certification described in subparagraph (A)(ii) shall be sufficient if the certification states that a serious health condition prevented the employee from being able to perform the functions of the position of the employee on the date that the leave of the employee expired.

(ii) LEAVE DUE TO SERIOUS HEALTH CONDITION OF FAMILY MEMBER.—The certification described in subparagraph (A)(i) shall be sufficient if the certification states that the employee is needed to care for the son, daughter, spouse, or parent who has a serious health condition on the date that the leave of the employee expired.

29 USC 2615.

SEC. 105. PROHIBITED ACTS.

(a) INTERFERENCE WITH RIGHTS.—

(1) EXERCISE OF RIGHTS.—It shall be unlawful for any employer to interfere with, restrain, or deny the exercise of or the attempt to exercise, any right provided under this title.

(2) DISCRIMINATION.—It shall be unlawful for any employer to discharge or in any other manner discriminate against any individual for opposing any practice made unlawful by this title.

(b) INTERFERENCE WITH PROCEEDINGS OR INQUIRIES.—It shall be unlawful for any person to discharge or in any other manner discriminate against any individual because such individual—

(1) has filed any charge, or has instituted or caused to be instituted any proceeding, under or related to this title;

(2) has given, or is about to give, any information in connection with any inquiry or proceeding relating to any right provided under this title; or

PUBLIC LAW 103-3—FEB. 5, 1993   107 STAT. 15

(3) has testified, or is about to testify, in any inquiry or proceeding relating to any right provided under this title.

SEC. 106. INVESTIGATIVE AUTHORITY.

29 USC 2616.

(a) IN GENERAL.—To ensure compliance with the provisions of this title, or any regulation or order issued under this title, the Secretary shall have, subject to subsection (c), the investigative authority provided under section 11(a) of the Fair Labor Standards Act of 1938 (29 U.S.C. 211(a)).

(b) OBLIGATION TO KEEP AND PRESERVE RECORDS.—Any employer shall make, keep, and preserve records pertaining to compliance with this title in accordance with section 11(c) of the Fair Labor Standards Act of 1938 (29 U.S.C. 211(c)) and in accordance with regulations issued by the Secretary.

(c) REQUIRED SUBMISSIONS GENERALLY LIMITED TO AN ANNUAL BASIS.—The Secretary shall not under the authority of this section require any employer or any plan, fund, or program to submit to the Secretary any books or records more than once during any 12-month period, unless the Secretary has reasonable cause to believe there may exist a violation of this title or any regulation or order issued pursuant to this title, or is investigating a charge pursuant to section 107(b).

(d) SUBPOENA POWERS.—For the purposes of any investigation provided for in this section, the Secretary shall have the subpoena authority provided for under section 9 of the Fair Labor Standards Act of 1938 (29 U.S.C. 209).

SEC. 107. ENFORCEMENT.

29 USC 2617.

(a) CIVIL ACTION BY EMPLOYEES.—

(1) LIABILITY.—Any employer who violates section 105 shall be liable to any eligible employee affected—

(A) for damages equal to—
(i) the amount of—
(I) any wages, salary, employment benefits, or other compensation denied or lost to such employee by reason of the violation; or
(II) in a case in which wages, salary, employment benefits, or other compensation have not been denied or lost to the employee, any actual monetary losses sustained by the employee as a direct result of the violation, such as the cost of providing care, up to a sum equal to 12 weeks of wages or salary for the employee;
(ii) the interest on the amount described in clause (i) calculated at the prevailing rate; and
(iii) an additional amount as liquidated damages equal to the sum of the amount described in clause (i) and the interest described in clause (ii), except that if an employer who has violated section 105 proves to the satisfaction of the court that the act or omission which violated section 105 was in good faith and that the employer had reasonable grounds for believing that the act or omission was not a violation of section 105, such court may, in the discretion of the court, reduce the amount of the liability to the amount and interest determined under clauses (i) and (ii), respectively; and
(B) for such equitable relief as may be appropriate, including employment, reinstatement, and promotion.

(2) RIGHT OF ACTION.—An action to recover the damages or equitable relief prescribed in paragraph (1) may be maintained against any employer (including a public agency) in any Federal or State court of competent jurisdiction by any one or more employees for and in behalf of—
    (A) the employees; or
    (B) the employees and other employees similarly situated.
(3) FEES AND COSTS.—The court in such an action shall, in addition to any judgment awarded to the plaintiff, allow a reasonable attorney's fee, reasonable expert witness fees, and other costs of the action to be paid by the defendant.
(4) LIMITATIONS.—The right provided by paragraph (2) to bring an action by or on behalf of any employee shall terminate—
    (A) on the filing of a complaint by the Secretary in an action under subsection (d) in which restraint is sought of any further delay in the payment of the amount described in paragraph (1)(A) to such employee by an employer responsible under paragraph (1) for the payment; or
    (B) on the filing of a complaint by the Secretary in an action under subsection (b) in which a recovery is sought of the damages described in paragraph (1)(A) owing to an eligible employee by an employer liable under paragraph (1),
unless the action described in subparagraph (A) or (B) is dismissed without prejudice on motion of the Secretary.
(b) ACTION BY THE SECRETARY.—
    (1) ADMINISTRATIVE ACTION.—The Secretary shall receive, investigate, and attempt to resolve complaints of violations of section 105 in the same manner that the Secretary receives, investigates, and attempts to resolve complaints of violations of sections 6 and 7 of the Fair Labor Standards Act of 1938 (29 U.S.C. 206 and 207).
    (2) CIVIL ACTION.—The Secretary may bring an action in any court of competent jurisdiction to recover the damages described in subsection (a)(1)(A).
    (3) SUMS RECOVERED.—Any sums recovered by the Secretary pursuant to paragraph (2) shall be held in a special deposit account and shall be paid, on order of the Secretary, directly to each employee affected. Any such sums not paid to an employee because of inability to do so within a period of 3 years shall be deposited into the Treasury of the United States as miscellaneous receipts.
(c) LIMITATION.—
    (1) IN GENERAL.—Except as provided in paragraph (2), an action may be brought under this section not later than 2 years after the date of the last event constituting the alleged violation for which the action is brought.
    (2) WILLFUL VIOLATION.—In the case of such action brought for a willful violation of section 105, such action may be brought within 3 years of the date of the last event constituting the alleged violation for which such action is brought.
    (3) COMMENCEMENT.—In determining when an action is commenced by the Secretary under this section for the purposes

PUBLIC LAW 103-3—FEB. 5, 1993   107 STAT. 17

of this subsection, it shall be considered to be commenced on the date when the complaint is filed.

(d) ACTION FOR INJUNCTION BY SECRETARY.—The district courts of the United States shall have jurisdiction, for cause shown, in an action brought by the Secretary—

    (1) to restrain violations of section 105, including the restraint of any withholding of payment of wages, salary, employment benefits, or other compensation, plus interest, found by the court to be due to eligible employees; or

    (2) to award such other equitable relief as may be appropriate, including employment, reinstatement, and promotion.

(e) SOLICITOR OF LABOR.—The Solicitor of Labor may appear for and represent the Secretary on any litigation brought under this section.

SEC. 108. SPECIAL RULES CONCERNING EMPLOYEES OF LOCAL EDUCATIONAL AGENCIES. 29 USC 2618.

(a) APPLICATION.—

    (1) IN GENERAL.—Except as otherwise provided in this section, the rights (including the rights under section 104, which shall extend throughout the period of leave of any employee under this section), remedies, and procedures under this title shall apply to—

        (A) any "local educational agency" (as defined in section 1471(12) of the Elementary and Secondary Education Act of 1965 (20 U.S.C. 2891(12))) and an eligible employee of the agency; and

        (B) any private elementary or secondary school and an eligible employee of the school.

    (2) DEFINITIONS.—For purposes of the application described in paragraph (1):

        (A) ELIGIBLE EMPLOYEE.—The term "eligible employee" means an eligible employee of an agency or school described in paragraph (1).

        (B) EMPLOYER.—The term "employer" means an agency or school described in paragraph (1).

(b) LEAVE DOES NOT VIOLATE CERTAIN OTHER FEDERAL LAWS.—A local educational agency and a private elementary or secondary school shall not be in violation of the Individuals with Disabilities Education Act (20 U.S.C. 1400 et seq.), section 504 of the Rehabilitation Act of 1973 (29 U.S.C. 794), or title VI of the Civil Rights Act of 1964 (42 U.S.C. 2000d et seq.), solely as a result of an eligible employee of such agency or school exercising the rights of such employee under this title.

(c) INTERMITTENT LEAVE OR LEAVE ON A REDUCED SCHEDULE FOR INSTRUCTIONAL EMPLOYEES.—

    (1) IN GENERAL.—Subject to paragraph (2), in any case in which an eligible employee employed principally in an instructional capacity by any such educational agency or school requests leave under subparagraph (C) or (D) of section 102(a)(1) that is foreseeable based on planned medical treatment and the employee would be on leave for greater than 20 percent of the total number of working days in the period during which the leave would extend, the agency or school may require that such employee elect either—

(A) to take leave for periods of a particular duration, not to exceed the duration of the planned medical treatment; or

(B) to transfer temporarily to an available alternative position offered by the employer for which the employee is qualified, and that—

(i) has equivalent pay and benefits; and

(ii) better accommodates recurring periods of leave than the regular employment position of the employee.

(2) APPLICATION.—The elections described in subparagraphs (A) and (B) of paragraph (1) shall apply only with respect to an eligible employee who complies with section 102(e)(2).

(d) RULES APPLICABLE TO PERIODS NEAR THE CONCLUSION OF AN ACADEMIC TERM.—The following rules shall apply with respect to periods of leave near the conclusion of an academic term in the case of any eligible employee employed principally in an instructional capacity by any such educational agency or school:

(1) LEAVE MORE THAN 5 WEEKS PRIOR TO END OF TERM.—If the eligible employee begins leave under section 102 more than 5 weeks prior to the end of the academic term, the agency or school may require the employee to continue taking leave until the end of such term, if—

(A) the leave is of at least 3 weeks duration; and

(B) the return to employment would occur during the 3-week period before the end of such term.

(2) LEAVE LESS THAN 5 WEEKS PRIOR TO END OF TERM.—If the eligible employee begins leave under subparagraph (A), (B), or (C) of section 102(a)(1) during the period that commences 5 weeks prior to the end of the academic term, the agency or school may require the employee to continue taking leave until the end of such term, if—

(A) the leave is of greater than 2 weeks duration; and

(B) the return to employment would occur during the 2-week period before the end of such term.

(3) LEAVE LESS THAN 3 WEEKS PRIOR TO END OF TERM.—If the eligible employee begins leave under subparagraph (A), (B), or (C) of section 102(a)(1) during the period that commences 3 weeks prior to the end of the academic term and the duration of the leave is greater than 5 working days, the agency or school may require the employee to continue to take leave until the end of such term.

(e) RESTORATION TO EQUIVALENT EMPLOYMENT POSITION.—For purposes of determinations under section 104(a)(1)(B) (relating to the restoration of an eligible employee to an equivalent position), in the case of a local educational agency or a private elementary or secondary school, such determination shall be made on the basis of established school board policies and practices, private school policies and practices, and collective bargaining agreements.

(f) REDUCTION OF THE AMOUNT OF LIABILITY.—If a local educational agency or a private elementary or secondary school that has violated this title proves to the satisfaction of the court that the agency, school, or department had reasonable grounds for believing that the underlying act or omission was not a violation of this title, such court may, in the discretion of the court, reduce the amount of the liability provided for under section 107(a)(1)(A)

PUBLIC LAW 103-3—FEB. 5, 1993   107 STAT. 19

to the amount and interest determined under clauses (i) and (ii), respectively, of such section.

SEC. 109. NOTICE.

29 USC 2619.

(a) IN GENERAL.—Each employer shall post and keep posted, in conspicuous places on the premises of the employer where notices to employees and applicants for employment are customarily posted, a notice, to be prepared or approved by the Secretary, setting forth excerpts from, or summaries of, the pertinent provisions of this title and information pertaining to the filing of a charge.

(b) PENALTY.—Any employer that willfully violates this section may be assessed a civil money penalty not to exceed $100 for each separate offense.

TITLE II—LEAVE FOR CIVIL SERVICE EMPLOYEES

SEC. 201. LEAVE REQUIREMENT.

(a) CIVIL SERVICE EMPLOYEES.—

(1) IN GENERAL.—Chapter 63 of title 5, United States Code, is amended by adding at the end the following new subchapter:

"SUBCHAPTER V—FAMILY AND MEDICAL LEAVE

"§ 6381. Definitions

"For the purpose of this subchapter—

"(1) the term 'employee' means any individual who—

"(A) is an 'employee', as defined by section 6301(2), including any individual employed in a position referred to in clause (v) or (ix) of section 6301(2), but excluding any individual employed by the government of the District of Columbia and any individual employed on a temporary or intermittent basis; and

"(B) has completed at least 12 months of service as an employee (within the meaning of subparagraph (A));

"(2) the term 'health care provider' means—

"(A) a doctor of medicine or osteopathy who is authorized to practice medicine or surgery (as appropriate) by the State in which the doctor practices; and

"(B) any other person determined by the Director of the Office of Personnel Management to be capable of providing health care services;

"(3) the term 'parent' means the biological parent of an employee or an individual who stood in loco parentis to an employee when the employee was a son or daughter;

"(4) the term 'reduced leave schedule' means a leave schedule that reduces the usual number of hours per workweek, or hours per workday, of an employee;

"(5) the term 'serious health condition' means an illness, injury, impairment, or physical or mental condition that involves—

"(A) inpatient care in a hospital, hospice, or residential medical care facility; or

"(B) continuing treatment by a health care provider; and

"(6) the term 'son or daughter' means a biological, adopted, or foster child, a stepchild, a legal ward, or a child of a person standing in loco parentis, who is—
"(A) under 18 years of age; or
"(B) 18 years of age or older and incapable of self-care because of a mental or physical disability.

"§ 6382. Leave requirement

"(a)(1) Subject to section 6383, an employee shall be entitled to a total of 12 administrative workweeks of leave during any 12-month period for one or more of the following:
"(A) Because of the birth of a son or daughter of the employee and in order to care for such son or daughter.
"(B) Because of the placement of a son or daughter with the employee for adoption or foster care.
"(C) In order to care for the spouse, or a son, daughter, or parent, of the employee, if such spouse, son, daughter, or parent has a serious health condition.
"(D) Because of a serious health condition that makes the employee unable to perform the functions of the employee's position.
"(2) The entitlement to leave under subparagraph (A) or (B) of paragraph (1) based on the birth or placement of a son or daughter shall expire at the end of the 12-month period beginning on the date of such birth or placement.

"(b)(1) Leave under subparagraph (A) or (B) of subsection (a)(1) shall not be taken by an employee intermittently or on a reduced leave schedule unless the employee and the employing agency of the employee agree otherwise. Subject to paragraph (2), subsection (e)(2), and section 6383(b)(5), leave under subparagraph (C) or (D) of subsection (a)(1) may be taken intermittently or on a reduced leave schedule when medically necessary. In the case of an employee who takes leave intermittently or on a reduced leave schedule pursuant to this paragraph, any hours of leave so taken by such employee shall be subtracted from the total amount of leave remaining available to such employee under subsection (a), for purposes of the 12-month period involved, on an hour-for-hour basis.

"(2) If an employee requests intermittent leave, or leave on a reduced leave schedule, under subparagraph (C) or (D) of subsection (a)(1), that is foreseeable based on planned medical treatment, the employing agency may require such employee to transfer temporarily to an available alternative position offered by the employing agency for which the employee is qualified and that—
"(A) has equivalent pay and benefits; and
"(B) better accommodates recurring periods of leave than the regular employment position of the employee.

"(c) Except as provided in subsection (d), leave granted under subsection (a) shall be leave without pay.

"(d) An employee may elect to substitute for leave under subparagraph (A), (B), (C), or (D) of subsection (a)(1) any of the employee's accrued or accumulated annual or sick leave under subchapter I for any part of the 12-week period of leave under such subsection, except that nothing in this subchapter shall require an employing agency to provide paid sick leave in any situation in which such employing agency would not normally provide any such paid leave.

"(e)(1) In any case in which the necessity for leave under subparagraph (A) or (B) of subsection (a)(1) is foreseeable based on an expected birth or placement, the employee shall provide the employing agency with not less than 30 days' notice, before the date the leave is to begin, of the employee's intention to take leave under such subparagraph, except that if the date of the birth or placement requires leave to begin in less than 30 days, the employee shall provide such notice as is practicable.

"(2) In any case in which the necessity for leave under subparagraph (C) or (D) of subsection (a)(1) is foreseeable based on planned medical treatment, the employee—

"(A) shall make a reasonable effort to schedule the treatment so as not to disrupt unduly the operations of the employing agency, subject to the approval of the health care provider of the employee or the health care provider of the son, daughter, spouse, or parent of the employee, as appropriate; and

"(B) shall provide the employing agency with not less than 30 days' notice, before the date the leave is to begin, of the employee's intention to take leave under such subparagraph, except that if the date of the treatment requires leave to begin in less than 30 days, the employee shall provide such notice as is practicable.

"§ 6383. Certification

"(a) An employing agency may require that a request for leave under subparagraph (C) or (D) of section 6382(a)(1) be supported by certification issued by the health care provider of the employee or of the son, daughter, spouse, or parent of the employee, as appropriate. The employee shall provide, in a timely manner, a copy of such certification to the employing agency.

"(b) A certification provided under subsection (a) shall be sufficient if it states—

"(1) the date on which the serious health condition commenced;

"(2) the probable duration of the condition;

"(3) the appropriate medical facts within the knowledge of the health care provider regarding the condition;

"(4)(A) for purposes of leave under section 6382(a)(1)(C), a statement that the employee is needed to care for the son, daughter, spouse, or parent, and an estimate of the amount of time that such employee is needed to care for such son, daughter, spouse, or parent; and

"(B) for purposes of leave under section 6382(a)(1)(D), a statement that the employee is unable to perform the functions of the position of the employee; and

"(5) in the case of certification for intermittent leave, or leave on a reduced leave schedule, for planned medical treatment, the dates on which such treatment is expected to be given and the duration of such treatment.

"(c)(1) In any case in which the employing agency has reason to doubt the validity of the certification provided under subsection (a) for leave under subparagraph (C) or (D) of section 6382(a)(1), the employing agency may require, at the expense of the agency, that the employee obtain the opinion of a second health care provider designated or approved by the employing agency concerning any information certified under subsection (b) for such leave.

"(e)(1) In any case in which the necessity for leave under subparagraph (A) or (B) of subsection (a)(1) is foreseeable based on an expected birth or placement, the employee shall provide the employing agency with not less than 30 days' notice, before the date the leave is to begin, of the employee's intention to take leave under such subparagraph, except that if the date of the birth or placement requires leave to begin in less than 30 days, the employee shall provide such notice as is practicable.

"(2) In any case in which the necessity for leave under subparagraph (C) or (D) of subsection (a)(1) is foreseeable based on planned medical treatment, the employee—

"(A) shall make a reasonable effort to schedule the treatment so as not to disrupt unduly the operations of the employing agency, subject to the approval of the health care provider of the employee or the health care provider of the son, daughter, spouse, or parent of the employee, as appropriate; and

"(B) shall provide the employing agency with not less than 30 days' notice, before the date the leave is to begin, of the employee's intention to take leave under such subparagraph, except that if the date of the treatment requires leave to begin in less than 30 days, the employee shall provide such notice as is practicable.

"§ 6383. Certification

"(a) An employing agency may require that a request for leave under subparagraph (C) or (D) of section 6382(a)(1) be supported by certification issued by the health care provider of the employee or of the son, daughter, spouse, or parent of the employee, as appropriate. The employee shall provide, in a timely manner, a copy of such certification to the employing agency.

"(b) A certification provided under subsection (a) shall be sufficient if it states—

"(1) the date on which the serious health condition commenced;

"(2) the probable duration of the condition;

"(3) the appropriate medical facts within the knowledge of the health care provider regarding the condition;

"(4)(A) for purposes of leave under section 6382(a)(1)(C), a statement that the employee is needed to care for the son, daughter, spouse, or parent, and an estimate of the amount of time that such employee is needed to care for such son, daughter, spouse, or parent; and

"(B) for purposes of leave under section 6382(a)(1)(D), a statement that the employee is unable to perform the functions of the position of the employee; and

"(5) in the case of certification for intermittent leave, or leave on a reduced leave schedule, for planned medical treatment, the dates on which such treatment is expected to be given and the duration of such treatment.

"(c)(1) In any case in which the employing agency has reason to doubt the validity of the certification provided under subsection (a) for leave under subparagraph (C) or (D) of section 6382(a)(1), the employing agency may require, at the expense of the agency, that the employee obtain the opinion of a second health care provider designated or approved by the employing agency concerning any information certified under subsection (b) for such leave.

"(2) Any health care provider designated or approved under paragraph (1) shall not be employed on a regular basis by the employing agency.

"(d)(1) In any case in which the second opinion described in subsection (c) differs from the original certification provided under subsection (a), the employing agency may require, at the expense of the agency, that the employee obtain the opinion of a third health care provider designated or approved jointly by the employing agency and the employee concerning the information certified under subsection (b).

"(2) The opinion of the third health care provider concerning the information certified under subsection (b) shall be considered to be final and shall be binding on the employing agency and the employee.

"(e) The employing agency may require, at the expense of the agency, that the employee obtain subsequent recertifications on a reasonable basis.

"§ 6384. Employment and benefits protection

"(a) Any employee who takes leave under section 6382 for the intended purpose of the leave shall be entitled, upon return from such leave—

"(1) to be restored by the employing agency to the position held by the employee when the leave commenced; or

"(2) to be restored to an equivalent position with equivalent benefits, pay, status, and other terms and conditions of employment.

"(b) The taking of leave under section 6382 shall not result in the loss of any employment benefit accrued prior to the date on which the leave commenced.

"(c) Except as otherwise provided by or under law, nothing in this section shall be construed to entitle any restored employee to—

"(1) the accrual of any employment benefits during any period of leave; or

"(2) any right, benefit, or position of employment other than any right, benefit, or position to which the employee would have been entitled had the employee not taken the leave.

"(d) As a condition to restoration under subsection (a) for an employee who takes leave under section 6382(a)(1)(D), the employing agency may have a uniformly applied practice or policy that requires each such employee to receive certification from the health care provider of the employee that the employee is able to resume work.

"(e) Nothing in this section shall be construed to prohibit an employing agency from requiring an employee on leave under section 6382 to report periodically to the employing agency on the status and intention of the employee to return to work.

"§ 6385. Prohibition of coercion

"(a) An employee shall not directly or indirectly intimidate, threaten, or coerce, or attempt to intimidate, threaten, or coerce, any other employee for the purpose of interfering with the exercise of any rights which such other employee may have under this subchapter.

"(b) For the purpose of this section—

PUBLIC LAW 103-3—FEB. 5, 1993   107 STAT. 23

"(1) the term 'intimidate, threaten, or coerce' includes promising to confer or conferring any benefit (such as appointment, promotion, or compensation), or taking or threatening to take any reprisal (such as deprivation of appointment, promotion, or compensation); and

"(2) the term 'employee' means any 'employee', as defined by section 2105.

"§ 6386. Health insurance

"An employee enrolled in a health benefits plan under chapter 89 who is placed in a leave status under section 6382 may elect to continue the health benefits enrollment of the employee while in such leave status and arrange to pay currently into the Employees Health Benefits Fund (described in section 8909), the appropriate employee contributions.

"§ 6387. Regulations

"The Office of Personnel Management shall prescribe regulations necessary for the administration of this subchapter. The regulations prescribed under this subchapter shall, to the extent appropriate, be consistent with the regulations prescribed by the Secretary of Labor to carry out title I of the Family and Medical Leave Act of 1993.".

(2) TABLE OF CONTENTS.—The table of contents for chapter 63 of title 5, United States Code, is amended by adding at the end the following:

"SUBCHAPTER V—FAMILY AND MEDICAL LEAVE

"6381. Definitions.
"6382. Leave requirement.
"6383. Certification.
"6384. Employment and benefits protection.
"6385. Prohibition of coercion.
"6386. Health insurance.
"6387. Regulations.".

(b) EMPLOYEES PAID FROM NONAPPROPRIATED FUNDS.—Section 2105(c)(1) of title 5, United States Code, is amended—

(1) by striking "or" at the end of subparagraph (C); and
(2) by adding at the end the following new subparagraph:

"(E) subchapter V of chapter 63, which shall be applied so as to construe references to benefit programs to refer to applicable programs for employees paid from nonappropriated funds; or".

TITLE III—COMMISSION ON LEAVE

SEC. 301. ESTABLISHMENT.   29 USC 2631.

There is established a commission to be known as the Commission on Leave (referred to in this title as the "Commission").

SEC. 302. DUTIES.   29 USC 2632.

The Commission shall—
(1) conduct a comprehensive study of—
(A) existing and proposed mandatory and voluntary policies relating to family and temporary medical leave, including policies provided by employers not covered under this Act;

PUBLIC LAW 103-3—FEB. 5, 1993

(B) the potential costs, benefits, and impact on productivity, job creation and business growth of such policies on employers and employees;
(C) possible differences in costs, benefits, and impact on productivity, job creation and business growth of such policies on employers based on business type and size;
(D) the impact of family and medical leave policies on the availability of employee benefits provided by employers, including employers not covered under this Act;
(E) alternate and equivalent State enforcement of title I with respect to employees described in section 108(a);
(F) methods used by employers to reduce administrative costs of implementing family and medical leave policies;
(G) the ability of the employers to recover, under section 104(c)(2), the premiums described in such section; and
(H) the impact on employers and employees of policies that provide temporary wage replacement during periods of family and medical leave.

Reports.
(2) not later than 2 years after the date on which the Commission first meets, prepare and submit, to the appropriate Committees of Congress, a report concerning the subjects listed in paragraph (1).

29 USC 2633.
SEC. 303. MEMBERSHIP.

(a) COMPOSITION.—
(1) APPOINTMENTS.—The Commission shall be composed of 12 voting members and 4 ex officio members to be appointed not later than 60 days after the date of the enactment of this Act as follows:
(A) SENATORS.—One Senator shall be appointed by the Majority Leader of the Senate, and one Senator shall be appointed by the Minority Leader of the Senate.
(B) MEMBERS OF HOUSE OF REPRESENTATIVES.—One Member of the House of Representatives shall be appointed by the Speaker of the House of Representatives, and one Member of the House of Representatives shall be appointed by the Minority Leader of the House of Representatives.
(C) ADDITIONAL MEMBERS.—
(i) APPOINTMENT.—Two members each shall be appointed by—
(I) the Speaker of the House of Representatives;
(II) the Majority Leader of the Senate;
(III) the Minority Leader of the House of Representatives; and
(IV) the Minority Leader of the Senate.
(ii) EXPERTISE.—Such members shall be appointed by virtue of demonstrated expertise in relevant family, temporary disability, and labor management issues. Such members shall include representatives of employers, including employers from large businesses and from small businesses.
(2) EX OFFICIO MEMBERS.—The Secretary of Health and Human Services, the Secretary of Labor, the Secretary of Commerce, and the Administrator of the Small Business Adminis-

tration shall serve on the Commission as nonvoting ex officio members.

(b) VACANCIES.—Any vacancy on the Commission shall be filled in the manner in which the original appointment was made. The vacancy shall not affect the power of the remaining members to execute the duties of the Commission.

(c) CHAIRPERSON AND VICE CHAIRPERSON.—The Commission shall elect a chairperson and a vice chairperson from among the members of the Commission.

(d) QUORUM.—Eight members of the Commission shall constitute a quorum for all purposes, except that a lesser number may constitute a quorum for the purpose of holding hearings.

SEC. 304. COMPENSATION. 29 USC 2634.

(a) PAY.—Members of the Commission shall serve without compensation.

(b) TRAVEL EXPENSES.—Members of the Commission shall be allowed reasonable travel expenses, including a per diem allowance, in accordance with section 5703 of title 5, United States Code, when performing duties of the Commission.

SEC. 305. POWERS. 29 USC 2635.

(a) MEETINGS.—The Commission shall first meet not later than 30 days after the date on which all members are appointed, and the Commission shall meet thereafter on the call of the chairperson or a majority of the members.

(b) HEARINGS AND SESSIONS.—The Commission may hold such hearings, sit and act at such times and places, take such testimony, and receive such evidence as the Commission considers appropriate. The Commission may administer oaths or affirmations to witnesses appearing before it.

(c) ACCESS TO INFORMATION.—The Commission may secure directly from any Federal agency information necessary to enable it to carry out this title, if the information may be disclosed under section 552 of title 5, United States Code. Subject to the previous sentence, on the request of the chairperson or vice chairperson of the Commission, the head of such agency shall furnish such information to the Commission.

(d) USE OF FACILITIES AND SERVICES.—Upon the request of the Commission, the head of any Federal agency may make available to the Commission any of the facilities and services of such agency.

(e) PERSONNEL FROM OTHER AGENCIES.—On the request of the Commission, the head of any Federal agency may detail any of the personnel of such agency to serve as an Executive Director of the Commission or assist the Commission in carrying out the duties of the Commission. Any detail shall not interrupt or otherwise affect the civil service status or privileges of the Federal employee.

(f) VOLUNTARY SERVICE.—Notwithstanding section 1342 of title 31, United States Code, the chairperson of the Commission may accept for the Commission voluntary services provided by a member of the Commission.

SEC. 306. TERMINATION. 29 USC 2636.

The Commission shall terminate 30 days after the date of the submission of the report of the Commission to Congress.

TITLE IV—MISCELLANEOUS PROVISIONS

29 USC 2651.

SEC. 401. EFFECT ON OTHER LAWS.

(a) FEDERAL AND STATE ANTIDISCRIMINATION LAWS.—Nothing in this Act or any amendment made by this Act shall be construed to modify or affect any Federal or State law prohibiting discrimination on the basis of race, religion, color, national origin, sex, age, or disability.

(b) STATE AND LOCAL LAWS.—Nothing in this Act or any amendment made by this Act shall be construed to supersede any provision of any State or local law that provides greater family or medical leave rights than the rights established under this Act or any amendment made by this Act.

29 USC 2652.

SEC. 402. EFFECT ON EXISTING EMPLOYMENT BENEFITS.

(a) MORE PROTECTIVE.—Nothing in this Act or any amendment made by this Act shall be construed to diminish the obligation of an employer to comply with any collective bargaining agreement or any employment benefit program or plan that provides greater family or medical leave rights to employees than the rights established under this Act or any amendment made by this Act.

(b) LESS PROTECTIVE.—The rights established for employees under this Act or any amendment made by this Act shall not be diminished by any collective bargaining agreement or any employment benefit program or plan.

29 USC 2653.

SEC. 403. ENCOURAGEMENT OF MORE GENEROUS LEAVE POLICIES.

Nothing in this Act or any amendment made by this Act shall be construed to discourage employers from adopting or retaining leave policies more generous than any policies that comply with the requirements under this Act or any amendment made by this Act.

29 USC 2654.

SEC. 404. REGULATIONS.

The Secretary of Labor shall prescribe such regulations as are necessary to carry out title I and this title not later than 120 days after the date of the enactment of this Act.

29 USC 2601 note.

SEC. 405. EFFECTIVE DATES.

(a) TITLE III.—Title III shall take effect on the date of the enactment of this Act.

(b) OTHER TITLES.—

(1) IN GENERAL.—Except as provided in paragraph (2), titles I, II, and V and this title shall take effect 6 months after the date of the enactment of this Act.

(2) COLLECTIVE BARGAINING AGREEMENTS.—In the case of a collective bargaining agreement in effect on the effective date prescribed by paragraph (1), title I shall apply on the earlier of—

(A) the date of the termination of such agreement; or

(B) the date that occurs 12 months after the date of the enactment of this Act.

PUBLIC LAW 103-3—FEB. 5, 1993   107 STAT. 27

TITLE V—COVERAGE OF CONGRESSIONAL EMPLOYEES

SEC. 501. LEAVE FOR CERTAIN SENATE EMPLOYEES.   2 USC 60m.

(a) COVERAGE.—The rights and protections established under sections 101 through 105 shall apply with respect to a Senate employee and an employing office. For purposes of such application, the term "eligible employee" means a Senate employee and the term "employer" means an employing office.

(b) CONSIDERATION OF ALLEGATIONS.—

(1) APPLICABLE PROVISIONS.—The provisions of sections 304 through 313 of the Government Employee Rights Act of 1991 (2 U.S.C. 1204–1213) shall, except as provided in subsections (d) and (e)—

(A) apply with respect to an allegation of a violation of a provision of sections 101 through 105, with respect to Senate employment of a Senate employee; and

(B) apply to such an allegation in the same manner and to the same extent as such sections of the Government Employee Rights Act of 1991 apply with respect to an allegation of a violation under such Act.

(2) ENTITY.—Such an allegation shall be addressed by the Office of Senate Fair Employment Practices or such other entity as the Senate may designate.

(c) RIGHTS OF EMPLOYEES.—The Office of Senate Fair Employment Practices shall ensure that Senate employees are informed of their rights under sections 101 through 105.

(d) LIMITATIONS.—A request for counseling under section 305 of such Act by a Senate employee alleging a violation of a provision of sections 101 through 105 shall be made not later than 2 years after the date of the last event constituting the alleged violation for which the counseling is requested, or not later than 3 years after such date in the case of a willful violation of section 105.

(e) APPLICABLE REMEDIES.—The remedies applicable to individuals who demonstrate a violation of a provision of sections 101 through 105 shall be such remedies as would be appropriate if awarded under paragraph (1) or (3) of section 107(a).

(f) EXERCISE OF RULEMAKING POWER.—The provisions of subsections (b), (c), (d), and (e), except as such subsections apply with respect to section 309 of the Government Employee Rights Act of 1991 (2 U.S.C. 1209), are enacted by the Senate as an exercise of the rulemaking power of the Senate, with full recognition of the right of the Senate to change its rules, in the same manner, and to the same extent, as in the case of any other rule of the Senate. No Senate employee may commence a judicial proceeding with respect to an allegation described in subsection (b)(1), except as provided in this section.

PUBLIC LAW 103-3—FEB. 5, 1993   107 STAT. 27

TITLE V—COVERAGE OF CONGRESSIONAL EMPLOYEES

SEC. 501. LEAVE FOR CERTAIN SENATE EMPLOYEES.   2 USC 60m.

(a) COVERAGE.—The rights and protections established under sections 101 through 105 shall apply with respect to a Senate employee and an employing office. For purposes of such application, the term "eligible employee" means a Senate employee and the term "employer" means an employing office.

(b) CONSIDERATION OF ALLEGATIONS.—

(1) APPLICABLE PROVISIONS.—The provisions of sections 304 through 313 of the Government Employee Rights Act of 1991 (2 U.S.C. 1204–1213) shall, except as provided in subsections (d) and (e)—

(A) apply with respect to an allegation of a violation of a provision of sections 101 through 105, with respect to Senate employment of a Senate employee; and

(B) apply to such an allegation in the same manner and to the same extent as such sections of the Government Employee Rights Act of 1991 apply with respect to an allegation of a violation under such Act.

(2) ENTITY.—Such an allegation shall be addressed by the Office of Senate Fair Employment Practices or such other entity as the Senate may designate.

(c) RIGHTS OF EMPLOYEES.—The Office of Senate Fair Employment Practices shall ensure that Senate employees are informed of their rights under sections 101 through 105.

(d) LIMITATIONS.—A request for counseling under section 305 of such Act by a Senate employee alleging a violation of a provision of sections 101 through 105 shall be made not later than 2 years after the date of the last event constituting the alleged violation for which the counseling is requested, or not later than 3 years after such date in the case of a willful violation of section 105.

(e) APPLICABLE REMEDIES.—The remedies applicable to individuals who demonstrate a violation of a provision of sections 101 through 105 shall be such remedies as would be appropriate if awarded under paragraph (1) or (3) of section 107(a).

(f) EXERCISE OF RULEMAKING POWER.—The provisions of subsections (b), (c), (d), and (e), except as such subsections apply with respect to section 309 of the Government Employee Rights Act of 1991 (2 U.S.C. 1209), are enacted by the Senate as an exercise of the rulemaking power of the Senate, with full recognition of the right of the Senate to change its rules, in the same manner, and to the same extent, as in the case of any other rule of the Senate. No Senate employee may commence a judicial proceeding with respect to an allegation described in subsection (b)(1), except as provided in this section.

107 STAT. 28   PUBLIC LAW 103-3—FEB. 5, 1993

(g) SEVERABILITY.—Notwithstanding any other provision of law, if any provision of section 309 of the Government Employee Rights Act of 1991 (2 U.S.C. 1209), or of subsection (b)(1) insofar as it applies such section 309 to an allegation described in subsection (b)(1)(A), is invalidated, both such section 309, and subsection (b)(1) insofar as it applies such section 309 to such an allegation, shall have no force and effect, and shall be considered to be invalidated for purposes of section 322 of such Act (2 U.S.C. 1221).

(h) DEFINITIONS.—As used in this section:

(1) EMPLOYING OFFICE.—The term "employing office" means the office with the final authority described in section 301(2) of such Act (2 U.S.C. 1201(2)).

(2) SENATE EMPLOYEE.—The term "Senate employee" means an employee described in subparagraph (A) or (B) of section 301(c)(1) of such Act (2 U.S.C. 1201(c)(1)) who has been employed for at least 12 months on other than a temporary or intermittent basis by any employing office.

2 USC 60n.   SEC. 502. LEAVE FOR CERTAIN HOUSE EMPLOYEES.

(a) IN GENERAL.—The rights and protections under sections 102 through 105 (other than section 104(b)) shall apply to any employee in an employment position and any employing authority of the House of Representatives.

(b) ADMINISTRATION.—In the administration of this section, the remedies and procedures under the Fair Employment Practices Resolution shall be applied.

(c) DEFINITION.—As used in this section, the term "Fair Employment Practices Resolution" means rule LI of the Rules of the House of Representatives.

TITLE VI—SENSE OF CONGRESS

SEC. 601. SENSE OF CONGRESS.

It is the sense of the Congress that:

(a) The Secretary of Defense shall conduct a comprehensive review of current departmental policy with respect to the service of homosexuals in the Armed Forces;

(b) Such review shall include the basis for the current policy of mandatory separation; the rights of all service men and women, and the effects of any change in such policy on morale, discipline, and military effectiveness;

Reports.   (c) The Secretary shall report the results of such review and consultations and his recommendations to the President and to the Congress no later than July 15, 1993;

PUBLIC LAW 103-3—FEB. 5, 1993   107 STAT. 29

(d) The Senate Committee on Armed Services shall conduct (i) comprehensive hearings on the current military policy with respect to the service of homosexuals in the military services; and (ii) shall conduct oversight hearings on the Secretary's recommendations as such are reported.

Approved February 5, 1993.

LEGISLATIVE HISTORY—H.R. 1 (S. 5):

HOUSE REPORTS: No. 103-8, Pt. 1 (Comm. on Education and Labor) and Pt. 2 (Comm. on Post Office and Civil Service).
SENATE REPORTS: No. 103-3 accompanying S. 5 (Comm. on Labor and Human Resources).
CONGRESSIONAL RECORD, Vol. 139 (1993):
    Feb. 2, S. 5 considered in Senate.
    Feb. 3, considered in Senate; H.R. 1 considered and passed House.
    Feb. 4, H.R. 1 considered and passed Senate, amended, in lieu of S. 5. House concurred in Senate amendment.
WEEKLY COMPILATION OF PRESIDENTIAL DOCUMENTS, Vol. 29 (1993):
    Feb. 5, Presidential remarks and statement.

Certification of Health Care Provider for
Employee's Serious Health Condition
(Family and Medical Leave Act)

U.S. Department of Labor
Wage and Hour Division

OMB Control Number: 1235-0003
Expires: 2/28/2015

SECTION I: For Completion by the EMPLOYER
INSTRUCTIONS to the EMPLOYER: The Family and Medical Leave Act (FMLA) provides that an employer may require an employee seeking FMLA protections because of a need for leave due to a serious health condition to submit a medical certification issued by the employee's health care provider. Please complete Section I before giving this form to your employee. Your response is voluntary. While you are not required to use this form, you may not ask the employee to provide more information than allowed under the FMLA regulations, 29 C.F.R. §§ 825.306-825.308. Employers must generally maintain records and documents relating to medical certifications, recertifications, or medical histories of employees created for FMLA purposes as confidential medical records in separate files/records from the usual personnel files and in accordance with 29 C.F.R. § 1630.14(c)(1), if the Americans with Disabilities Act applies.

Employer name and contact: _____

Employee's job title: _____ Regular work schedule: _____

Employee's essential job functions: _____

Check if job description is attached: _____

SECTION II: For Completion by the EMPLOYEE
INSTRUCTIONS to the EMPLOYEE: Please complete Section II before giving this form to your medical provider. The FMLA permits an employer to require that you submit a timely, complete, and sufficient medical certification to support a request for FMLA leave due to your own serious health condition. If requested by your employer, your response is required to obtain or retain the benefit of FMLA protections. 29 U.S.C. §§ 2613, 2614(c)(3). Failure to provide a complete and sufficient medical certification may result in a denial of your FMLA request. 20 C.F.R. § 825.313. Your employer must give you at least 15 calendar days to return this form. 29 C.F.R. § 825.305(b).

Your name: _____
First   Middle   Last

SECTION III: For Completion by the HEALTH CARE PROVIDER
INSTRUCTIONS to the HEALTH CARE PROVIDER: Your patient has requested leave under the FMLA. Answer, fully and completely, all applicable parts. Several questions seek a response as to the frequency or duration of a condition, treatment, etc. Your answer should be your best estimate based upon your medical knowledge, experience, and examination of the patient. Be as specific as you can; terms such as "lifetime," "unknown," or "indeterminate" may not be sufficient to determine FMLA coverage. Limit your responses to the condition for which the employee is seeking leave. Please be sure to sign the form on the last page.

Provider's name and business address: _____

Type of practice / Medical specialty: _____

Telephone: (___) _____ Fax: (___) _____

Page 1   CONTINUED ON NEXT PAGE   Form WH-380-E Revised January 2009

74 • *Maternity Leave: Policy and Practice*

PART A: MEDICAL FACTS
1. Approximate date condition commenced: _____

   Probable duration of condition: _____

   Mark below as applicable:
   Was the patient admitted for an overnight stay in a hospital, hospice, or residential medical care facility?
   ___No ___Yes. If so, dates of admission:

   _____

   Date(s) you treated the patient for condition:

   _____

   Will the patient need to have treatment visits at least twice per year due to the condition? ___No ___Yes.

   Was medication, other than over-the-counter medication, prescribed? ___No ___Yes.

   Was the patient referred to other health care provider(s) for evaluation or treatment (e.g., physical therapist)?
   ___No ___Yes. If so, state the nature of such treatments and expected duration of treatment:

   _____

2. Is the medical condition pregnancy? ___No ___Yes. If so, expected delivery date: _____

3. Use the information provided by the employer in Section I to answer this question. If the employer fails to provide a list of the employee's essential functions or a job description, answer these questions based upon the employee's own description of his/her job functions.

   Is the employee unable to perform any of his/her job functions due to the condition: ____ No ____ Yes.

   If so, identify the job functions the employee is unable to perform:

   _____

4. Describe other relevant medical facts, if any, related to the condition for which the employee seeks leave (such medical facts may include symptoms, diagnosis, or any regimen of continuing treatment such as the use of specialized equipment):

   _____
   _____
   _____
   _____
   _____
   _____
   _____

PART B: AMOUNT OF LEAVE NEEDED

5. Will the employee be incapacitated for a single continuous period of time due to his/her medical condition, including any time for treatment and recovery? ___No ___Yes.

   If so, estimate the beginning and ending dates for the period of incapacity: _____

6. Will the employee need to attend follow-up treatment appointments or work part-time or on a reduced schedule because of the employee's medical condition? ___No ___Yes.

   If so, are the treatments or the reduced number of hours of work medically necessary?
   ___No ___Yes.

   Estimate treatment schedule, if any, including the dates of any scheduled appointments and the time required for each appointment, including any recovery period:

   _____

   Estimate the part-time or reduced work schedule the employee needs, if any:

   _____ hour(s) per day; _____ days per week from _____ through _____

7. Will the condition cause episodic flare-ups periodically preventing the employee from performing his/her job functions? ___No ___Yes.

   Is it medically necessary for the employee to be absent from work during the flare-ups?
   ___ No ___ Yes. If so, explain:

   _____
   _____

   Based upon the patient's medical history and your knowledge of the medical condition, estimate the frequency of flare-ups and the duration of related incapacity that the patient may have over the next 6 months (e.g., 1 episode every 3 months lasting 1-2 days):

Frequency   : _____ times per _____ week(s) _____ month(s)

           Duration: _____ hours or ___ day(s) per episode

ADDITIONAL INFORMATION: IDENTIFY QUESTION NUMBER WITH YOUR ADDITIONAL ANSWER.

_____
_____
_____
_____
_____
_____

Signature of Health Care Provider   **Date**

PAPERWORK REDUCTION ACT NOTICE AND PUBLIC BURDEN STATEMENT
If submitted, it is mandatory for employers to retain a copy of this disclosure in their records for three years. 29 U.S.C. § 2616; 29 C.F.R. § 825.500. Persons are not required to respond to this collection of information unless it displays a currently valid OMB control number. The Department of Labor estimates that it will take an average of 20 minutes for respondents to complete this collection of information, including the time for reviewing instructions, searching existing data sources, gathering and maintaining the data needed, and completing and reviewing the collection of information. If you have any comments regarding this burden estimate or any other aspect of this collection information, including suggestions for reducing this burden, send them to the Administrator, Wage and Hour Division, U.S. Department of Labor, Room S-3502, 200 Constitution Ave., NW, Washington, DC 20210. **DO NOT SEND COMPLETED FORM TO THE DEPARTMENT OF LABOR; RETURN TO THE PATIENT.**

Certification of Health Care Provider for
Family Member's Serious Health Condition
(Family and Medical Leave Act)

U.S. Department of Labor
Wage and Hour Division

OMB Control Number: 1235-0003
Expires: 2/28/2015

SECTION I: For Completion by the EMPLOYER
INSTRUCTIONS to the EMPLOYER: The Family and Medical Leave Act (FMLA) provides that an employer may require an employee seeking FMLA protections because of a need for leave to care for a covered family member with a serious health condition to submit a medical certification issued by the health care provider of the covered family member. Please complete Section I before giving this form to your employee. Your response is voluntary. While you are not required to use this form, you may not ask the employee to provide more information than allowed under the FMLA regulations, 29 C.F.R. §§ 825.306-825.308. Employers must generally maintain records and documents relating to medical certifications, recertifications, or medical histories of employees' family members, created for FMLA purposes as confidential medical records in separate files/records from the usual personnel files and in accordance with 29 C.F.R. § 1630.14(c)(1), if the Americans with Disabilities Act applies.

Employer name and contact: _____

SECTION II: For Completion by the EMPLOYEE
INSTRUCTIONS to the EMPLOYEE: Please complete Section II before giving this form to your family member or his/her medical provider. The FMLA permits an employer to require that you submit a timely, complete, and sufficient medical certification to support a request for FMLA leave to care for a covered family member with a serious health condition. If requested by your employer, your response is required to obtain or retain the benefit of FMLA protections. 29 U.S.C. §§ 2613, 2614(c)(3). Failure to provide a complete and sufficient medical certification may result in a denial of your FMLA request. 29 C.F.R. § 825.313. Your employer must give you at least 15 calendar days to return this form to your employer. 29 C.F.R. § 825.305.

Your name: _____
              First   Middle   Last

Name of family member for whom you will provide care: _____
                                            First   Middle   Last
Relationship of family member to you: _____

    If family member is your son or daughter, date of birth: _____

Describe care you will provide to your family member and estimate leave needed to provide care:

_____
_____
_____
_____

_____   _____
Employee Signature   Date

CONTINUED ON NEXT PAGE   Form WH-380-F Revised January 2009

78 • *Maternity Leave: Policy and Practice*

SECTION III: For Completion by the HEALTH CARE PROVIDER
INSTRUCTIONS to the HEALTH CARE PROVIDER: The employee listed above has requested leave under the FMLA to care for your patient. Answer, fully and completely, all applicable parts below. Several questions seek a response as to the frequency or duration of a condition, treatment, etc. Your answer should be your best estimate based upon your medical knowledge, experience, and examination of the patient. Be as specific as you can; terms such as "lifetime," "unknown," or "indeterminate" may not be sufficient to determine FMLA coverage. Limit your responses to the condition for which the patient needs leave. Page 3 provides space for additional information, should you need it. Please be sure to sign the form on the last page.

Provider's name and business address: _____

Type of practice / Medical specialty: _____

Telephone: (_____) _____ Fax:(_____) _____

PART A: MEDICAL FACTS

1. Approximate date condition commenced: _____

   Probable duration of condition: _____

   Was the patient admitted for an overnight stay in a hospital, hospice, or residential medical care facility?
   ___ No ___ Yes. If so, dates of admission: _____

   Date(s) you treated the patient for condition: _____

   Was medication, other than over-the-counter medication, prescribed? ___ No ___ Yes.

   Will the patient need to have treatment visits at least twice per year due to the condition? ___ No ___ Yes

   Was the patient referred to other health care provider(s) for evaluation or treatment (e.g., physical therapist)?
   ____ No ____ Yes. If so, state the nature of such treatments and expected duration of treatment:
   _____
   _____

2. Is the medical condition pregnancy? ___ No ___ Yes. If so, expected delivery date: _____

3. Describe other relevant medical facts, if any, related to the condition for which the patient needs care (such medical facts may include symptoms, diagnosis, or any regimen of continuing treatment such as the use of specialized equipment):
   _____
   _____
   _____

Background • 79

PART B: AMOUNT OF CARE NEEDED: When answering these questions, keep in mind that your patient's need for care by the employee seeking leave may include assistance with basic medical, hygienic, nutritional, safety or transportation needs, or the provision of physical or psychological care:

4. Will the patient be incapacitated for a single continuous period of time, including any time for treatment and recovery? ___No ___Yes.

   Estimate the beginning and ending dates for the period of incapacity: _____

   During this time, will the patient need care? __ No __ Yes.

   Explain the care needed by the patient and why such care is medically necessary:

   _____
   _____
   _____
   _____
   _____

5. Will the patient require follow-up treatments, including any time for recovery? ___No ___Yes.

   Estimate treatment schedule, if any, including the dates of any scheduled appointments and the time required for each appointment, including any recovery period:

   _____

   Explain the care needed by the patient, and why such care is medically necessary: _____

   _____

6. Will the patient require care on an intermittent or reduced schedule basis, including any time for recovery? __ No __ Yes.

   Estimate the hours the patient needs care on an intermittent basis, if any:

   _____ hour(s) per day; _____ days per week   from _____ through _____

   Explain the care needed by the patient, and why such care is medically necessary:

   _____
   _____
   _____
   _____

80 • *Maternity Leave: Policy and Practice*

7. Will the condition cause episodic flare-ups periodically preventing the patient from participating in normal daily activities? ____No ____Yes.

Based upon the patient's medical history and your knowledge of the medical condition, estimate the frequency of flare-ups and the duration of related incapacity that the patient may have over the next 6 months (e.g., 1 episode every 3 months lasting 1-2 days):

Frequency: _____ times per _____ week(s) _____ month(s)

Duration: _____ hours or ___ day(s) per episode

Does the patient need care during these flare-ups? ____ No ____ Yes.

Explain the care needed by the patient, and why such care is medically necessary: _____

_____
_____
_____
_____

ADDITIONAL INFORMATION: IDENTIFY QUESTION NUMBER WITH YOUR ADDITIONAL ANSWER.

_____
_____
_____
_____
_____
_____
_____

Signature of Health Care Provider   **Date**

PAPERWORK REDUCTION ACT NOTICE AND PUBLIC BURDEN STATEMENT

If submitted, it is mandatory for employers to retain a copy of this disclosure in their records for three years. 29 U.S.C. § 2616; 29 C.F.R. § 825.500. Persons are not required to respond to this collection of information unless it displays a currently valid OMB control number. The Department of Labor estimates that it will take an average of 20 minutes for respondents to complete this collection of information, including the time for reviewing instructions, searching existing data sources, gathering and maintaining the data needed, and completing and reviewing the collection of information. If you have any comments regarding this burden estimate or any other aspect of this collection information, including suggestions for reducing this burden, send them to the Administrator, Wage and Hour Division, U.S. Department of Labor, Room S-3502, 200 Constitution Ave., NW, Washington, DC 20210.
DO NOT SEND COMPLETED FORM TO THE DEPARTMENT OF LABOR; RETURN TO THE PATIENT.

REFERENCES

Anthony, D. 2008. The hidden harms of the family and medical leave act: Gender-neutral versus gender equal. *American University Journal of Gender, Social Policy and the Law* 16 (4): 459–501.

Brill, S. 2007. Strengthen paternity leave by encouraging voluntary standards for businesses. *Policy Studies Journal* 35 (3): 540–541.

Carter, J. 1978. Occupational discrimination based on pregnancy statement on signing S. 995 into law. The American Presidency Project developed by G. Peters and J. T. Woolley. http://www.presidency.ucsb.edu/ws/?pid=30079 (accessed August 25, 2012).

Childress, M. 1999. *Childcare in Kentucky: Current Status and Future Improvements.* Frankfort, KY: The Kentucky Long-Term Policy Research Center.

Clinton, W. 1993. Statement on signing the Family and Medical Leave Act of 1993. The American Presidency Project developed by G. Peters and J. T. Woolley. http://www.presidency.ucsb.edu/ws/?pid=46777 (accessed August 26, 2012).

Connelly, R., and K. Ghodsee. 2011. *Professor Mommy: Finding Work-Family Balance in Academia.* Lanham, MD: Rowman and Littlefield Publishers, Inc.

Dunbar, A. 2012. Child care credit. http://www.taxpolicycenter.org/taxtopics/encyclopedia/Child-care-credit.cfm (accessed August 25, 2012).

Edelman, M. 1985. *The Symbolic Uses of Politics.* Urbana, IL: University of Illinois Press.

Esenwein, G. 2012. Child tax credit. http://www.taxpolicycenter.org/taxtopics/encyclopedia/child-tax-credit.cfm (accessed August 25, 2012).

Family and Medical Leave Act of 1993. February 5, 1993. Public Law 103-3. http://library.clerk.house.gov/reference-files/PPL_FamilyMedicalLeaveAct.pdf (accessed October 26, 2012).

Frederickson, H. G. 1997. *The Spirit of Public Administration.* San Francisco, CA: Jossey-Bass.

Grossman, J. 2008. The thirtieth anniversary of the Pregnancy Discrimination Act: Cause for celebration, but also reflection on the progress yet to be made. http://writ.lp.findlaw.com/grossman (accessed August 24, 2012).

Hallett, T. 2003. Symbolic power and organizational culture. *Sociological Theory* 21 (2): 128–149.

Hallstein, D. L. 2008. Silences and choice: The legacies of white second wave feminism in the new professoriate. *Women's Studies in Communication* 31 (2): 143–150.

Karoly, L. A., P. W. Greenwood, S. S. Everingham, J. Houbé, M. R. Kilburn, C. P. Rydell, M. Sanders, and J. Chiesa. 1998. *Investing in Our Children: What We Know and Don't Know about the Costs and Benefits of Early Childhood Interventions.* Santa Monica, CA: RAND.

Kleba, K., and L. Batchis. 2011. Reasonable break time for nursing mothers clarified. *Legal Report: Society for Human Resources Management*: 1–4. http://www.shrm.org/law (accessed July 1, 2011).

Lenhoff, D. 2004. Family and medical leave in the United States: Historical and political reflections. Paper presented at conference at University of Minnesota.

McGlen, N., and K. O'Connor. 1998. *Women, Politics and American Society.* Upper Saddle River, NJ: Prentice-Hall.

Murtagh, L., and A. Moulton. 2011. Strategies to protect vulnerable populations: Working mothers, breastfeeding and the law. *Government, Politics and Law* 101 (2): 217–223.

Nadler, J. May 8, 2012. Introductory remarks to the House of Representatives on Pregnant Workers Fairness Act.

National Association of Child Care Resources and Referral Agencies. 2011. Child Care in America: 2011 State Fact Sheets. http://www.NACCRRA.org (accessed August 14, 2012).

National Association of Child Care Resources and Referral Agencies. 2012. Child Care in America: 2012 State Fact Sheets. http://www.NACCRRA.org (accessed August 27, 2012).

O'Leary, A. 2007. How family leave laws left out low-income workers. *Berkeley Journal of Employment and Labor Law* 28 (1): 1–62.

Patient Protection and Affordable Care Act. March 23, 2010. Public Law 111–148. http://www.gpo.gov/fdsys/pkg/PLAW-111publ148/pdf/PLAW-111publ148.pdf (accessed October 26, 2012).

Pregnancy Discrimination Act. October 31, 1978. Public Law 95–955. http://infousa.state.gov/government/branches/docs/pregact.pdf (accessed August 24, 2012).

Rawls, J. 1971. *A Theory of Justice*. Cambridge, MA: Harvard University Press.

Skafida, V. 2012. Juggling work and motherhood: The impact of employment and maternity leave on breastfeeding duration: A survival analysis on growing up in Scotland data. *Maternal and Child Health Journal* 16: 519–527.

Sloan Work and Family Research Network. 2007. 2007 Legislative summary sheet: Survey of bills related to breastfeeding and the workplace introduced into state legislatures. http://www.bc.edu/wfnetwork.

Stone, D. 2002. *Policy paradox: The Art of Political Decision Making*. New York, NY: W. W. Norton and Company.

U.S. Congress. House of Representatives. *Pregnant Workers Fairness Act*. HR 5647. 112th Congress, 2nd session.

U.S. Chamber of Commerce. 2005. Real experiences administering the FMLA: Why the regulations need reform. http://www.uschamber.com.

U.S. Department of Labor. Employment Standards Administration. Wage and Hour Division. June 28, 2007. Proposed Rules: 29 CFR Part 825, Family and Medical Leave Act Regulations: A Report on the Department of Labor's Request for Information. *Federal Register* 72 (124): 35,550–35,638. http://www.dol.gov/esa/whd/fmla2007report.htm.

U.S. Department of Labor. Wage and Hour Division. 2008. Final rule on Family and Medical Leave: Providing military family leave and updates to the regulations. http://www.wagehour.dol.gov.

U.S. Department of Labor. Wage and Hour Division. February 2010. Fact sheet #28: The Family and Medical Leave Act of 1993. http://www.wagehour.dol.gov.

U.S. Department of Labor. Wage and Hour Division. December 2010. Fact sheet #73: Break time for nursing mothers under the FLSA. http://www.wagehour.dol.gov.

U.S. Equal Employment Opportunity Commission. February 2, 2007. Discussion letter on Title VII pregnancy discrimination in job interviews. http://www.eeoc.gov/eeoc/foia/letters/2007/pregnancy_discrimination.html (accessed August 24, 2012).

U.S. Equal Employment Opportunity Commission. 2012a. Pregnancy discrimination charges, EEOC and Fair Employment Practices Agencies, combined FY 1997–FY 2011. http://www.eeoc.gov/eeoc/statistics/enforcement/pregnancy.cfm (accessed August 24, 2012).

U.S. Equal Employment Opportunity Commission. 2012b. Pregnancy discrimination charges, EEOC and Fair Employment Practices Agencies, combined FY 1992–FY 1996. http://www.eeoc.gov/eeoc/statistics/enforcement/pregnancy-a.cfm (accessed August 24, 2012).

Vandell, D. L., J. Belsky, M. Burchinal, L. Steinberg, N. Vandergrift, and NICHD Early Child Care Research Network. 2010. Do effects of early childcare extend to age 15 years? Results from the NICHD study of early child care and youth development. *Child Development* 81: 737–756.

———. May 7, 2012. Letter of support for *Pregnant Workers Fairness Act* addressed to all members of Congress. http://nadler.house.gov/sites/nadler.house.gov/files/documents/PregnantWorkersFairnessActSign-OnLetter050812.pdf (accessed October 26, 2012).

3

The Evolution and Devolution of Maternity Leave as an Employee Benefit

In this chapter, we continue on the journey toward an understanding of maternity leave as an organizational policy. First, we review the birthrate and fertility rate for the United States and the relationship of trends in these rates to employment patterns of women. Second, we examine the types of leave benefits offered by employers in higher education and in the pharmaceutical industry, as these policies are typical of those of the employers of the women interviewed for this project. Finally, we explore how these benefits first evolved and then devolved over the past 40 years, how women and men have utilized these policies, and how organizational actions and attitudes toward maternity leave policies have changed.

TRENDS IN BIRTHRATES, FERTILITY RATES, EMPLOYMENT PATTERNS, AND USE OF MATERNITY LEAVE BENEFITS

The U.S. Census Bureau continually collects data about births, fertility, family structure, and employment of women. Specifically, the Census Bureau asks of women aged 15 to 44, "How many children have you ever had?" and "What is the date of birth of your last child?" From these two questions, the bureau calculates the fertility rate, or the number of births per 1,000 women aged 15 to 44, which in 2011 stood at 63.2. This is the lowest general fertility rate *ever* reported for the United States and is the fourth consecutive year that the rate has declined.

86 • *Maternity Leave: Policy and Practice*

Childbearing in the U.S. 1920–2011

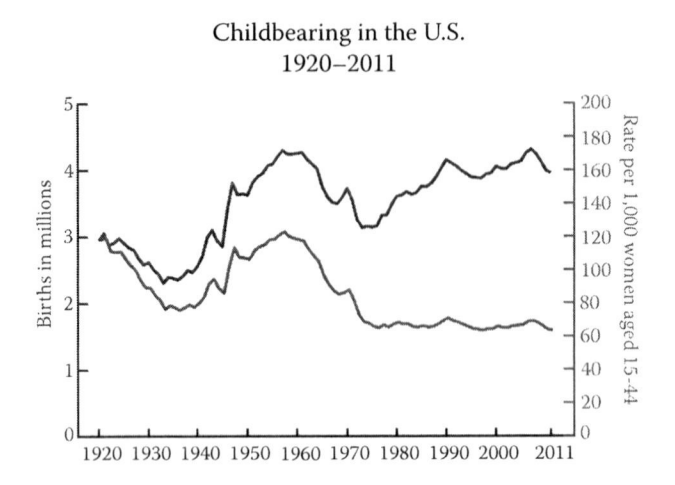

[Figure: line graph showing births in millions (left axis, 0–5) and rate per 1,000 women aged 15–44 (right axis, 0–200) from 1920 to 2011]

FIGURE 3.1
Childbearing in the United States 1920–2011. (From National Center for Health Statistics, CDC/NCHS, National Vital Statistics System. http://www.census.gov/newsroom/cspan/childbearing_patterns_slides_3.pdf (December 2, 2012).

Fertility and birthrates are also calculated from data collected from state depositories of vital records and birth certificates, and these calculations are made available through the National Center for Health Statistics (NCHS). Figure 3.1 depicts the number of births and the fertility rate for years 1920 through 2011 as compiled by the NCHS. According to the NCHS, the number of births in the United States for 2011 was 3,953,593. The birthrate, which is the total births per 1,000 of total population, as reported by the NCHS in October 2012 for the year 2011, was 12.7. The birthrate is down from 2010. In 2011, births to teens were down to the lowest rate recorded in 70 years. Births to women in their 20s were down; births to women in their early 30s and in their late 40s remained unchanged; and births to women in their late 30s and early 40s rose (Hamilton, Martin, and Ventura, October 3, 2012, 1–4).

Utilizing vital records data and U.S. Census Bureau data, the NCHS calculates and reports birthrates and fertility rates by race and ethnicity of mother, age of mother, and marital status of mother. The NCHS also tracks these rates over time.

Table 3.1 presents the NCHS's preliminary data for 2011 for number of births, birthrates, and fertility rates by place of residence of the mother (Hamilton et al., October 3, 2012, 25). These birthrates and fertility rates are calculated based on population estimates as of July 1, 2011. The data shown are for all races.

TABLE 3.1

Births, Birthrate, and Total Fertility Rate, United States and by State, 2011

	Number of Births All Races and Origins	Birth Rate All Races	Total Fertility Rate All Races
United States	3,953,593	12.7	63.2
Alabama	59,347	12.4	61.8
Alaska	11,455	15.8	78.5
Arizona	85,543	13.2	67.3
Arkansas	38,713	13.2	67.8
California	502,118	13.3	63.4
Colorado	65,055	12.7	62.7
Connecticut	37,280	10.4	54.3
Delaware	11,257	12.4	62.9
Florida	213,344	11.2	59.6
Georgia	132,488	13.5	63.8
Hawaii	18,957	13.8	71.9
Idaho	22,305	14.1	72.3
Illinois	161,312	12.5	61.5
Indiana	83,702	12.8	65.0
Iowa	38,213	12.5	66.1
Kansas	39,642	13.8	71.2
Kentucky	55,377	12.7	64.7
Louisiana	61,889	13.5	66.4
Maine	12,704	9.6	53.1
Maryland	73,086	12.5	61.3
Massachusetts	73,225	11.1	54.4
Michigan	114,004	11.5	59.9
Minnesota	68,411	12.8	65.5
Mississippi	39,856	13.4	66.0
Missouri	76,117	12.7	64.8
Montana	12,069	12.1	66.7
Nebraska	25,720	14.0	72.0
Nevada	35,295	13.0	64.2
New Hampshire	12,852	9.7	51.9
New Jersey	105,886	12.0	61.3
New Mexico	27,289	13.1	68.2
New York	241,290	12.4	59.8
North Carolina	120,385	12.5	61.5
North Dakota	9,527	13.9	72.4
Ohio	137,916	11.9	62.1
Oklahoma	52,274	13.8	70.4

Continued

TABLE 3.1 (Continued)

Births, Birthrate, and Total Fertility Rate, United States and by State, 2011

	Number of Births All Races and Origins	Birth Rate All Races	Total Fertility Rate All Races
Oregon	45,157	11.7	59.4
Pennsylvania	143,148	11.2	58.8
Rhode Island	10,960	10.4	51.5
South Carolina	57,368	12.3	61.8
South Dakota	11,849	14.4	77.1
Tennessee	79,588	12.4	62.3
Texas	377,449	14.7	69.8
Utah	51,223	18.2	83.6
Vermont	6,078	9.7	51.8
Virginia	102,648	12.7	61.9
Washington	86,976	12.7	63.7
West Virginia	20,720	11.2	60.7
Wisconsin	67,811	11.9	62.0
Wyoming	7,398	13.0	69.1

Source: Hamilton B., J. Martin, and S. Ventura. October 3, 2012. Births: Preliminary data for 2011. *National Vital Statistics Reports* 61 (5): 1–29. Hyattsville, MD: National Center for Health Statistics.

If a generation of U.S. citizens is to replace itself, the fertility rate needs to be 2,100 births per 1,000 women. The fertility rate for 2011 was below that replacement level at 1,894.5 births per 1,000 women. The rate was below the replacement rate during the period 1972 through 2005, and then rose above replacement rate in 2006 and 2007. Since then, the rate has dropped below the replacement level (Hamilton et al., October 3, 2012, 5).

Information on birthrates and fertility rates is important to understand because it also helps us to understand the implications on employment patterns for women in the workforce. For example, if a woman chooses to leave the workforce on a temporary basis to have or care for her children, then that affects the available female labor supply. Some researchers believe this movement in and out of the workforce is one contributing factor to the overall wage gap between men and women. Another consideration might be the timing of when a woman decides to have a child. If she waits until later in life, and then has fertility issues, that decision may affect how many children she has in her lifetime, and that may also affect her participation in the workforce, and therefore her overall lifetime earnings (Cristia 2006, 3). Further, understanding birthrates and fertility rates may also lead us to a greater understanding of the role that employer-provided benefits may play in both the decision to have children and in the number of children a family decides to have. While this chapter focuses primarily on maternity leave benefits, it is important to keep in mind that employer-provided health insurance, infertility treatment coverage, and subsidized child care are also important considerations, as are a woman's economic status, job security, educational attainment, and work experience. All of these factors play into a woman's decision on whether and when to start a family, how long she will work during pregnancy, and how soon she may return to work after giving birth (Laughlin 2011, 2).

Since 1920, the U.S. Department of Labor (2012) has been charged with monitoring the role of women in the workplace. Over the past 90 years, the DOL's Women's Bureau has reported on working conditions, minimum wages, maximum working hours, equal pay, child-care issues, work-family issues, and employment opportunities. The Women's Bureau also from time to time works with the Bureau of Labor Statistics and the U.S. Census Bureau to collect information related to the labor force, employment, unemployment, and earnings. The information presented in Tables 3.2, 3.3, and 3.4 is taken from the Current Population Survey, a national monthly sample survey of approximately 60,000 households and reported by the DOL.

Participation of mothers in the workforce has increased substantially over the past 30 years, and more women are employed full time, and are likely to work during their entire adult lives, rather than move in and out of the workforce (Laughlin 2011, 1). In 2009, 59.2% of women were in the labor force (U.S. Department of Labor 2010, 1). While the number of women in the workforce has increased since 1970, the percentage of women that work full time remains nearly the same at 73.5% in 2009 as compared to 73.9% in 1970 (2, 73). "In January 2010, the median number of years that female wage and salary workers had been with their employer was 4.2 years, compared with 4.6 years for their male counterparts. Among both men and women, tenure at a job was greater for workers age 45 and older" (3).

Table 3.2 presents the participation rates of women over age 16 in the civilian workforce for selected years from 1970 to 2009. In 1970, 43.3% of women were in the workforce. This participation rate grew to 59.2% in 2009. The overall unemployment rate for women for 2009 was 8.1%, up over previous years due to the economic downturn of 2008 (U.S. Department of Labor 2010, 8).

Table 3.3 presents the employment status of women by presence and age of youngest child for selected years from 1975 to 2009. In 1975, the labor

TABLE 3.2

Employment Status of the Civilian Noninstitutional Population, Women 16 Years of Age and Over, for Selected Years 1970–2009, Annual Averages (Numbers in Thousands)

Year	Civilian Noninstitutional Population	Total Civilian Labor Force and Percent of Population	Total Employed and Percent of Population	Total Unemployed and Percent of Population	Not in Labor Force
1970	72,782	31,543 (43.3)	29,688 (40.8)	1,855 (5.9)	41,239
1980	88,348	45,487 (51.5)	42,117 (47.7)	3,370 (7.4)	42,861
1990	98,787	56,829 (57.5)	53,689 (54.3)	3,140 (5.5)	41,957
2000	110,613	66,303 (59.9)	63,586 (57.5)	2,717 (4.1)	44,310
2009	121,665	72,019 (59.2)	66,208 (54.4)	5,811 (8.1)	49,646

Source: Current Population Survey, U.S. Department of Labor, U.S. Bureau of Labor Statistics 2010.

force participation rate of mothers with children under the age of 18 was 47.4% and by 2009 this percentage was 71.6. Women with children over the age of 6 are more likely to work than mothers with younger children (U.S. Department of Labor 2010, 15, 18–20).

The percentage of the contribution of a woman's earnings to her family's income has increased from 26.6% in 1970 to 36% in 2008. Data on the contribution of a woman's earnings to her family for selected years are presented in Table 3.4 (U.S. Department of Labor 2010, 77). Women who make more than their husbands, in families with two wage earners, is reported at 26.6% for 2008. This is an increase over the 18.1% of women who earned more than their husbands in families with two wage earners in 1988 (78).

The Census Bureau has collected data on employment patterns and use of maternity leave since the early 1960s. In its most recent comprehensive report, the Census Bureau reports on trends of childbearing, employment, maternity leave, hours worked, pay level, and job skill level of women after the birth of their first child (Laughlin 2011). The average age at which women gave birth to their first child was 21.4 years in 1970 and 25 years in 2007. In 1970, only 9% of all mothers had completed a bachelor's degree, and that percentage increased to 24% by 2007 (2).

TABLE 3.3

Employment Status of Women in Civilian Labor Force by Presence and Age of Youngest Child, for Selected Years 1975–2009 (Numbers in Thousands)

Presence and Age of Youngest Child	Year	Total Civilian Labor Force	Percentage of Population	Employed	Total Unemployed	Percentage of Labor Force Unemployed
Age 18 and younger	1975	14,616	47.4	13,069	1,548	11.0
	1980	17,790	56.6	16,526	1,264	7.1
	1990	22,196	66.7	20,865	1,331	6.0
	2000	25,795	72.9	24,693	1,102	4.3
	2009	26,122	71.6	24,079	2,043	7.8
Age 6 to 17, none younger	1975	8,917	54.9	8,218	700	7.9
	1980	11,252	64.3	10,640	612	5.4
	1990	12,799	74.7	12,133	666	5.2
	2000	15,479	79.0	14,931	549	3.5
	2009	15,625	78.2	14,562	1,063	6.8
Under age 6	1975	5,699	39.0	4,851	848	14.9
	1980	6,538	46.8	5,886	652	10.0
	1990	9,397	58.2	8,732	664	7.1
	2000	10,316	65.3	9,763	553	5.4
	2009	10,497	63.6	9,517	980	9.3
Under age 3	1975	2,824	34.3	2,326	500	17.7
	1980	3,565	41.9	3,167	398	11.2
	1990	5,216	53.6	4,823	393	7.5
	2000	5,670	61.0	5,350	320	5.6
	2009	5,960	61.1	5,401	559	9.4
No children under age 18	1975	22,365	45.1	20,381	1,984	8.9
	1980	27,144	48.1	25,375	1,769	6.5
	1990	33,942	52.3	32,391	1,551	4.6
	2000	40,142	54.8	38,408	1,733	4.3
	2009	45,649	53.8	42,343	3,306	7.2

Source: Current Population Survey, U.S. Department of Labor, U.S. Bureau of Labor Statistics 2010.

As noted in Chapter 2, in the 1960s and the 1970s, both the expectation and the reality were that working women who became pregnant would willingly or unwillingly leave the workforce. For example, at Western Kentucky University, Board of Regents' meeting minutes from the 1970s reflect the approval of female staff and faculty (usually female faculty were part-time employees with no eligibility for benefits) going on maternity leave, and often a few months later, meeting minutes show the acceptance of resignations from those same women, with a notation that the female employee had been on maternity leave for the period leading up to the date

TABLE 3.4

Contribution of Wives' Earnings to Family Income, Selected Years 1970–2008

Year	Contribution to Family Income (Median Percentage)
1970	26.6
1975	26.3
1980	26.7
1985	28.3
1990	30.7
1995	31.9
2000	33.5
2005	35.1
2008	36.0

Source: Current Population Survey, U.S. Department of Labor, U.S. Bureau of Labor Statistics 2010.

of resignation (Western Kentucky University, September 29, 1973). This common occurrence began to change as more families became economically dependent on a second income, and this change was also supported by the enactment of legislation that prohibited discrimination against women who became pregnant while working, and amendments to the tax code that allowed for tax credits for child care (Laughlin 2011, 3).

Table 3.5 shows the employment history of women before they first gave birth for selected years 1961 to 2008. These data indicate that 60% of women who first gave birth in 1961 to 1965 had worked for at least six months prior to the birth, and for the period 2006 to 2008 this had increased to 72.3%. The percentage of women who worked during pregnancy of a first child was 44.4% during the period 1961 to 1965, increasing to 65.6% for the period 2006 to 2008. These percentages were slightly less for those women working full time during their pregnancies for each respective time period (Laughlin 2011, 4).

For the period 2006 to 2008, 88% of all first-time mothers worked into their third trimester. Older women worked longer toward the end of their pregnancies than did their younger counterparts. During the period 1961–1965, 35% of first-time mothers worked into their last month of pregnancy, and this increased to 82% for first-time mothers during the period 2006–2008 (Laughlin 2011, 6). Laughlin suggests these recent trends may indicate that women work longer into their pregnancies for reasons other

TABLE 3.5

Employment History of Women before First Birth, 1961 to 2008 (Numbers in Thousands)

Year of First Birth	Number of Women with a First Birth	Percentage Ever Worked for Six or More Months Continuously	Percentage Worked during Pregnancy	Percentage Worked Full-Time during Pregnancy
1961–1965	6,306	60.0	44.4	39.7
1966–1970	6,956	66.4	49.4	44.2
1971–1975	6,920	68.9	53.5	47.6
1976–1980	7,192	73.1	61.4	53.1
1981–1985	8,129	75.2	64.5	54.0
1986–1990	8,568	75.5	67.2	58.3
1991–1995	8,599	73.8	66.8	54.5
1996–2000	8,558	74.0	67.2	56.6
2001–2005	8,215	75.0	69.2	58.7
2006–2008	5,127	72.3	65.6	56.1

Source: Laughlin, L. 2011. Maternity leave and employment patterns of first time mothers: 1961–2008. *Current Population Report*, 4. Washington, D.C.: U.S. Census Bureau.

than strictly economic need, perhaps due to jobs being seen as an investment in their family's future, and perhaps due to the personal commitment of the women to both their career and to their employer (8). This is counter to trends in the 1960s and 1970s when women who were economically disadvantaged—teens, black women, and women with premarital first births—were more likely to return to work more quickly after giving birth (16). Women may also work longer into the pregnancy in order to utilize more accrued paid leave after the baby arrives.

TYPES OF MATERNITY LEAVE TAKEN— PAID AND UNPAID

The U.S. Census Bureau has only asked questions about maternity leave arrangements for first-time mothers since 1980, so trend data for types of leave taken by women covers a relatively short time span. During these most recent decades, we also saw the enactment of the Family and Medical Leave Act, which impacted the types of leave offered by employers. Many working women use any and all types of leave, both paid and unpaid, available to them for maternity leave—including accrued personal, vacation, sick, and short-term disability. Some women report quitting, or being fired or laid off as the "type" of leave taken, although this is much less likely to occur today (Laughlin 2011, 8). Generally, the percentage of women who quit their jobs upon giving birth is much lower, while those who use some combination of paid, unpaid, and disability leave is much greater than what was reported in the early 1980s.

Since the mid-1970s, it appears that "increasing levels of education go hand-in-hand with the use of paid leave benefits. Sixty-six percent of women with a bachelor's degree or more used paid leave, compared with 19 percent of women who had less than a high school education," and the age of a woman, along with her corresponding years of work experience, also is related to her having access to paid leave benefits (Laughlin 2011, 12).

Having an education allows women to gain entry into organizations and to work in positions where they are able to have access to paid leave benefits. Table 3.6 shows the leave arrangements by type that were used by first-time mothers for periods from 1981 to 2008, and Table 3.7 shows greater detail about the types of leave taken by first-time mothers from 2006 to 2008 (Laughlin 2011, 9). In the period 2006 to 2008, 41% of first-time mothers received paid maternity leave, and 36% of them received unpaid maternity leave (10). For this same time period, 51% of women who gave birth for the first time and who worked while pregnant used some type of paid leave, 42% used some type of unpaid leave, and 10% used disability leave (9, 19).

As noted previously, working mothers return to work quickly after giving birth for a variety of reasons. In the 1960s, the return to work was slower, with 14% of all mothers with newborns returning to work by the sixth month. Since the 1980s, women have tended to work longer into their pregnancies and return to work sooner, with 44% returning to work by the sixth month after giving birth. Since the mid-1990s, 57% of mothers with newborns have returned to work by the sixth month (Laughlin 2011, 14). More than 80% of working mothers who gave birth during the period 2005 to 2007 returned to their prebirth employer after maternity leave (19).

There have been some studies undertaken to gauge whether FMLA legislation has had an impact on the length of leave time taken by new mothers. It is important to remember that FMLA does not apply to all workers or organizations. Baum (2004) found that, overall, family leave legislation

TABLE 3.6

Selected Leave Arrangements Used by Women Who Worked during Pregnancy Preceding First Birth, 1981–2008 (Numbers in Thousands)

Year of First Birth	Number of Women Who Worked during Pregnancy	Percentage of Women Who Quit Job	Percentage of Women Who Used Paid Leave	Percentage of Women Who Used Unpaid Leave	Percentage of Women Who Used Disability Leave	Percentage of Women Let Go from Job
1981–1985	5,147	35.7	37.3	33.7	6.3	3.5
1986–1990	5,758	26.5	43.3	41.0	7.5	2.3
1991–1995	5,740	26.9	42.7	40.3	11.2	4.2
1996–2000	5,749	25.6	42.0	45.0	6.9	2.2
2001–2005	5,686	21.5	49.4	38.3	7.8	4.0
2006–2008	3,363	21.9	50.8	42.4	9.5	4.7

Source: Laughlin, L. 2011. Maternity leave and employment patterns of first time mothers: 1961–2008. *Current Population Report*, 9. Washington, D.C.: U.S. Census Bureau.

96 • *Maternity Leave: Policy and Practice*

TABLE 3.7

Detailed Leave Arrangement Used by Women Who Worked during Pregnancy Preceding First Birth, 2006–2008 (Percentages Based on 3,363,000 Women)

Type of Leave	Before or After Birth	Before Birth	After Birth
Quit job	21.9	15.9	6.0
Paid leave	50.8	21.4	45.3
Maternity leave	40.7	16.9	35.1
Sick leave	9.8	2.9	8.1
Vacation leave	10.8	3.1	9.2
Other paid leave	1.8	0.9	1.0
Unpaid leave	42.4	19.1	36.5
Maternity leave	35.5	16.0	30.6
Sick leave	3.4	0.9	2.6
Vacation leave	3.2	1.3	2.4
Other unpaid leave	3.1	1.1	2.3
Disability leave	9.5	3.2	8.1
Other leave	8.4	3.4	6.2
Self-employed	0.9	0.4	0.7
Employer went out of business	0.1	0.1	0.0
Other	7.4	3.0	5.5
Let go from job	4.7	3.2	3.1

Source: Laughlin, L. 2011. Maternity leave and employment patterns of first time mothers: 1961–2008. *Current Population Report*, 9. Washington, D.C.: U.S. Census Bureau.

had little effect on the number of mothers taking leave or on the length of leave taken (94, 109). Baum suggests this may be explained by the fact that many women simply cannot afford to take the leave mandated by the legislation because it is unpaid leave (112, 113). Baum suggests that if the mandated leave were paid, his study results might have showed a much greater correlation between leave available to women and leave time they take (114).

TYPES OF PATERNITY AND PARENTAL LEAVE POLICIES

Within the discussion of maternity leave, it is important to note that in recent years some organizations have officially replaced paid and unpaid maternity leave benefits with nonpaid leave under FMLA, while others have added paternity leave to the selection of employer-provided benefits. Some organizations offer paternity leave to new fathers. The length of this leave is usually shorter than maternity leave, an acknowledgment that this is a non-medical-related leave, but this leave may run concurrently with FMLA. For this leave to be paid, some organizations require the father to use accumulated leave. Other organizations recognize and support the importance of the father bonding with the baby, and offer this as paid leave.

Some organizations have simply changed the name from maternity leave to parental leave or family leave, perhaps in an effort to make employee benefits more gender neutral and to be perceived as being more family-friendly to all employees. As we will explore in later chapters, this approach of renaming this leave "parental" may do little except penalize the female employees who are giving birth—in terms of reducing the length of paid time off allowed for mothers. For example, in the higher education setting, there is the misconception that all faculty members have autonomy and flexibility, and therefore the organization is inherently family friendly. Following from this notion, it is believed that there is no need to treat men and women differently in order to be family friendly (Wyatt-Nichol 2011, 48). And yet, women who take advantage of stopping the tenure clock or asking for modified duties are often penalized financially and professionally. Women are often perceived as "not as dedicated" or viewed as "not carrying their weight" in terms of job responsibilities (59). As explained by Acker (1992), ingrained stereotypes and assumptions about women are created and reproduced even when organizations try to adopt and implement gender-neutral policies. These stereotypes and assumptions are then further perpetuated and result in women with children being blocked from advancement opportunities. As long as the culture within an organization does not support leave policies for giving birth, women may continue to be penalized no matter how we frame it.

As noted in Chapter 2, FMLA applies to both the mother and father of a newborn, but this is simply a job protection assurance that an employee can return to his or her position after taking unpaid leave. It is difficult for one parent, let alone two, to take unpaid leave. There are some states that have "parental" leave policies that offer paid leave at least on a short-term, partial-pay or wage-replacement basis (Ray, Gornick, and Schmitt 2009, 4). These state-level requirements still fall short as compared to benefits offered usually to both parents of newborns in other countries, which will be explored in Chapter 9.

Some universities offer employees a combination of paid and unpaid parental leave. For example, Cornell University (2008) offers to qualifying employees 16 weeks of parental leave for nonacademic staff. This leave runs concurrently with leave under FMLA in terms of job protection for 12 weeks, and the university extends job protection for the full 16 weeks as part of its organizational policy. Under this leave plan, the employee may take parental leave at any time during the 12-month period following the birth or adoption of a child. Half pay is provided for a consecutive 4-week period for the parent. The remaining 12 weeks of the 16-week parental leave can be taken as unpaid, but all accrued vacation time may be used to replace some of this unpaid leave, and up to 10 days of accrued sick leave may be used.

Duke University (2012) provides parental leave for the birth or adoption of a child for up to 3 consecutive weeks at full pay, but the leave takes effect 3 weeks after a "waiting period." During this waiting period, the eligible employee can use any accrued sick, vacation, or paid-time-off leave, or he or she may take the time off without pay. This leave runs concurrently with FMLA. Both of these schools extend these benefits to same-sex partners or spousal equivalents. Montana State University (2012) differentiates between maternity and parental leave. It offers birth fathers and adoptive parents the option of taking parental leave for a period of 15 working days immediately following the birth or adoption. Eligible employees may use accumulated sick or annual leave or may take the leave without pay.

EXAMPLES OF MATERNITY LEAVE POLICIES

Providing maternity leave as an employee benefit first evolved and then subsequently devolved over the past 40 years. At a minimum, most policies are difficult to read and complicated to understand. Some benefit policies that list maternity leave in their table of contents only direct the employee to the FMLA provisions within the document. To further complicate the issue, maternity leave in institutions of higher learning present some unique administrative challenges as staff usually earn and accrue sick and vacation leave, but faculty often do not. Further, faculty maternity leave is often a negotiated arrangement between the faculty member and her supervisor. This results in two-tiered and sometimes three-tiered systems within the same organization. In this section, several examples of maternity leave policies of both universities and pharmaceutical companies are presented. It is important to note that it is rare to find two maternity leave policies that are identical. These examples presented are not intended to be viewed as "model" or exemplary policies. They are presented simply as examples.

The first example traces the changes to maternity policies over a period of more than 30 years at Western Kentucky University. At present, for faculty positions at the university, the university's policy indicates that the maternity leave will be a negotiated arrangement between the faculty member and department head or dean. In contrast, in 1980, the maternity leave policy at Western Kentucky University covered both faculty and staff and read as follows:

> Pregnancy and childbearing justify a leave of absence for members of the faculty and staff for a reasonable length of time, and for reinstatement following childbirth without loss of accrued benefits. Approved absences related to pregnancy and confinement is chargeable to sick leave or any combination of sick leave, annual vacation, and sick leave without pay.... While the University does not specify any period for maternity leave, up to four weeks before delivery and six weeks after delivery are considered to be a reasonable length of time.... After accrued sick leave is exhausted, maternity absence shall be charged to accrued annual vacation or leave without pay.... A staff employee should report pregnancy as soon as it is known, so that necessary staffing adjustments may be planned. Female faculty members expecting delivery during the semester or term should consult with the Department Head and Dean to make arrangements for classes.

Before this policy was implemented in 1980, it appears that there was no maternity leave in place for faculty according to correspondence in the archive records at Western Kentucky University. A memorandum dated November 7, 1979, from James L. Davis, Vice President for Academic Affairs, to Western Kentucky University President, Donald W. Zacharias, reads as follows.

> I concur with the recommendation that Dr. (*name omitted*) be granted maternity leave during the second bi-term of the spring semester 1980. The date for this leave will be March 24, 1980 for the remainder of the semester. Dr. (*name omitted*) will teach a full load of two bi-term classes during the first bi-term. No replacement for her during this period is requested.
>
> It is my understanding from Mr. Tomes (*in personnel*) that due to procedures used for other faculty illness situations, we are under obligation to provide this benefit. We normally carry faculty for a reasonable period of illness without reduction in salary. This is the first request for this type that

I am aware of. Perhaps there needs to be a study of the "sick leave" policy for nine-month faculty.

Ten years later, Western Kentucky University (August 14, 1991) amended the 1980 maternity policy to add provisions for the adoption of children, and to state that eligible employees will continue to accrue sick and vacation days during the leave. The terminology about "reasonable length of leave" was amended as follows: "while the University does not specify any period for maternity leave, up to a total of ten weeks taken before and/or after delivery, the time to be determined by the individual, is considered to be a reasonable length of time" (1). Less than a decade after this, the only mention of maternity leave in the employee benefits summary document was found in the section explaining the provisions of FMLA, which called for 12 weeks of leave for the birth or adoption of a child (Western Kentucky University, July 1, 2000). There was no mention about antenatal leave, indicating that the university had backtracked on acknowledging that this might be a needed type of leave for its pregnant employees.

The current policy and procedures document regarding sick and medical leave applicable for faculty at Western Kentucky University became effective in 2007. The policy first addresses FMLA provisions in brief, and refers the faculty member to the full FMLA policy found in a separate document, and then further reads in part:

> Western Kentucky University has historically pursued informal arrangements and practices which enabled student needs to be met or essential faculty services to be provided when individual faculty members are unable to fulfill assigned duties and responsibilities due to the faculty member's own illness or incapacity. While the majority of these informal practices and arrangements have proven satisfactory, there are basic constraints that exist for faculty who need such informal leave and are unable to fulfill their instructional, service, and research duties. (Western Kentucky University, April 17, 2007, 1)

The policy, which states that a faculty member may have up to a semester off with pay, also addresses pregnancy and maternity leave specifically and appears to be much more limited in terms of the length of paid leave allowed. This section of the policy and procedure document reads as follows:

> Absences related to childbirth and adoption, are qualified under FMLA leave.... FMLA leave shall run concurrently with any paid time authorized

under these provisions. Faculty members are eligible for uninterrupted pay continuance for absences associated with pregnancy/maternity. The intent is to treat pregnancy/maternity absences in a manner similar to those for medical or health related causes (of the faculty member) unrelated to pregnancy/maternity. Faculty members shall continue to be paid their regular salary and corresponding benefits for a period of six weeks (traditional period of medical disability associated with pregnancy). In situations where a temporary medical disability extends beyond six weeks, affected faculty members shall continue to receive their regular salary and benefits up to a maximum of one academic semester, as certified by a qualified health care provider. In cases where a faculty member may request time off beyond the initial six weeks for reasons unrelated to the faculty member's own health status, time off without pay will be granted within the provisions of the University's FMLA policy. (Western Kentucky University 2007, 2)

Under this policy, six weeks of paid maternity leave is all that is granted to faculty, although a semester is 16 weeks long, but FMLA provides for 12 weeks of leave. The "glitch" in the system seems to be the requirement that longer paid time off that is allowed up to the length of one semester requires certification by a qualified health care provider regarding the mother's health. If the mother is released from her doctor's care after 6 weeks, it appears the remainder of her leave would be unpaid, unless an arrangement is reached through negotiation.

Conversely, at Notre Dame there is a reference to 6 weeks of paid leave, but also an acknowledgment that the faculty member is relieved of teaching duties for the whole semester. This type of proviso seems to be a workable compromise. At Notre Dame University, faculty members are to take FMLA for leave required for pregnancy and childbirth. The policy found in the University of Notre Dame's faculty handbook (2008) states that leave

related to childbirth and recovery is normally for at least six weeks.... no ... duties are required during the period of the leave. In addition, a faculty member whose due date for the birth of her child is any time during the semester is relieved from all teaching responsibilities during that semester.

The revised policy also allows for the faculty member to contact the provost if her due date falls outside of the regular semester dates, for a determination of whether she will be relieved of her teaching duties, presumably for either the semester before or after the due date.

In 1967, the Notre Dame faculty manual did not mention maternity leave specifically. The university's senior archivist notes that this is not surprising since there were only a handful of women on faculty then. The 1967 policy reads as follows:

> Leave of absence is also granted to members for reasons of incapacitating sickness... . The University obligates itself to pay a member's salary for a period of six months... . Leave of absence officially granted by the University with or without remuneration is counted as service for purpose of tenure and promotion. (University of Notre Dame 1967, 14)

In 1974, the leave of absence policy was amended to read as follows: "Leave of absence is also granted to members for reason of childbearing... . The University obligates itself to pay a member's salary for a period of six months" (University of Notre Dame 1973, 32). This policy remained unchanged until 1985, when the faculty handbook was amended to add a section on medical leaves of absence. The added section allows for a pregnant faculty member to be granted 4 weeks of compensated leave without applying for a medical leave of absence. The section reads in part as follows:

> Several months prior to the expected beginning of the four-week leave the faculty member should advise the departmental chairperson or the appropriate academic officer so that provision can be made for her responsibilities. (University of Notre Dame 1985, 52–53)

In another example, at the University of Colorado, the "parental" leave policy was changed in 1990, twice in 2000, and again in 2003 and 2005. The policy has different provisions based on the type of position one holds—staff, 9-month faculty, or 12-month faculty and administrative personnel. Faculty at this school do accrue sick leave and can use it for leave after giving birth. If the accrued sick leave is not sufficient to cover an entire semester, then the faculty member can take the remainder of the semester off at half pay with full benefits (University of Colorado, June 6, 2005, 1).

Westminster College (2012) addresses both paternity leave and maternity leave under "pregnancy-related absences" in its faculty handbook. For faculty, the policy states "a new mother is eligible for family and medical leave. Any accrued, paid benefits such as sick leave, personal days, and vacation days are to be used first before the employee is placed on unpaid family and medical leave" (53). The language is identical for covered staff but is located in a separate employee handbook. The language in this policy seems to indicate that a faculty member would be eligible to take more than 12 weeks of leave allowed under FMLA if she had accrued leave available.

Within the pharmaceutical industry, paid maternity leave benefits are often generous, both in an effort to be supportive of female employees and their families and to ensure that these employees do not leave the organization. Organizations that rate "best places to work" often point to pharmaceutical companies such as Merck and Pfizer as those that offer exemplary benefits, especially as it relates to maternity and paternity leave (Working Mother Network 2012). Interestingly, some of these companies have reduced leave benefits under both paternity and maternity policies in the past year. Pfizer, for example, reduced paid maternity leave from 15 weeks to 12 weeks, and eliminated provisions under paternity leave that had previously provided for up to 6 weeks of paid leave for fathers (Working Mother Network 2012). It should be noted that the number of weeks of maternity leave referred to on the website of Working Mother Network does not match Pfizer's current written policy, which indicates that the 12 weeks of leave reported on the website may have been reduced to a total of 9 weeks of paid leave, 3 weeks before delivery and 6 weeks after (Pfizer 2012). Pfizer (2012) did institute a new "caregiver" leave policy for all employees that allows for up to 5 days of paid leave to care for a child of any age.

Pharmaceutical companies often provide for and utilize short-term disability policies in conjunction with provisions under FMLA and with the use of paid leave accrued by employees. Some companies also offer unpaid additional non-medical-related leaves of absence after the birth of a child, which only become effective when all paid leave has been exhausted.

As an example, Pfizer's (2012) document that outlines the use of the short-term disability policy in conjunction with FMLA states:

> short-term disability benefits for childbirth generally begin three weeks before your projected due date and continue for six weeks after the birth of your child.... This period will be paid at 100% base pay and will not reduce the 26-week short-term disability benefit allowed in a rolling 12-month period. (Pfizer 2012, 14)

Further, the document states that accrued vacation leave does not run concurrently with leave taken under the short-term disability policy, and therefore, accrued vacation leave will not be used until all short-term disability and any other additional paid leave is exhausted (Pfizer 2012, 22).

Additionally, an employee may return to work on a transitional return-to-work schedule, while still receiving benefits under short-term disability leave (25). In conjunction, these provisions may potentially lengthen the time a woman is off work for pregnancy and maternity leave, which is an attractive recruitment and retention tool.

ANTENATAL LEAVE AND SHORT-TERM DISABILITY LEAVE

Traditionally, taking leave before delivery was a common occurrence for women in the United States, and it was supported by many employers. Many organizations allowed for antenatal or prenatal leave, usually about a month before the delivery due date. At Western Kentucky University (1982, 1989), the policy of offering 4 weeks of leave for "mothers-to-be" as a reasonable length of time allowed for antenatal leave was touted all through the 1970s and 1980s under employee benefits. In other countries, this is still today a normal practice and is supported as a way to ensure the health and well-being of the baby and mother.

In the United States, "mandated" antenatal leave was challenged in the courts as a discriminatory practice. Some of these cases in the mid-1970s involved pregnant public school teachers who were required under school policy to take leave at a set time during the pregnancy. These policies were declared by the courts to be in conflict with the due process clause of the Fourteenth Amendment, but in some cases, the courts suggested compromises that would allow for a shorter mandatory leave time at the end of the pregnancy. These compromises were intended to protect the rights of the individual but allow for some administrative control by the schools (Grenig 1975, 851).

As noted above, in the pharmaceutical industry it is common for the expectant mother to be allowed to stop working three weeks before delivery as a matter of practice, and sometimes earlier under the terms of short-term disability policies. For pharmaceutical sales representatives, who are typically in and out of a car for more than eight hours a day, this is a welcome employee leave benefit.

In California, qualifying employees may take up to four weeks of paid antenatal leave. Research conducted by Guendelman, Pearl, Graham, Angulo, and Kharrazi (2006) indicates that in California this leave taking is usually pursued as a result of medical issues, stress, and fatigue or if the woman has other young children at home to care for during the last month of pregnancy. While not all eligible women take antenatal leave, providing the option may be beneficial for the employer. Offering paid antenatal leave may serve as a strategy for organizations to retain workers and therefore reduce turnover costs, while promoting the health of the mother (63, 71).

The use of short-term disability or temporary disability leave is one way that some states have provided for maternity leave beyond FMLA or other employer-provided paid leave provisions. Some of this leave is covered by organizational policy as described in the Pfizer example, and some is covered by the purchase of an insurance coverage policy for short-term disability. For example, in California, temporary disability insurance is required of employers with more than five employees. The benefit is paid for through a tax on wages and is used to provide partial pay for mothers unable to work owing to pregnancy or maternity disabilities for periods of up to four months. In Hawaii and New York, businesses are required to offer enrollment in temporary disability insurance programs that give partial wage replacement for pregnancy- and maternity-related medical conditions (Ray 2008, 32, 33).

Other states may allow for short-term disability insurance but do not mandate that employers offer it to employees, or may require that the employee pay the full premium for this insurance. Some of these policies that purport to cover pregnancy- and maternity-related medical conditions may be so restrictive or limited in terms of what is considered to be a continuous short-term disability that it may be impossible to utilize this benefit for these conditions. For those companies that allow for pregnancy- and maternity-related short-term disability coverage to be utilized, there are varying time periods and levels at which the wage or salary are paid to the employee, and there must be continuing physician involvement and approval for time allowed and utilized under this coverage.

NO LEAVE AND PERMANENT EXIT FROM THE WORKPLACE

Most working women take some leave from work due to the physical stress that giving birth places on the mother's body. However, as more women work in professional jobs that allow for and require working from home, those who take a "complete" leave from work responsibilities during maternity leave are harder to identify. Technology has made this demarcation line between work and home fuzzier. Even when employers do not expect a woman to check her e-mail or stay in touch with what is going on at her workplace, women may feel compelled to do so. Some do not want to be perceived as being less committed than their male counterparts. For example, new Yahoo CEO Marissa Mayer chose not to take a lengthy formal maternity leave, saying that she would "work throughout it" in an effort to stay in touch with day-to-day operations (Gootman and Saint Louis 2012, 1). However, her previous employer, Google, recently amended its maternity leave policy and lengthened it from partial pay for three months to full pay for five months. Google was concerned about the number of women who were leaving employment after giving birth, and the company now reports that attrition among these employees has decreased by 50% (Miller, August 22, 2012). However, increasing benefits are the exception rather than the rule.

At the other end of the leave spectrum, some women decide to completely leave employment. During the period 2005–2007, 794,000 women who gave birth to their first child reported that they quit work around the time of their child's birth. Of these women, 52% of them did not work at all during the first year after their child's birth. The fact that they were not working a year after the birth may have been a deliberate decision so they could stay home with their child or it may have something to do with finding a new job, which might be complicated by the challenges of having a newborn (Laughlin 2011, 15, 16).

The initial decision to quit may be due to several factors: no health insurance available through the employer, no paid maternity leave available, unacceptable length of paid and unpaid leave, unacceptable pay, and unacceptable working hours. Conversely, satisfaction with these factors may influence a woman's decision to return to work rather than quit, and if she returns to the same employer she does not have the added stress of looking for work (Laughlin 2011, 18, 19). Guendelman et al. (2006) found in their study of California employees that the lack of maternity leave benefits was associated with the decision to quit, but the decision to quit was only made by 9% of the 1,214 study participants. Guendelman et al. concluded that when women do not have maternity leave benefits or affordable health insurance benefits, it may create a work disincentive (71).

Over the past decade, state legislators in Massachusetts have looked at expanding job-protected paid leave in an effort to encourage workers to return to work rather than permanently exiting the labor force. Proponents of this kind of policy change say workers will be more productive when they return to work and that both employer and employee will benefit from the employee returning to work when the employee is both physically and mentally ready. Further, they suggest mandatory paid leave would help the economically disadvantaged as they are typically the employees who do not have access to paid leave to begin with (Albelda and Clayton-Matthews 2006, 5, 17). The employer benefits as well, as explained by Albelda and Clayton-Matthews (2006) because

> returning to work reduces turnover, lowering employer costs, both the direct costs of advertising, interviewing, orientation, training, and processing ... and indirect costs associated with losing employees who understand internal networks, specific customers, or coworkers' abilities, and decreased morale or efficiency associated with working with inexperienced new employees. (5)

A woman's decision to quit her job has several potentially negative implications. First, her lifetime earnings will be reduced, which ultimately impacts contributions to lifetime savings, retirement, and social security funds. Second, she may forego advancement and promotion opportunities by leaving her current employer, and when she is ready to return to work it may be hard to convince a future employer of her commitment to her career and to the new organization she joins. Certainly, some jobs and careers are easier to move in and out of than others, but a woman's sense of professional identity may suffer. Sometimes, women just miss the daily contact with other adults that working affords and staying home does not (Stone 2007, 147).

Third, it may reinforce stereotypical gender roles in the responsibilities of home and with parenting because when women quit their jobs to stay home, often the sharing of responsibilities ceases, and the responsibilities fall disproportionately on the woman (Galtry 2002, 266; Stone 2007, 183). Fourth, when women choose to opt out of the workforce, organizations lose the benefit of their expertise and experience. There are experiences unique to women, and based on those experiences women pose different questions than their male counterparts (Madsen 2012, 133). Younger women in the workforce also lose the benefit of learning from these talented women (Stone 2007, 3). That is not to say that society loses out, because many women will use those talents and put their energies into volunteer work that benefits their community and into investing in their children (173, 174). However, by opting out, their voices are absent from the discussions and debate within the workforce about why women, families, and children should be valued (235).

There are myriad benefits to mother and baby when a woman makes the decision to stay home, and those benefits will be addressed in following chapters. The reality is that most women utilize leave options that lie between taking no leave and quitting. Many women would welcome the opportunity and the choice to transition back just a little more slowly to their jobs after having a baby. Transitional options include working part-time, working a reduced number of hours per day or per week, or utilizing flextime or job sharing (Galtry 2002, 271; Stone 2007, 233), but the availability of paid maternity leave is perhaps the most realistic and helpful alternative for women trying to balance the demands of work with having a newborn. In the next chapter, we explore the issue of women's mental and physical health as it relates to childbearing and the workplace.

REFERENCES

Acker, J. 1992. Gendering organizational theory. In *Gendering Organizational Analysis*, ed. A. J. Mills and P. Tancred, 248–260. Thousand Oaks, CA: Sage Publications.

Albelda, R., and A. Clayton-Matthews. 2006. Sharing the costs, reaping the benefits: Paid family and medical leave in Massachusetts. *Labor Resource Center Publications*, Paper 1. http://scholarworks.umb.edu/lrc_pubs/1 (accessed October 14, 2012).

Baum, C. 2004. Has family leave legislation increased leave taking? *Washington University Journal of Law and Policy* 15: 93–114. http://digitalcommons.law.wust.edu (accessed October 13, 2012).

Cornell University Division of Human Resources. 2008. Parental leave for non-academic staff. *Employee Brochure*. Ithaca, NY: Cornell University.

Cristia, J. 2006. The effect of a first child on female labor supply: Evidence from women seeking fertility services. Washington, D.C.: Congressional Budget Office.

Duke University Human Resources. 2012. Benefit policy. Durham, NC: Duke University. http://www.hr.duke.edu/benefits (accessed October 10, 2012).

Galtry, J. 2002. Child health: An underplayed variable in parental leave policy debates? *Community, Work and Family* 5 (3): 257–277.

Gootman, E., and C. Saint Louis. July 20, 2012. Maternity leave? It's more like a pause. *New York Times*. http://www.nytimes.com/2012/07/22fashion (accessed August 23, 2012).

Grenig, J. 1975. Public education: Maternity leave. *The Urban Lawyer* 7: 851–855. http://scholarship.law.marquette.edu/facpub/460 (accessed October 13, 2012).

Guendelman, S., M. Pearl, S. Graham, V. Angulo, and M. Kharrazi. 2006. Utilization of pay in antenatal leave among working women in southern California. *Maternal and Child Health Journal* 10 (1): 63–73.

Hamilton B., J. Martin, and S. Ventura. October 3, 2012. Births: Preliminary data for 2011. *National Vital Statistics Reports* 61 (5): 1–29. Hyattsville, MD: National Center for Health Statistics.

Laughlin, L. 2011. Maternity leave and employment patterns of first time mothers: 1961–2008. *Current Population Report*, P70-128. Washington, D.C.: U.S. Census Bureau.

Madsen, S. 2012. Women and leadership in higher education: Current realities, challenges, and future directions. *Advances in Developing Human Resources* 14 (2): 131–139.

Miller, C. August 22, 2012. In Google's inner circle, a falling number of women. *New York Times*. http://www.nytimes.com/2012/08/23/technology (accessed October 13, 2012).

Montana State University. 2012. Family advocacy. *Employee Brochure*. Bozeman, MT: Montana State University.

Pfizer. January 1, 2012. The Pfizer short-term disability policy and the Family and Medical Leave Act. *Employee brochure*.

Ray, R. 2008. A detailed look at parental leave policies in 21 OECD countries: Washington, D.C.: Center for Economic and Policy Research. http://www.cepr.net (accessed October 12, 2012).

Ray, R., J. Gornick, and J. Schmitt. 2009. Parental leave policies in 21 countries: Assessing generosity and gender equality. Washington, D.C.: Center for Economic and Policy Research. http://www.cepr.net (accessed October 10, 2012).

Stone, P. 2007. *Opting Out? Why Women Really Quit Careers and Head Home.* Berkeley and Los Angeles, CA: University of California Press.

University of Colorado. June 6, 2005. Administrative policy statement. https://www.cu.edu/policies/aps/hr/5019.pdf (accessed October 14, 2012).

University of Notre Dame. 1967. *Faculty Manual.* The Archives of the University of Notre Dame.

University of Notre Dame. 1973. *Faculty Handbook.* The Archives of the University of Notre Dame.

University of Notre Dame. 1985. *Faculty Handbook.* The Archives of the University of Notre Dame.

University of Notre Dame. 2008. Faculty family and medical leave policy. *Faculty handbook*. http://facultyhandbook.nd.edu/university-policies/fmla (accessed October 14, 2012).

U.S. Department of Labor. Women's Bureau. 2012. Our history: An overview 1920–2012. http://www.dol.gov/wb/info about_wb/interwb/htm (accessed October 7, 2012).

U.S. Department of Labor. Bureau of Labor Statistics. 2010. Women in the labor force: A databook. http://www.bls.gov/cps/wlf-databook-2010.pdf (accessed October 7, 2012).

Western Kentucky University. September 29, 1973. Minutes of meeting of board of regents. WKU Archives Records.

Western Kentucky University. November 7, 1979. Memorandum to president, Donald W. Zacharias from James L. Davis. WKU Archives Records.

Western Kentucky University. July 1, 1980. Maternity leave policy. *Personnel policies and procedures manual.*

Western Kentucky University. August 14, 1991. Maternity leave policy. *Personnel policies and procedures manual.*

Western Kentucky University. July 1, 2000. Family and medical leave. *Employee benefits summary.*

Western Kentucky University. April 17, 2007. Explanation of academic administrative procedures for sick/medical leave. Policy and procedure document 4.6350. http://www.wku.edu/policies/hr_policies/hrpolicy4_6350.pdf (accessed October 15, 2012).

Western Kentucky University. Human Resources. 1982. UA28/1 The personnel file. *Paper 1422.* WKU Archives Records. http://digitalcommons.wku.edu/disc_ua_records/1422 (accessed October 4, 2012).

Western Kentucky University. Human Resources. 1989. UA28/1 The personnel file. *Paper 1473.* WKU Archives Records. http://digitalcommons.wku.edu/disc_ua_records/1473 (accessed October 4, 2012).

Westminster College. 2012. *Faculty Handbook.* http://www.westminster-mo.edu/explore/offices/business/hr/Documents/FacultyHandbookAugust2012.pdf (accessed October 14, 2012).

Working Mother Network. 2012a. 2011 Working mother 100 best companies. http://www.workingmother.com/best-companies/ (accessed October 15, 2012).

Working Mother Network. 2012b. 2012 Working mother 100 best companies. http://www.workingmother.com/best-companies/ (accessed October 15, 2012).

Wyatt-Nichol, H. 2011. Case study: Female-friendly policies in the academe. In *Women in Public Administration: Theory and Practice,* ed. M. D'Agostino and H. Levine, 45–65. Sudbury, MA: Jones and Bartlett.

4

Women's Health Care and the Workplace

In this chapter, we explore women's maternal health care issues, particularly as they relate to women in the workforce. This chapter focuses on the issues important to women who are pregnant while working, and who then return to work postpartum. We also present the perspective of health-care professionals who treat women and infants. Finally, this chapter touches on the important issue of what is best for the baby's health with regard to maternity leave policies, and the importance of the baby's health to the mother's overall health and well-being. We conclude this chapter with a discussion of why it is so hard to approach women's health from a holistic viewpoint.

HEALTH INSURANCE FOR WOMEN OF CHILDBEARING AGE

Health insurance for many working women is provided through an employer or a family member's employer. In 2010, 167 million people, 54.9% of the civilian noninstitutionalized population, had employer-based health insurance. When there is a downturn in the economy, employer-based health insurance availability may decline, as an employee may lose coverage due to a layoff or job loss. Most employees are eligible to continue group health plan coverage under provisions of the *Consolidated Omnibus Budget Reconciliation Act* (COBRA), but often the employee cannot afford the premiums. The cost of purchasing an individual health insurance plan from a private provider can be prohibitive. Also, women of childbearing age may pay higher premiums for individual plans that include maternity coverage. If an employee transitions to part-time work, he or she may not be eligible for employer-based health insurance coverage (Brault and Blumenthal 2011, 1–8).

After the economic downturn that started in 2008 in the United States, there was a decrease in the number of workers aged 18 to 64 who were employed full time, year round. Many of these workers who lost their full-time jobs also lost their employer-based health insurance. Of all workers aged 18 to 64 in the civilian noninstitutionalized population, the number of employees with employer-based health insurance decreased from 105,477,000 (69.2% of all workers) in 2008 to 99,018,000 (67.1%) in 2010. From 2008 to 2010, the number of employees with non-employer-provided insurance increased, as did the number of uninsured (Brault and Blumenthal 2011, 1–8).

The U.S. Census Bureau reports that approximately 84.3% of the U.S. population had some type of health insurance coverage in 2011, with the remaining 15.7% uninsured (DeNavas-Walt, Proctor, and Smith 2012, 21). The Congressional Budget Office (CBO) and the Joint Committee on Taxation (JCT) have estimated that the current number of persons who have coverage through an employer-based health insurance plan may decrease by about 3 to 5 million persons in light of the anticipated changes to the health care system under the Affordable Care Act (ACA), which is set to go into effect over the next several years. The ACA refers to The Patient Protection and Affordable Care Act (Public Law 111-148), as amended by the health-care provisions of the Health Care and Education Reconciliation Act of 2010 (Public Law 111-152). Many of these persons who may lose employer-based coverage will be eligible to obtain coverage through government-sponsored programs such as Medicaid or State Children's Health Insurance Programs (SCHIP) or through new exchange networks that will be established. It is anticipated that the ACA will have significant impacts on small employers and employers that employ low-wage earners (Congressional Budget Office, March 2012).

In June 2012, the U.S. Supreme Court issued a ruling that made the expansion of the Medicaid program under the ACA a state option. The CBO and the JCT then updated their estimates of the budgetary effects of the health insurance coverage provisions of the ACA. As a result, they now expect that fewer people will be allowed to access coverage under Medicaid, which will mean more people will have to utilize coverage through the new exchanges or will be uninsured. The full impact of the

ACA will not be determined for several years, but the CBO predicts that most employers will continue to provide health insurance benefits for their employees (Congressional Budget Office, July 2012). That is hopeful news for gainfully employed women, but many underemployed women will continue to work for employers who do not provide access to health insurance, and therefore as part-time or low-wage earners, there is a great possibility that these women will be uninsured.

FERTILITY ISSUES

One factor important to many women in our study is the issue of fertility. Many women, especially if they have delayed childbearing until later in life, may need to undergo fertility treatments to become pregnant. There are also risks associated with women having children later in life: risk of birth defects such as Down syndrome, and medical risks for the mother, including greater risk of miscarriage. Other factors that may affect a woman's ability to become pregnant are education, smoking status, use of recreational drugs, obesity, and sexual frequency. Some infertility issues can be addressed with simple and inexpensive procedures (Cristia 2006, 6), but others require a lot of time, money, and effort.

In an interview, Dr. Dawn Charles-Heizman, a postgraduate, year-four resident in the University of Missouri–Kansas City School of Medicine Residency Program, and a health-care professional specializing in obstetrics and gynecology, shared her thoughts about patients seeking treatment for infertility:

> At our clinic, we see people with infertility and for preconception counseling. Anyone over the age of thirty should not try more than six months to become pregnant without seeking the help of an ob-gyn. If you are older, then you should seek help sooner. Of course, the male factor of infertility plays into this as well, but we see women of all ages. We see women who have a decreased or diminished ovarian reserve, meaning a decreased amount of eggs because of their age. We see women who have polycystic ovarian syndrome (PCOS), who are slightly overweight. We see women who are really thin with PCOS. We see women with structural anomalies from either STDs or endometriosis—those can happen at any age. Women in their 20s have their fair amount of problems. The way the world has changed with regard to nutrition, we often see patients with PCOS and

insulin resistance. These all play into ovulatory dysfunction and infertility. I think with younger people, we may start to see the prevalence of STDs—specifically chlamydia, and its role in causing mutations and blocking fallopian tubes.

If a woman needs help in conceiving, some of the costs associated with more invasive fertility treatments are paid for through health insurance, but many women must pay for these costs out of pocket. According to Dr. Charles-Heizman:

> We see many women in their mid-30s, who are trying to have their career or profession established and be financially secure when they start a family, but the flip side to that is the older you get the higher the rate of infertility, and the more it costs to get pregnant. So all the planning to be financially secure before starting a family could just put you in a situation to pay out more money. Infertility is not typically covered by insurance. However, some of the medicines to start treatment are relatively inexpensive. If you have to increase treatment into something like intrauterine insemination (IUI), that is probably $300 to $500. If you have to advance to *in vitro* fertilization (IVF), that is probably $8000.

The U.S. Census Bureau (2012, 75) reports on the outcomes of assisted reproductive technology. Data for the years 2000 through 2006 are shown in Table 4.1, which details the growing number of procedures over this time period and the outcomes of those procedures.

INTENDED AND UNINTENDED PREGNANCIES

In order to present a complete picture of women's health issues, here we'll address information on intended and unintended pregnancies. While the entirety of this book rests on the premise that babies who enter this world should always be wanted and welcomed, it must be acknowledged that abortions do occur every day in the United States, although the abortion rate per 1,000 women in the United States has decreased significantly over the past 20 years. The U.S. Census Bureau (2012, 76) reports that in 1990 the abortion rate was 27.4 per 1,000 women, in 2000 it was 21.3, and in 2007 it was 19.5. The reported number of abortions was 1,609,000 in 1990, 1,313,000 in 2000, and 1,210,000 in 2007.

TABLE 4.1

Outcomes of Assisted Reproductive Technology (ART) by Procedures, 2000–2006

Year	Procedures Started	Number of Pregnancies	Live Birth Deliveries (Defined as One or More Live Born Infants	Live Born Infants
2000	99,629	30,557	25,228	35,025
2001	107,587	35,726	29,344	40,687
2002	115,392	40,046	33,141	45,751
2003	122,872	43,503	35,785	48,756
2004	127,977	44,774	36,760	49,458
2005	134,260	47,651	38,910	52,041
2006	138,198	50,571	41,343	54,656

Source: U.S. Census Bureau. 2012. Outcomes of assisted reproductive technology (ART) by procedures: 2000–2006. *Statistical Abstract of United States:* 2012: 75. Washington, D.C.

Note: ARTs include infertility treatments in which both eggs and sperms are handled in the laboratory for the purpose of establishing a pregnancy—i.e., *in vitro* fertilization and related procedures.

In a related strand of literature, Mosher, Jones, and Abma (2012) studied pregnancy trends between 1982 and 2010, and examined specifically whether pregnancies that ended in a live birth were planned or unintended. Their results show that in the United States

> about 37% of births ... were unintended at the time of conception. The overall proportion unintended has not declined significantly since 1982.... Unmarried women, black women, and women with less education or income are still much more likely to experience unintended births compared with married, white, college-educated, and high-income women (1).

Some studies have shown that when births are unintended, there are adverse social, financial, and health consequences, and in some cases, adverse effects for both mother and child. Some research has shown an association between unintended pregnancies "and delayed prenatal care, smoking during pregnancy, not breastfeeding the baby, poorer health during childhood, and poorer outcomes for the mother, and the mother-child relationship" (Mosher et al. 2012, 2). These mothers may have financial difficulties in paying for prenatal care, and if they are uninsured the costs of having a baby may be insurmountable and may have lasting effects on the family's finances.

Conversely, sometimes even when a couple is not trying to have a baby, the unintended pregnancy may be met with happiness. In Table 4.2, results

TABLE 4.2

Mean Value "Happy to Be Pregnant" (on Scale of 1 to 10, with 1 Being Very Unhappy to Be Pregnant and 10 Being Very Happy to Be Pregnant)

Characteristic	Number of Births (in Thousands)	Mean Scale Value
Total	14,532	8.0
Intent at conception		
Intended	9,098	9.4
Unwanted	1,885	4.8
Mistimed	3,549	6.3
Less than 2 years too soon	1,361	7.2
2 years or more too soon	2,152	5.8
Whether mother wanted a baby with that partner		
Definitely yes	10,823	8.8
Probably yes	1,632	6.4
Probably no	767	5.5
Definitely no	1,292	4.7
Mother's perception of baby's father intent		
Intended	9,399	9.1
Unwanted	1,879	5.8
Mistimed	2,700	6.5
Don't know	554	5.5

Source: Mosher, W., J. Jones, and J. Abma. 2012. Intended and unintended births in the United States: 1982–2010. Division of Vital Statistics. *National Vital Statistics Reports* 55: 23. Hyattsville, MD: National Center for Health Statistics.

are presented of the "happiness" attitudinal factor based on a woman's positive and negative feelings toward pregnancy as identified in the study by Mosher, Jones, and Abma (2012, 11, 23). The mean value of happiness on a scale of 1 to 10 was 8.0 for this group of women. These data are further delineated by the woman's intention to become pregnant at conception; whether the mother wanted a baby with that partner; and the mother's perception of the baby's father's intention to have a child. These emotions about pregnancy—negative or positive—may impact and complicate how women feel about their work, too.

PREGNANCY AND WORK

Other studies, including Buzzanell and Liu (2005), have examined the role of a woman's feelings when finding out she is pregnant and the reaction to her pregnancy by her coworkers and supervisors in the workplace. In their study, many women became discouraged by the reactions and attitudes of their bosses, and many eventually left employment, which is an atypical outcome. Even when maternity leave was available as a standard benefit for employees, there was an attitude from supervisors that the leave was a "burden" on the company (11). Buzzanell and Liu reported that half of the women in their study believed that their pregnancies and subsequent maternity leaves were the reasons that their bosses demoted them or denied raises or promotions to them, and these women believed that these actions ultimately impacted their incomes and their potential for career advancement (12).

In addition to the feelings women have about finding out they are pregnant, it does not take long for other emotional and physical changes to begin. Buzzanell and Liu (2005, 13) state that "the pregnant body is one of excess, hormonal and emotional changes, and sexuality. Most participants talked about morning sickness, discomfort because of weight gain and swelling, and tiredness." As an example, in the higher education setting, O'Meara and Campbell (2011, 469) reported that one faculty member told them that what she most wanted was to not be noticed. "Being pregnant visually "screamed" that she was female every day in an environment where there were very few females. She wanted more privacy and invisibility than her body gave her" (469). So, while women in higher education may not be faced with extreme physical challenges or obstacles to doing their job while pregnant, they still perceive that their physical condition will impact how others view their commitment to their work (470). This in turn takes a toll on how a woman views her employer, supervisor, and coworkers, and it impacts the amount of maternity leave she may actually decide to take.

In our interview with Dr. Charles-Heizman, we asked about work restrictions that a pregnant woman might be placed under by her physician. She said:

> During pregnancy we don't typically put any work restrictions on pregnant women. It depends on the individual, and there are certainly high-risk pregnancies, but for a typical-normal pregnancy, no restrictions. The only thing we might do in terms of work is give lifting restrictions, if the patient has a job with heavy-lifting requirements. This would usually be a ten-pound weight limit restriction. We normally encourage a woman to work until her due date, because it is not that we necessarily feel that it is

better for the pregnancy, although it is not harmful, but FMLA is a finite period of time. Giving a patient a work restriction that says that they cannot work, that eats into their postpartum recovery time. A lot of times, our patients rely on their jobs to pay their bills, and so for them to be not getting paid going into having a newborn, it is not something that we want to see either. Obviously, if they are high-risk then they may be on bed rest, and we certainly would fill out FMLA paperwork and/or short-term disability forms, if that is an available option for the patient. Short-term disability may be partially paid. For example, a patient who breaks her water early on, may have to be on bed rest in the hospital until she delivers.

PREGNANCY AND FACTORS IMPACTING INFANT MORTALITY

Generally, we are focusing on working women as it relates to our specific study, and most of the women in our study have good-paying jobs and adequate health insurance benefits. However, it is also important to remember that approximately 15% of the U.S. population lives in poverty (DeNavas-Walt, Proctor, and Smith 2012), and even though some of those persons have health insurance they may not be able to afford the out-of-pocket expenses necessary for doctor visits, preventive tests, and medication. For all families, out-of-pocket nonpremium medical expenses do significantly impact the family's budget, and lack of care may affect the long-term health of children in those families (Smith and O'Hara 2011).

Further, a lack of insurance and/or a lack of prenatal care can be factors that result in higher rates of low-weight babies, preterm babies, and infant mortality. Many women who have no insurance or who cannot afford out-of-pocket expenses seek out health-care services through public health agencies. Other women fall through the cracks and do not get any medical attention. Of course, there are other health risk factors to both mother and baby, such as when prenatal care begins, maternal smoking status, and maternal educational attainment (Mathews and MacDorman 2012). Table 4.3 presents infant mortality rates for 2008 as related to these three factors.

Infant mortality rates in the United States in 2008 were 6.61 per 1,000 live births. This rate was down from the 2007 rate of 6.75. As reported in a study by the National Center for Health Statistics:

TABLE 4.3

Infant Mortality Rates for 2008 by Selected Characteristics for 22 States Reporting as of January 1, 2007

Characteristic	Rate
Prenatal care	
Prenatal care beginning in the 1st trimester	5.31
Prenatal care beginning after the 1st trimester or no care	7.37
Prenatal care beginning in the 2nd trimester	6.09
Prenatal care beginning in the 3rd trimester	5.60
No prenatal care	27.25
Smoking status during pregnancy	
Smoker	9.68
Nonsmoker	5.68
Maternal educational attainment	
Less than high school diploma	7.74
High school diploma	7.22
Some college/technical school	5.71
Bachelor's degree or higher	3.74

Source: Mathews, T. J., and M. MacDorman. 2012. Infant mortality statistics from the 2008 period linked birth/infant death data set. Division of Vital Statistics. *National Vital Statistics Reports* 60 (5): 24. Hyattsville, MD: National Center for Health Statistics.

Note: Rates per 1,000 live births in specified group.

Infant mortality was higher for male infants and infants born preterm or at low birth weight. Infant mortality rates were also higher for those infants who were born in multiple deliveries and to mothers who were unmarried.... Preterm and low-birth-weight infants had the highest infant mortality rates and contributed greatly to the overall U.S. infant mortality. The three leading causes of infant death—congenital malformations, low birth weight, and sudden infant death syndrome—accounted for 46 percent of all infant deaths (Mathews and MacDorman 2012, 2).

DELIVERY

In our interview with Dr. Charles-Heizman, we asked about delivery, the time the patient would be in the hospital, how long the patient might be relieved of work duties, and when the patient would be seen for a follow-up visit. Dr. Charles-Heizman said:

For FMLA purposes, we as a general or standard practice, fill out the length of time for the patient to be off on the paperwork as six weeks from delivery date. Six weeks is the standard—for normal delivery and for cesarean. It is the same for a hysterectomy too. In terms of gynecology, many procedures and techniques are becoming far more advanced. We are using minimally invasive techniques—laparoscopic hysterectomies, robot-assisted hysterectomies. The recovery time on those procedures is significantly less. In fact, many women can return to work sooner. We allow them six weeks, though. In terms of obstetric patients, even if women feel better earlier, they still have a new baby at home. That is a period of adjustment. If an employer allows longer, we certainly encourage that, if they can financially afford it.... But we don't as a rule have a conversation with the patient about what she wants or what is available or allowed at her place of work.

Typically, if it is a normal, uncomplicated vaginal delivery, we keep the patient in the hospital for two days postpartum, and then let the patient go home on postpartum day two, and we would see her back six weeks later. For C-sections we keep her until post-operative day number three or four, and insurance will pay up until post-operative day four. About a week after the C-section we bring her back to look at the incision. That might involve removing staples or just looking at the incision to make sure it is healing well. If it looks good then she would return six weeks from the delivery date. If a problem for the mom arises medically, even if it is not recognized until later after she goes home, then insurance would probably cover any issue within the global fee of pregnancy. Postpartum care is usually very easy and quick to obtain.

Obviously, women who have cesarean sections for delivery do stay longer in the hospital and are normally not released from their doctor's care for at least six weeks after the birth. In the United States, the rate of cesarean deliveries had increased substantially for about 15 years, but has now leveled off. From 1996 through 2009, the percentage of cesarean births rose 60%. In 2009, the cesarean delivery rate was 32.9 per 100 live births. The cesarean delivery rate for all births in the United States in both 2010 and 2011 was 32.8 per 100 live births (Hamilton, Martin, and Ventura, October 3, 2012).

Taking time off before delivery can help reduce the likelihood of a cesarean delivery. In a study of women in California who were allowed to take paid antenatal leave, Guendelman, Pearl, Graham, Hubbard, Hosang, and Kharrazi (2009) found that "after adjusting for gestational age, infant gender, maternal race, pre-pregnancy BMI, height, and occupation, women who took antenatal leave had almost four times lower odds of a primary cesarean delivery as women who continued working" (33). Preventing the need for a cesarean is important because a first-birth cesarean can be a predictor for cesareans in subsequent births due to increased risks of placenta previa and placental abruption (31). Women who are allowed to take time off before delivery can reduce their stress and anxiety levels, may get more rest and sleep, and may forestall in part the need for a cesarean, and therefore reduce the chance of complications (31).

MATERNITY LEAVE AND INFANT MORTALITY

In an international study covering 141 countries and which examined the relationship between maternity leave and infant mortality rate, Heymann, Raub, and Earle (2011, 127) found that "an increase of ten full-time-equivalent weeks of paid maternity leave was associated with a 10 percent lower neonatal and infant mortality rate … and a 9 percent lower rate of mortality in children younger than five years of age." The study controlled for total national health expenditures as a percentage of gross domestic product, the percentage of health expenditures that were made by the government and overall resources available to meet basic needs, female literacy, and basic public health measures (129).

Based on their results, Heymann, Raub, and Earle (2011) conclude that longer paid maternity leaves lead to longer periods of breast-feeding, which lowers infant and child morbidity by lowering risks of infection (128). Further, in addition to breast-feeding, prenatal care, quality care during delivery and immediately after, immunizations, postnatal health care, adequate sanitation, and nutrition all can have a positive impact on a child's health (128). These authors acknowledge that the ability for a woman to work, in the countries they studied, leads to positive outcomes for a family, in terms of income and gender equity. However, working or poor working conditions may lead women to cease breast-feeding due to the obstacles they face in the workplace, which is a negative effect (128). Early return to work after delivery or the inability to take time off for doctor's visits may lead to both poorer nutrition and poorer health outcomes for the baby (128, 129). Heymann et al. conclude that paid leave helps the family income and contributes to a woman's decision to remain with her employer after the birth of the baby, which in turns positively contributes to the woman's lifetime earnings (132).

MOTHER'S RETURN TO WORK AND BREAST-FEEDING

A mother's return to work and the issue of breast-feeding are intertwined. There are several studies that show a correlation between length of maternity leave and the duration of breast-feeding. The World Health Organization and the American Academy of Pediatrics has recommended that babies be fed only breast milk for the first six months of life (Galtry 2002, 259). Despite this recommendation, a national study by Ryan, Zhou, and Arensberg (2006, 248, 249) found that breast-feeding to six months of age was shortened by the mother's return to work full time. Further, they found that participation in the federally funded Women, Infants and Children (WIC) nutrition program "had a large, negative effect on the initiation and duration of breastfeeding, regardless of employment status." This finding raises the question as to whether the provision of free baby formula may be a disincentive to breast-feeding.

There are also studies that investigate why women do not initiate breast-feeding. A study of women in Arkansas reported that women did not initiate breast-feeding for the following reasons: not wanting to be tied down; not liking breast-feeding; being embarrassed; wanting the body back to oneself; household responsibilities; other children to care for; and going back to work or school. Some women reported that a lack of instruction by staff while in the hospital played a significant role in their decision to initiate breast-feeding. The age of the mother also played a role in the decision, with very young mothers being more likely to not initiate breast-feeding (Ogbuanu, Probst, Laditka, Liu, Baek, and Glover 2009, 275). Ogbuanu et al. cite concerns that public attitudes are not supportive of breast-feeding and call for public information campaigns to correct these negative attitudes (275). They also call for support for paid maternity leave in an effort to encourage mothers to initiate and continue breast-feeding (277). Finally, they express concern that hospital staff need to play a more proactive role in breast-feeding instruction, and they call for hospitals to offer support after the mother and baby leave the hospital (277). Ryan, Zhou, and Arensberg (2006) recommend that employers need to support breast-feeding mothers through workplace policies that support lactation. They suggest that this support in the workplace may lead to lower absenteeism, higher productivity, greater morale, and company loyalty (249, 250).

One meta-analysis of 31 studies related to breast-feeding support identified several aspects of women's experiences and their perceptions about breast-feeding support (Schmied, Beake, Sheehan, McCourt, and Dykes 2011). In their assessment, Schmied et al. defined the following types or styles of support: authentic, facilitative, reductionist, and disconnected. Authentic support reflects a trusting relationship. Help is offered in a supportive, not undermining, manner. The supporter listens in a positive way, and gives the mother time to feel relaxed, comfortable, and not pressured. The supporter affirms and acknowledges the experiences of the mother, without presuming or telling (51–53). Facilitative support is more of a partnership between mother and supporter. Mothers want to hear about personal and practical aspects of breast-feeding, along with potential challenges and difficulties. These mothers want detailed and accurate information. They want encouragement, but not pressure from the supporter (53, 54). The reductionist approach reflects a more difficult arrangement. The supporter may give conflicting information or oversimplified information to the point of the mother feeling unsatisfied with the support. This approach causes confusion and distress, and undermines the confidence of the mother (56). Finally, the disconnected approach seems to result in the most problems. Mothers report feeling a lack of confidence, guilt, disempowered, and undermined. The supporter is seen as too busy, disengaged, and too critical of the mother's efforts. While this may not have been the intention of the supporter, at a time when the mother is vulnerable, uncertain about her ability to breast-feed, feeling pressured and physically tired, the interaction leads to the mother feeling overwhelmed. Many mothers being supported with a disconnected approach gave up breast-feeding due to the perceived lack of support (57). This analysis supports the idea that the decision to breast-feed can be helped along if appropriate support is provided by health-care providers, and if women have access to this type of support. Further, health-care providers have to recognize that different women may perceive their instruction and support differently, and the lactation specialist may need to adjust the approach accordingly (58).

WELL-BABY DOCTOR VISITS

The ob-gyn can play a significant role in the baby's health and the success of breast-feeding too. Dr. Charles-Heizman reports that when patients return for an initial checkup after delivery, one of the issues discussed is the baby's health. Dr. Charles-Heizman says:

> We check in with how breast-feeding is going. Usually by six weeks after delivery patients are doing really well with breast-feeding, or they have abandoned it because they really struggled so much. We want to see how the baby is, how the health of the baby is, and make sure the baby has a pediatrician. We want to make sure the baby has gotten appropriate care.

With regard to the mother's return to work and her child's well-baby doctor visits, Hamman (2011) investigated the association between these two factors and the influence of other factors, including the mother's FMLA eligibility. Hamman states that the recommended number of visits to the doctor for a newborn is six visits by age 1. She reports that only 10% of infants meet those recommended number of visits. These well-baby checkups also serve to screen for possible conditions that might be corrected easily if caught early. Hamman, building upon the work of previous researchers, posits that mothers who return to work are under time constraints that limit the time off they have to take the baby for these checkups. Hamman reports that "mothers who work full-time take their children to 0.18 fewer visits than those who have quit their jobs.... Mothers with employer-provided paid vacation leave take their children to 0.20 more visits than other working mothers" (1,029). However, her findings suggest that even if mothers work for employers who provide paid sick or vacation leave, the accrued leave may have been exhausted during maternity leave, and so they may not actually have any of this type of paid leave available to use to take their child to the well-baby visits during the child's first year. Hamman suggests that employers should provide more paid leave in order to ensure that newborns meet the recommended number of visits to the doctor.

POSTPARTUM ISSUES

In the interview with Dr. Charles-Heizman, we asked about what occurs at the patient's six week follow-up visit after delivery. Dr. Charles-Heizman said:

> At six weeks, most patients want to talk about whether they are they released for work. They want to know if they can resume normal activities. They want to know if they can resume intercourse, and they want to understand what their options are for postpartum contraception, especially if

breast-feeding. We try to talk about nutrition and exercise, and encourage them to take care of themselves as well as baby.

We also asked about more serious issues that might arise at the six-week follow-up visit. Dr. Charles-Heizman reports that:

> One of the most unfortunate things we see is postpartum depression. We try to catch those patients with true postpartum depression, not just the baby blues, which is a more transient, normal emotional state after pregnancy. It doesn't mean everyone has it, but with the baby blues the mom is still functional, she is still caring for her baby, she is taking family support. She is not withdrawn. She is very involved. If those kinds of feelings worsen or progress, then we need to know and we need to catch it. Typically at that six-week checkup, every woman has to fill out a postpartum screening survey, and she is scored on that. The purpose is to identify problems. We have social workers who work in our clinic to find support and resources for her. We can start the patient on an antidepressant, or give her resources to find and follow-up with a psychiatrist. We see her back within a week of starting medication, and weekly thereafter until we ensure that she gets psychiatric follow up. At this point we might find it necessary to sign off on FMLA for the husband. We encourage men to take paternity leave if his employment allows for it. We normally sign off on FMLA for the father and for paternity leave because we feel the mothers need the care to recover after delivery or cesarean. Usually, we sign off on two weeks for the father from a medical perspective. But if there is a patient with severe depression, then we might sign off for six weeks for the husband or sometimes if there is no spouse we also sign off for another primary caregiver in the household—the grandmother, the sister, or other family member to help and support the mother.

Two interview subjects who are nurses—a pediatric emergency room nurse and a nurse with extensive experience in obstetrics—first stated that when women have good prenatal care they usually have better outcomes in terms of delivery as well as postpartum. When the nurses were asked about postpartum issues that they see in their professional roles, both women reported that "you see new moms that are sleep deprived, anxious, tired, exhausted, with dark circles under their eyes, and sometimes they have hormone imbalances." One of the problems that exacerbate these conditions is that "new moms think they are supposed to be invincible, and they don't feel that they can tell anyone how they are feeling especially if they are depressed, so by the time they get to us things are really bad." This can result in the baby being endangered even with the mother because of the mother's exhaustion, and it may result in injury to the baby. A worst-case scenario example seen by the ER nurse was a baby who was suffocated by the sleeping mother who rolled over on the baby. Interviewee 24 said:

> I have seen four cases in the last six months of women rolling over on their child in bed, because they are exhausted and they suffocated the child. The last mom—she was exhausted. She tried to go back to work too soon, and she put the baby in bed with her, rather than get up. I just don't know how you get over that.

When women are released to return to work, some workplace accommodation issues still arise. One issue that was mentioned by Dr. Charles-Heizman involved both pregnant women and women returning to work postpartum. Dr. Charles-Heizman said:

> One breast-feeding issue and return-to-work issue is the need to write notes or orders for a patient to have water at her desk. Or sometimes I have to write a note that a patient must be allowed to eat and drink frequently. Milk production strongly correlates to the amount of water you drink or consume, and your diet, the fat in your diet. Patients have to be able to meet their caloric intake needs, and they must be able to snack appropriately at their jobs and stay hydrated. That is also true for pregnant women, and for women with diabetes during pregnancy that must eat six small meals during the day. If they have one lunch break, they can't do that. There are some employers who, for safety concerns or OSHA regulations, for example, in a manufacturing job, don't allow the employee to have food or drink while they work. Even at a grocery store, the cashier may not be allowed to have a water bottle, or she may be given only very short and limited number of breaks. For women who want to pump at work, they need the time and the facilities to do so. I have heard from a lot of patients who have to go to a bathroom stall to pump. Resuming normal life and breast-feeding is hard.

Research on workplace accommodations for breast-feeding has shown that while most coworkers may view accommodations as reasonable, at the same time there are some employees who may feel resentful and view the accommodations as unfair (Seijts 2004, 162). In the study by Seijts, both males and females who had children were most likely to view accommodations as reasonable more so than employees who did not have children (163). Breast-feeding accommodations are minimal, and one of the most cost-effective benefits an employer can offer in the workplace (162).

Other studies have shown that mothers who breast-feed actually miss less work than mothers who formula feed their newborns, which supports the idea that there is a health benefit to breast-feeding for baby (151). Further, the U.S. Surgeon General supports longer breast-feeding because of the health benefits to the mother in terms of reduced incidence of breast and ovarian cancer. In a recent report, the U.S. Surgeon General states:

> Similarly, the risk of ovarian cancer was found to be 27 percent higher for women who had never breastfed than for those who had breastfed for some period of time. In general, exclusive breastfeeding and longer durations of breastfeeding are associated with better maternal health outcomes. (U.S. Department of Health and Human Services 2011, 1)

OPTIMAL LENGTH OF MATERNITY LEAVE

There are several studies that show the health benefits of taking time off after childbirth, and 12 to 20 weeks seems to be the optimum time for the mother's physical recovery. Of course, more time off is also important for mother–child bonding. For physical healing, Dr. Charles-Heizman reports that six weeks should be sufficient for most mothers to recover. However, the length of time a woman takes off of work varies by several factors: amount of paid leave available, her partner's earnings, total family income, work environments, birth outcomes—such as multiple births—and babies with health complications. In a study of new mothers in Minnesota before the enactment of FMLA, McGovern, Dowd, Gjerdingen, Moscovice, Kochevar, and Murphy (2000) found that for all women in their study the average length of the leave was 10 weeks. For women with some access to any type of paid leave (maternity, sick, vacation), the average was 10.5 weeks leave taken, and for women with no access to paid leave, the average time off was 6.6 weeks (547). This study supports the idea that having a lower-paying job, which typically provides fewer benefits, has an impact on the length of maternity leave taken.

Anthony (2008, 485, 486) supports extended maternity leave benefits, and she argues for the leave to be paid. She suggests that when parents has time off, they can be more attentive to the physical, emotional, and developmental needs of their children. Further, Anthony states that reduced work hours increases mental health; longer time off work after giving birth decreases depression and anger and leads to lower levels of anxiety, while reducing job turnover; schedule flexibility is linked to less depression, physical complaints ...; and social support systems at work reduce the work/family conflict. (485–486)

THE BABY'S PERSPECTIVE

Galtry (2002) suggests that any discussion of what the optimal length of maternity leave should be must include the perspective of the baby, specifically the child's health, education, and care (258). Consistent with the studies discussed above, breast-feeding can have positive health outcomes for the infant and the mother, and as other studies have shown, if returning to work full time limits the duration of breast-feeding, then we as a society may not be placing enough value on the importance of a longer maternity leave. Further, if we want to follow recommended breast-feeding guidelines, maternity leaves should be six months in duration or women should be allowed to return to work part time (259).

Galtry (2002) also suggests that because of breast-feeding alone, parental leave is not gender-neutral, and perhaps the United States should reconsider, reassess, and redesign a maternity leave period that would allow for breast-feeding to be continued at least until the child is six months old. Galtry does suggest that this leave be extended to both parents so that the family has control over child-care arrangements for their child (271). Employers could support this through temporary arrangements of part-time work, shorter workdays, flextime, or other ways to let the mother return to work on a gradual basis (266). An alternative or a complementary arrangement might be for the employer to support the mother's efforts to pump at work so that the caregiver could continue to feed breast milk to the baby (266). Of course, this particular arrangement would do nothing to enhance the mother–child bond (267).

When women do return to work, then one of the issues is the placement of the child in day care. Research is mixed with regard to the negative or positive effects on the development of infants and toddlers who attend child care out of the home (Galtry 2002, 260). Aside from the cognitive development, there is a health risk to babies who attend day care in terms of infectious diseases, minor as they may be. Generally, babies in day care

are two to three times more likely to experience upper respiratory tract and otitis media infections than babies who are cared for only at home (261). Of course, being at home does not ensure an environment free of germs or other potentially hazardous conditions (264). However, if a child is sick and cannot go to day care, there is still a need for someone to be with the child, and additional costs will be incurred by the family (264). Interviewee 24, a pediatric emergency room nurse, supports the idea that babies should be at home for the first three months. She says:

> If moms go back to work at six weeks, you don't have time to establish a routine. So, we have moms coming in the ER who are freaking out over things that are not a big deal, but then others, you think "why weren't you here days ago?" We see newborns in the ER, that when they first hit day care they are exposed to a lot. These are exposures that newborns should not be exposed to. In the ER if we see a baby that comes in with any kind of fever or unusual fussiness, and they are under three months of age, they are absolutely going to be admitted to the hospital—no question. They may get a spinal tap, and urine and blood tests. At less than three months, they are at a way higher risk for so many things, so that is another reason for moms to stay home for three months. We need to send the message to moms that it is okay not to rush back to work.

The development of a baby's brain structure and the subsequent development and learning potential of the baby is affected by interactions with the caregiver. The quality of care babies receive also influences the ability to form attachments (Lally 2010, 17). In the United States, babies go to formal day care very early as compared to babies in other countries (19). Child care is usually paid for by the family, and there is very little if any governmental support to offset the costs. Further, quality of care is hard to regulate, and there is great turnover of day-care workers, primarily because of the low pay. This turnover contributes to the lack of consistency in quality of care and in care from the same caregiver (20). These are additional reasons that a longer maternity leave would benefit both the health of mother and child, and the baby's continued long-term development. Support for the emotional connections and exchanges between mother and child also benefit society (19, 20).

The nurses interviewed for this chapter agreed that new mothers need to spend time with their babies in order to understand the rhythms and routines of their newborns. When the baby goes to day care too soon, for example, or is not with the same caregiver day in and day out, there is a chance that health problems will be overlooked or not identified because no one notices or sees a change in the infant that might be an indication of a developing problem. Plotka's (2012, 1) study of 3,850 working women and their infants supports this and showed that "the length of maternity leave had a significant effect on the quality of mother–child interactions measured when the infants were nine months." Plotka suggests that "the amount of time a mother is able to spend with her infant before she negotiates separation and reentry to work" plays a role in the way a mother learns to read her infant's cues and affects the attachment relationship formed.

Another related issue identified by the nurses interviewed is a lack of recognition that women do not always have immediate success with breast-feeding. The health care professionals interviewed recounted examples of women who for a variety of reasons—such as having complications with a vaginal or cesarean birth—may not have been given any instruction on breast-feeding while in the hospital, or they may have had a negative experience with breast-feeding while still in the hospital. Many times these women "fall through the cracks" and then give up on breast-feeding. These minor problems could have been corrected with just a little instruction.

One of the overarching issues is a gap in care because women are told to visit their ob-gyn in a few weeks, and the baby too is scheduled to see the pediatrician a few weeks after discharge. It is during those first few weeks that professional health-care intervention could make the difference in how a new mom is feeling and in how successful she is with breast-feeding. There is a need for follow-up care during this time so that women have the opportunity to ask questions even if everything is going well. As described by Interviewee 24:

> There is a gap between delivery and helping mom through that first couple of weeks. There is a gap there, because the pediatrician is not covering the mom, and the ob-gyn is not covering the baby, and really they are one and the same for a little while. Mom's health and baby's health are very connected, whether it be with nursing or getting used to their circadian rhythms together. Sometimes I don't think ob's are very good at recognizing problems or asking the right questions or explaining how not to get mastitis, or how to recognize it if you do. When the baby gets there, no matter how much education the lactation specialist has provided, it is just a whole different deal when baby actually arrives.

Dr. Charles-Heizman, also responded with a similar concern about breast-feeding support. She said:

> There really is a big time gap when the mother is just at home with the newborn. If they have a problem, they might see a lactation consultant that they saw while still here at the hospital, or they might come in for a class. Babies can get weighed, and we can troubleshoot any issues that might be going on.

More than 20 years ago, the U.S. General Accounting Office (1990), now the Government Accountability Office (both abbreviated as GAO), investigated the possibility of using visiting nurses for the purpose of offering services in the home to new mothers and babies in order to improve maternal and child health. The GAO report read:

> home visiting is a promising strategy for delivering or improving access to early intervention services that can help at-risk families become healthier and more self-sufficient. Evaluations have demonstrated that such services are particularly useful when families both face barriers to needed services and are at risk of such poor outcomes as low birth weight, child abuse and neglect, school failure, and welfare dependency (2).

Lally (2010) points to the record of other countries in providing government-funded prenatal care and postpartum care in the home as a way to support the development of the baby and the health and well-being of the mother. One example is taken from Victoria, Australia, where a nurse-educator visits each mother and newborn five days after birth, and then stays in touch with the family until the baby is 18 months old. Lally states that

> the home nurses report that they not only help with normal questions about breastfeeding and sleep, but they also address issues that arise early in the life of a baby that can derail emotional attunement, such as the ability to read the child's cues and respond accordingly (19).

In 1996, the U.S. GAO researched the growing trend of releasing mother and baby rather quickly after normal delivery, and the concern that this early discharge might lead to serious disorders not being identified appropriately. The findings of this report were inconclusive as to whether shorter hospital stays did or did not have adverse health consequences for babies or their mothers. However, the report did acknowledge that

> Many health professionals believe that short hospital stays increase the risk that neonatal problems will go undetected or that babies will leave

the hospital before accurate health screening results are obtained. Some pediatricians and obstetricians report seeing many more babies with jaundice, infection, and dehydration caused by difficulty in breast-feeding. Clinicians also express concern that mothers need more time to recuperate and learn how to care for their newborns, as they see new mothers struggling with breast-feeding, fatigued, and suffering from strep and urinary infections that could have been detected with an extra day in the hospital. (U.S. General Accounting Office 1996, 8)

While longer hospital stays after a normal delivery would not necessarily correct deficiencies in identifying problems, this particular study did identify some of the issues faced by new moms when they go home with the baby, many of which were recounted by the health care professionals interviewed for this project.

THE NEED FOR A HOLISTIC APPROACH TO WOMEN'S HEALTH

Anthony (2008, 485) suggests that when a woman's work and family responsibilities are in conflict it may manifest itself in "physical and mental health ailments ... depression, physical distress, sleep disorders, decreased concentration, decreased alertness." In a longitudinal study in the Minneapolis–St. Paul area, Grice, McGovern, Alexander, Ukestad, and Hellerstedt (2011) followed the experiences of new mothers over 18 months following the births of their children. Grice et al. wanted to understand the work–family conflict experiences of these mothers and how those conflicts impacted the mental and physical health of the mothers (20). These mothers participated in work duties such as checking e-mail and answering calls, while on maternity leave (21). Among the findings of this study, Grice et al. found that women experienced lower mental health when they had high levels of job spillover into their home lives; as did women who experienced home responsibilities spilling over into work (25). Grice et al. suggest that new mothers have to look for support and learn to ask for help from health-care providers, colleagues, and community support groups (25). Grice et al. state:

> On average, women's mental health outlook was also more positive when she perceived that her family was satisfied with the way she balanced both

work and family. When family members affirm how the mother balances both work and family they are also offering a form of emotional support. (25)

In the area of higher education, if women are untenured when they decide to have a baby, they may have the option to stop the tenure clock or extend the time to apply for tenure. This distinction is important, as the American Association of University Professors recommends the former. Stopping the clock sends the message that the mother's attention will be diverted elsewhere; extending the tenure period does not send the same message, and may be perceived by colleagues that the mother is somehow gaining an unfair advantage (Sotirin 2008, 264).

Perhaps because of this perceived bias, many women deliberately do not take advantage of these policies, and many universities report that this particular policy of stopping the tenure clock is underused (O'Meara and Campbell 2011, 447). In an extreme example found in the O'Meara and Campbell (2011, 464, 465) study, one faculty member recounted being told to not stop the tenure clock by a senior colleague and her department chair. They told her, "It will look bad for the department. It would look like you can't get your research done." The young woman said the message they conveyed was that "it would not be a good thing for my career." These administrators and others do not seem to recognize or acknowledge that for many women the years for childbearing and for attaining tenure occur simultaneously in a woman's life, and they do not seem to understand the added emotional and physical pressure they are putting on women by their insensitive comments or lack of understanding (Armenti 2004, 226). Further, these attitudes and actions of administrators persist because institutional policies do not allow for women to take a career path that might differ from that of their male colleagues (229). Whether women decide to delay applying for tenure or not, women still feel work-related pressure before, during, and after having a child and are torn between work and family responsibilities.

It is this author's considered opinion, although a gross overgeneralization, that some women often find it difficult to compartmentalize; that is, it is difficult even in the best of circumstances to divide the many components of life into separate areas or categories and even more difficult to keep them separated. This is not a disadvantage; rather, this capacity for seeing the whole rather than the parts is a distinct and positive advantage. While I also believe that women can manage the multifaceted aspects of their lives with style, grace, and aplomb, it can be difficult and sometimes overwhelming. If something is out of sync in one area it may affect other areas. This tension between work and family must be a consideration in any discussion of women's health. As one author wrote, after reading a humorous book entitled, *Men Are Like Waffles, Women Are Like Spaghetti* (Farrel and Farrel 2001), "the book compared men to waffles, with compartmentalized thinking and roles, and women to spaghetti, with ideas and roles that were interwoven" (Mills 2008, 216). This book resonated with Mills, and she suggested that her view and ideas of how to blend her work and family were interwoven, but the men she worked with saw those as separate realms of responsibility and, consequently, made both realms more difficult to manage (216).

An example of trying to manage competing demands is best summarized in the words of one mother in higher education:

> I loved my work and I loved my kids. But, I didn't love … always feeling behind, overwhelmed, and fearful that all of the fragile glass balls I juggled would come cascading down if I ever stopped moving. I rarely admitted my fatigue, concerns about inadequacy, or fear of failure. (Short-Thompson 2008, 255)

If we are to approach women's health holistically, we must "ask new questions about women's participation in society and what health means to women … and involve women in the process of generating knowledge" (Raftos, Mannix, and Jackson 1997, 1,147). We must listen to women. We must recognize the complexities of women's social, political, economic, and cultural realities and the role that each aspect plays in a woman's health (1,142, 1,147). We must look at the whole, rather than try to compartmentalize women's health into maternal health, reproductive health, child health, or family health.

In our interview with Dr. Dawn Charles-Heizman, we asked about her perspective on approaching women's health from a holistic viewpoint. We asked if the typical medical professional tries to understand all of the competing stressors and issues that are going on in a woman's life at the time she is having a baby. We asked if she thought medical professionals are looking at the whole picture. Surprisingly, among the first words she used to describe the current approach to women's health was "compartmentalized." Dr. Charles-Heizman responded as follows:

> I would say that we have compartmentalized women's health, which makes my job easier as an ob-gyn. If I was the one who had to say you get six weeks

off for maternity leave, or no, because you are having more trouble adjusting at home you get ten weeks off. That is a hard decision for a health-care provider to make. And then to be responsible for the financial impact that might result from the decision of keeping someone off work that is very difficult, especially if the leave is unpaid. Obviously, things are being missed. If you look at other countries, they take way more than six weeks off for maternity leave to be home with their babies. In the United States there are certain employers who allow 12 weeks at home. I think any woman who is given that opportunity and who has the financial means should take that leave. That is my view as a woman.

So, the doctor is charged with clearing the patient from a surgical and physical health perspective, and of course part of her health is the emotional aspect too, especially if the woman is showing signs of depression. Depression is not the only emotion that can be a factor after delivery. Debilitating stress, lack of focus or concentration at work can be issues, especially if the patient is thinking about her baby at home, while she is at work. Reliable day care can factor into how the patient feels too.

I don't think that there is any one person that is charged with taking care of the entire well-being of a patient. I think most ob-gyn's would like to think that we do that. We try to work women up from a primary care perspective. We take care of their needs in terms of women's health, but at the same time, we are restricted by the economy, the state of how we do business in our nation, whether that is dictated by the government, the employer, or the insurance companies. We have to work in and around those systems just as much as the patient does.

I always try to err on the side of what is right for the patient. Every physician has to work within those constraints—insurance companies tell us how long the patient can stay in the hospital after delivery, or how many visits they can come back for. Everything is done within the confines of the bigger structure—insurance companies, government, and FMLA—it protects your job, but it doesn't give you money to live on.

Perhaps it is these types of institutional constraints that have kept us from making meaningful changes to maternity leave policies in the past. As a society, we need to recognize that new mothers are facing myriad challenges the first few weeks after giving birth—lack of sleep; breast-feeding; healing the body; caring for a newborn; trying to fit in exercise and good nutrition; attending to the father's emotional and, eventually, physical needs; and in some cases attending to other children's needs. Did I mention the laundry, cooking, dishes, walking the dog, paying bills, and running errands? Where is work supposed to fit into this schedule during the first few weeks after giving birth? Should it? Is it so impossible to think that organizations might consider offering a valuable employee a paid maternity leave? Can we support what is healthy for the employee and her baby, without imposing on her the consideration of what is healthy for her career? (Short-Thompson 2008, 254).

In Chapter 5, we continue the journey of understanding maternity leave, and we describe the rationale for using a qualitative approach for this research project. We describe the participants who were interviewed, and present the questions used to guide the interviews.

REFERENCES

Anthony, D. 2008. The hidden harms of the family and medical leave act: Gender-neutral versus gender equal. *American University Journal of Gender, Social Policy and the Law* 16 (4): 459–501.

Armenti, C. 2004. May babies and posttenure babies: Maternal decisions of women professors. *The Review of Higher Education* 27 (2): 211–231.

Brault, M., and L. Blumenthal. 2011. Health insurance coverage of workers aged 18 to 64, by work experience: 2008 and 2010. American Community Survey Briefs #10-11. Washington, D.C.: U.S. Census Bureau. http://www.census.gov/prod/2011pubs/acsbr10-11.pdf (accessed November 3, 2012).

Buzzanell, P., and M. Liu. 2005. Struggling with maternity leave policies and practices: A poststructuralist feminist analysis of gendered organizing. *Journal of Applied Communication Research* 33 (1): 1–25.

Congressional Budget Office. March 2012. CBO and JCT's estimates of the effects of the affordable care act on the number of people obtaining employment-based health insurance. http://www.cbo.gov/sites/default/files/cbofiles/attachments/03-15-ACA_and_Insurance_2.pdf (accessed November 3, 2012).

Congressional Budget Office. July 2012. Estimates for the insurance coverage provisions of the affordable care act updated for the recent Supreme Court decision. http://www.cbo.gov/sites/default/files/cbofiles/attachments/43472-07-24-2012-CoverageEstimates.pdf (accessed November 3, 2012).

Cristia, J. 2006. The effect of a first child on female labor supply: Evidence from women seeking fertility services. Washington, D.C.: Congressional Budget Office.

DeNavas-Walt, C., B. Proctor, and J. Smith. 2012. Income, poverty, and health insurance coverage in the United States: 2011. Current Population Reports P60-243. Washington, D.C.: U.S. Census Bureau.

Farrel, B., and P. Farrel. 2001. *Men Are Like Waffles—Women Are Like Spaghetti: Understanding and Delighting in Your Differences*. Eugene, OR: Harvest House Publishers.

Galtry, J. 2002. Child health: An underplayed variable in parental leave policy debates? *Community, Work and Family* 5 (3): 257–277.

Grice, M., P. McGovern, B. Alexander, L. Ukestad, and W. Hellerstedt. 2011. Balancing work and family after childbirth: A longitudinal analysis. *Women's Health Issues* 21: 19–27.

Guendelman, S., M. Pearl, S. Graham, A. Hubbard, N. Hosang, and M. Kharrazi. 2009. Maternity leave in the ninth month of pregnancy and birth outcomes among working women. *Women's Health Issues* 19: 30–37.

Hamilton B., J. Martin, and S. Ventura. October 3, 2012. Births: Preliminary data for 2011. *National Vital Statistics Reports* 61 (5): 1–29. Hyattsville, MD: National Center for Health Statistics.

Hamman, M. 2011. Making time for well-baby care: The role of maternal employment. *Maternal Child Health Journal* 15: 1029–1036.

Heymann, J., A. Raub, and A. Earle. 2011. Creating and using new data sources to analyze the relationship between social policy and global health: The case of maternal leave. *Public Health Reports* 26: 127–134.

Lally, J. R. 2010. School readiness begins in infancy: Social interactions during the first two years of life provide the foundation for learning. *Kappan* 92 (3): 17–21.

Mathews, T. J., and M. MacDorman. 2012. Infant mortality statistics from the 2008 period linked birth/infant death data set. Division of Vital Statistics. *National Vital Statistics Reports* 60 (5): 1–28. Hyattsville, MD: National Center for Health Statistics.

McGovern, P., B. Dowd, D. Gjerdingen, I. Moscovice, L. Kochevar, and S. Murphy. 2000. The determinants of time off work after childbirth. *Journal of Health Politics* 25 (3): 527–564.

Mills, M. B. 2008. Interactions between work and family: When a playpen can be office furniture. *Women's Studies in Communication* 31 (2): 213–217.

Mosher, W., J. Jones, and J. Abma. 2012. Intended and unintended births in the United States: 1982–2010. Division of Vital Statistics. *National Vital Statistics Reports* 55: 1–28. Hyattsville, MD: National Center for Health Statistics.

Ogbuanu, C., J. Probst, S. Laditka, J. Liu, J. Baek, and S. Glover. 2009. Reasons why women do not initiate breastfeeding: A southeastern state study. *Women's Health Issues* 19: 268–278.

O'Meara, K., and C. Campbell. 2011. Faculty sense of agency in decisions about work and family. *The Review of Higher Education* 34 (3): 447–476.

Plotka, R. 2012. Maternity leave, mother-child interactions, and attachment. Dissertation. New York: Fordham University.

Raftos, M., J. Mannix, and D. Jackson. 1997. More than motherhood? A feminist exploration of "women's health" in papers indexed by CINAHL 1993-1995. *Journal of Advanced Nursing* 26: 1142–1149.

Ryan, A., W. Zhou, and M. Arensberg. 2006. The effect of employment status on breastfeeding in the United States. *Women's Health Issues* 16: 243–251.

Schmied, V., S. Beake, A. Sheehan, C. McCourt, and F. Dykes. 2011. Women's perceptions and experiences of breastfeeding support: A metasynthesis. *Birth: Issues in Perinatal Care* 38: 49–60.

Seijts, G. 2004. Coworker perceptions of outcome fairness of breastfeeding accommodation in the workplace. *Employee Responsibilities and Rights Journal* 16 (3): 149–166.

Short-Thompson, C. 2008. A parenting odyssey: Shouldering grief, welcoming joy. *Women's Studies in Communication* 31 (2): 249–257.

Smith, J., and B. O'Hara. 2011. The financial burden of paying for non-premium medical expenses for children. Social, Economic and Housing Statistics Division Working Paper #2011-12. Washington, D.C.: U.S. Census Bureau.

Sotirin, P. 2008. Academic momhood: In for the long haul. *Women's Studies in Communication* 31 (2): 258–267.

U.S. Census Bureau. 2012. Abortions by selected characteristics: 1990–2007. *Statistical Abstract of the United States: 2012*: 76. Washington, D.C.

U.S. Census Bureau. 2012. Outcomes of assisted reproductive technology (ART) by procedures: 2000–2006. *Statistical Abstract of the United States: 2012*: 75. Washington, D.C.

U.S. Department of Health and Human Services. 2011. *The Surgeon General's Call to Action to Support Breastfeeding*. Washington, D.C.: U.S. Department of Health and Human Services, Office of the Surgeon General.

U.S. General Accounting Office. 1990. Home visiting: A promising early intervention strategy for at-risk families. GAO Report #HRD-90-83. Washington, D.C.

U.S. General Accounting Office. 1996. Maternity care: Appropriate follow-up services critical with short hospital stays. GAO Report #HEHS-96-207. Washington D.C.

5

Research Approach

THE METHODOLOGY: WHY QUALITATIVE RESEARCH?

This research project utilizes a qualitative approach for gathering data. For this project, the qualitative approach gives the researcher an opportunity to understand, to get to the heart of this very complex issue, and to understand the meaning of the experience of utilizing maternity leave. As Miles and Huberman (1994) point out, the first question skeptics ask a qualitative researcher is, why did you not use a survey to collect data? Even the best survey instrument would have been difficult to distribute to women who had given birth recently and had taken maternity leave. There are some studies of maternity leave that have tried this approach, but I wanted to approach data gathering in a way that would get to responses beyond what five point Likert-scale questions might offer on a traditional survey instrument.

In order to address the obstacle of finding persons who had recently utilized maternity leave, the individuals who were asked to participate were based on a purposive sample. I set out to interview women who had become a mother while working, and utilized a snowball or referral type of sampling. Each participant was asked to refer others who might also be a relatively new parent, and whom a participant thought might be willing to participate. These referrals, of course, led to both similar and more dissimilar interviewees, but all were helpful for making comparisons across the data and for enriching the data collected. One of the dangers of qualitative research is to sample too narrowly, so it is helpful to explore all referrals to ensure that one has a sample that is wide, deep, and contrasting (Miles and Huberman 1994, 34).

Each referral was first contacted by the recommending participant to ascertain whether the person was agreeable to actually being contacted by the researcher. E-mail addresses or phone numbers were then exchanged, and contact was made by the researcher. None of the referrals declined to participate. Although some referrals were not sure initially what they could contribute, by the end of the interviews, it is hoped they understood that all stories were worthy of being told and included in the research project.

Most of the interviews were conducted in person, usually lasting from 45 to 90 minutes, and were done at a location of the interviewee's choice. A very limited number of interviews were conducted via telephone if scheduling difficulties made an in-person interview unattainable. As noted above, the in-depth interviews provided a more diverse and richer type of probing than another data collection method might have allowed, which was a primary goal of this research project. All interviews were conducted by the author.

The very nature of qualitative research demands that the researcher listen to the interviewee and let the "words" of the interviewee speak for her or him. The words represent the individual's perspective, and each person adds a meaningful layer to understanding the phenomena under study (Miles and Huberman 1994, 5). The text—the transcribed words—is the data with which the researcher works. It is bulky and cumbersome, and the researcher must be careful not to overweigh or underweigh his or her understanding of the words. Words can be organized so that the researcher can compare, contrast, analyze, and find patterns (Miles and Huberman 1994, 7).

Further, reliability and validity in qualitative research include factors such as quality control, triangulation, member checking, peer debriefing, credibility, dependability, and authenticity. Although computer software was used for this project, using software does not ensure reliability or validity. Rather, it is more important to build into the process factors such as interviewing multiple people across differing organizations, interviewing people with different perspectives, accurately transcribing the audiotapes, preserving the data collected, allowing interviewees to check their own words, and acknowledging any biases of the researcher. The author fully acknowledges that the interviews were in part an act of collaboration toward an understanding of the use of maternity leave benefits, more than a completely detached data-gathering mission (Miles and Huberman 1994, 8). Further, all researchers must acknowledge that they may see more than is there, and must be careful not to lose their perspective. This is why it is so critical to let the words of these women speak for them, and then let the reader interpret and learn something from each story.

Each interviewee was promised confidentiality and anonymity. Measures used to protect the interviewees include (1) referring to each participant by number; (2) separating demographic data from participant comments and from participant identification numbers; (3) storing audiotapes and written field notes in a secure location and separate from identifying data; (4) committing to destroying audiotapes, field notes, and identifying information at a date in the future; and (5) allowing participants to withdraw from the study at any time.

Each interviewee was given the opportunity to review her words and retract anything she said that she was not comfortable with upon review. It is of interest that, when given this opportunity, some women were afraid to share some of the stories they had provided, even knowing that their identity would be protected. They feared retaliation within their own organizations. One interviewee, upon review of the written transcript of her interview, asked for a paragraph to be deleted because she was afraid her employer could identify her. There was absolutely not one identifying word or phrase in that entire paragraph. Another interviewee at the end of the interview said, "I hate almost to say this, but I don't want to be identifiable... . It is so depressing. I wish I could be different about it. It does make me a little nervous, even with tenure. You never know." This fear is perhaps the most poignant and most telling finding to come out of the interviews and this project.

ANALYSIS OF THE INTERVIEWS

Miles and Huberman (1994, 44) suggest several uses of software in qualitative research. The uses include making notes in the field; transcribing field notes; editing or correcting field notes; coding; storage or organizing; search and retrieval of key words and phrases, quotes, and themes; data linking between and among interviews or transcripts; content analysis; data display; conclusion drawing or verification; creating diagrams; and preparing preliminary and summary reports.

When choosing a software program to aid in a project, the researcher should think about the needs for the analysis process, and the functions and flexibility that the software can provide (Miles and Huberman 1994, 312). QSR NVivo software helps to code, index, and summarize data and themes. The use of content analysis software in qualitative research is meant to strengthen and support the findings of the researcher. At a minimum, the researcher has a tool for storing, organizing, processing, retrieving, and displaying data. The real usefulness provided by content analysis software to qualitative research is in the coding and identification of themes and patterns in the data (Gordon 2009).

For this project, the content of the transcribed interviews was first analyzed phenomenologically using a constant comparative method to look for statements of similarity and dissimilarity for the purpose of understanding the perceptions and experiences of the utilization of maternity leave benefits. Then, to build upon the results of the constant comparative method of analyzing the transcripts, QSR NVivo content analysis software was utilized to explore and code the data for the purpose of looking for further similarities and dissimilarities. While software helps the researcher make sense of the data, no tool can be a substitute for gaining understanding through listening to the interviewees.

Early steps taken in the data analysis process allow the researcher time to think about new questions to ask in subsequent interviews; correct any misconceptions or poorly worded questions; add any follow-up questions that are deemed appropriate to the study; and consider any surprises that might come out of the initial interviews. It is important for the researcher to have time to reflect and to ask questions such as (1) does it make sense? (2) is it plausible? (3) are there rival or counterexplanations for what I am hearing? (4) is what I am hearing supported in the literature? (5) are there inconsistencies across the interviews, and what might these inconsistencies mean? (Miles and Huberman 1994, 50–56, 246, 268, 270).

It is also helpful if transcription is done as soon as possible after the interviews so that field notes can be used to augment any questions the transcriptionist has or to address any problems with the taped interviews. Any nonverbal observations made during the interviews can also be incorporated into the preliminary analysis, and any nonessential information can be discounted. Further, by conducting a preliminary and ongoing analysis, the danger of the researcher becoming overwhelmed by the volume of information collected, or forgetting what meaningful information was heard in each interview, is eliminated. Taking these steps can result in the researcher doing a better job of tracking related themes and patterns found in the transcripts, which in turn adds to the quality of the research project and which may serve to energize the researcher (Miles and Huberman 1994, 50–56).

Based on a careful reflection and analysis of the results, this researcher developed an understanding of the perceptions and experiences of the utilization of maternity leave benefits. The findings, as presented in the following chapters, are in no way meant to be generalized. They do, however, provide a crucial first step in providing a fresh perspective to an ongoing concern that seems to be overlooked and understated in the literature and in the workplace. This oft-silent topic has been given voice through the words of these women.

Miles and Huberman (1994) suggest that looking at a cross section of organizations and at a variety of persons interviewed allows us some ability to generalize the results because we are able to deepen our understanding of the perceptions of these individuals about a particular phenomenon, an issue, or a theme—in this case, the utilization of maternity leave benefits. Without overstating the results, at the very least, we can find value in the lessons learned from listening to the experiences of others. Although the results of this research cannot be fully generalized, they can be shared with others so that they may use the information to make improvements within their own organizations in the area of employee benefits—especially in a research area such as this where understanding the words and perceptions of individuals can be very important and meaningful.

STUDY LIMITATIONS

As with all qualitative research projects, critics interested in strictly quantitative analysis point to the lack of the generalizability of the results as a deficiency of qualitative research. As noted above, the best way to ensure that this study is presenting reliable and valid results is to listen to these women and pursue high standards of accuracy and verifiability in the presentation of their words, and in the conclusions drawn from these interviews. Another limitation of qualitative research as expressed by critics is the lack of the ability to replicate the research. By presenting specific detail on how the study was structured and the procedures by which the study was conducted, this limitation is overcome. Finally, it is impossible to ever interview as many people as someone else might suggest is necessary in order to fully understand such a complex subject. However, based on previous experience with qualitative research, 20 interviews are usually sufficient to reach the point at which you have developed a good sense of what is going on and what is meaningful within a particular topic area.

It must be noted that there are missing voices. This study does not include disadvantaged or underemployed women, so we must acknowledge that generally well-informed and educated women are those who are included in this study. The study is limited to women in higher education and in the pharmaceutical industry. These are women who typically are adequately paid, qualify for benefits, and are generally eligible for coverage under the FMLA. Further, while women of differing ethnic and cultural backgrounds are included, the voices of women of color are missing, and this is a concern, but one that will be addressed in future research. These deficiencies do not mean that the experiences of these particular women who were interviewed should not be valued.

Limitations of resources—time constraints and lack of an unlimited travel budget—also had an impact on the number of interviews conducted. As noted previously, when possible the interviews were conducted in person so that all of the nuances of body language and facial expressions could be understood by the researcher. The fact that some interviews had to be conducted by telephone is considered by the researcher to be a limitation of this study.

Availability and use of maternity leave benefits are universal and continuing issues of importance for women, men, families, and organizations. Only by understanding the experiences and perceptions of women can we start to address these issues and make meaningful improvements on an institutional and societal level.

THE PARTICIPANTS: WHO ARE THESE WOMEN?

For this study, 18 women were interviewed about their experiences with maternity leave. Interviews were conducted over the course of a year or so across eight states—California, Colorado, Connecticut, Indiana, Kentucky, Missouri, New York, and Rhode Island. Table 5.1 presents selected demographic information on each interviewee. Any information that could potentially identify participants has been removed from this table. The interviewees included four at private universities, nine at public universities, and five in the private sector, employed primarily in pharmaceutical companies. The women ranged in age from 29 to 44 years at the time of interviews. The

TABLE 5.1

Demographic Information on Interviewees

Number of Children	Ages of Children at Time of Interview	Degree Attained	Year Degree Earned	Tenure Status (if applicable)	Annual Base Salary
2	9, 5	MASTER	1996	Nontenure track	$36,000
4	16, 13, 8, 6	PHD	2009	Nontenure track	$46,000
1	13 weeks	MASTER	2010	Nontenure track	$45,000
2	13, 7 months	PHD	2002	Tenure track	$42,000
3	14, 12, 8	PHD	2009	Tenure track	$42,000
3	8, 7, 4	PHD	2013	Private	$126,000
2	3, 18 months	BACHELOR	2001	Private	$0
1	Under a year	PHD	2008	Nontenure track	$93,000
2	4, 22 months	BACHELOR	2002	Private	$92,000[a]
1	1	BACHELOR	2002	Private	$83,081[a]
2	2½, 2 months	BACHELOR	2005	Nontenure track staff	$44,000
2	27 months, 6 months	PHD	2006	Tenure track	$70,000
1	3 months	MASTER	1994	Nontenure track staff	$42,792
1	4 months	PHD	2004	Tenured	$56,136
2	9, 3	PHD	2007	Tenure track	$72,000
2	5, 3	PHD	2004	Tenured	$63,000
1	3½	PHD	2006	Tenure track	$60,000
1	9 months	BACHELOR	2000	Private	$105,000[a]

[a] Salary reported includes bonuses.

ages of their children at the time of the interviews ranged from 2 months to 16 years. Ten of the women hold a PhD, and the others have master's or bachelor's degrees. Only two of these women were tenured. The annual salaries of these women ranged from $0 for those not working to $126,000.

Eight other individuals were interviewed for this project on topics related to personnel or administrative issues, maternity leave benefits, paternity leave benefits, or some aspect of women's health, but they had not taken maternity leave in the recent past. These individuals on the periphery of our central topic of the utilization of maternity leave are not included in the table that presents demographic information.

DESCRIPTION OF THE IN-DEPTH INTERVIEW QUESTIONS

In-depth interviews using a set of semistructured questions were used to guide the interviews, but spontaneity was encouraged. Follow-up questions were interjected by the author when appropriate. For example, initially there was no question included about breast-feeding, but the first interview demonstrated that breast-feeding and pumping at work were issues critical to the successful return of the mother to the workplace, so questions were added to address this topic. Interviews were recorded on tape and transcribed verbatim. Each transcript was reviewed in triplicate to ensure accuracy and completeness. The questions used to guide the interviews were

- What was your experience like in terms of making the decision to have or adopt a child? What professional concerns did you have?
- At what point in the process did you seek out or investigate organizational policies on maternity/paternity leave? Health insurance benefits? Other benefits?
- What professional concerns did you have?
- What was your experience like in terms of conceiving/adopting a child?
- What professional concerns did you have? (reactions of colleagues, supervisors)
- What was your experience like in terms of delivery?
- What was your experience like in terms of utilizing maternity leave, paternity leave, parental leave, and family leave?
- Did your spouse take leave? At the same time? At a different time?
- If you took time off, when did you return to work?
- What was your experience like in terms of returning to work?
- Did you return to work full time or part time?
- Did you ask for reduced or modified (teaching load or) duties?

- Did you ask for the tenure clock to be stopped? (for higher education interviewees)
- After you had a child, what was your experience like in terms of balancing home and work responsibilities?
- Upon returning to work, what was your child-care decision like? Problems, issues, concerns?
- What has your experience with child care been like?
- What impact has the decision to have a child or not have a child had on your (tenure and promotion or) employment promotion process?
- Overall, how has having a child affected your commitment to your institution or employer?
- Looking back, what might you have handled differently?
- Looking back, what might you have wanted to see your employer do differently?

In the next chapter, profiles of each interviewee are presented. The chapter is organized and the interviewees are divided by the type of institution each woman works for—public institutions of higher learning, private institutions of higher learning, and the private sector's pharmaceutical industry. Their stories are told in their own words. Chapter 7 summarizes some of the themes and patterns that developed out of the collection of interviews.

REFERENCES

Gordon, V. 2009. Perceptions of regional economic development: Can win-lose become win-win? *Economic Development Quarterly* 23: 317–328.

Miles, M., and A. M. Huberman. 1994. *Qualitative Data Analysis*. Thousand Oaks, CA: Sage.

6

The Interviews: Profiles of Women and Their Perceptions and Experiences

Rarely when reporting on qualitative data is one given the opportunity to present the entire content of multiple interviews. Usually, the researcher must summarize, organize, or give some context within which to place the interviewee's words (Sandelowski 1998). In this chapter, the interviewees of this study tell their own stories in their own voices, although only partial content of each of the interviews is presented. Then, in Chapter 7, selected passages from the interviews are presented with the intent of identifying, illustrating, and illuminating the common themes and patterns that have become evident to the researcher. In this chapter, there is minimal interpretive and analytical intrusion (377), and the reader has the luxury of listening to the words of the interviewees and learning about their maternity leave experiences directly from these remarkable women. With very few exceptions, no content of the interviews presented in this chapter is repeated again in Chapter 7.

This chapter and the interviews are organized into three parts: first, public university employees, then, private university employees, and finally, pharmaceutical industry employees. This division allows the similarities and differences among the experiences of women to be compared and contrasted by the reader. Identifying comments such as names of places, organizations, and individuals are eliminated, and demographic information is omitted from the profiles to protect the privacy of the individuals. The profiles are presented in a question and answer format.

EMPLOYEES OF PUBLIC UNIVERSITIES

Interviewee 13 is employed in a full-time, year-round, staff position at a public university. We met in her campus office for the interview. We began our conversation with a discussion of her very recent return to work after maternity leave.

> Q. What professional concerns did you have upon returning to work?
> A. Interviewee 13.
>> I still struggle with working full time. It is not being there for him you know during the day, and then also being able to focus and being fully available at work. I think that you are torn either way. At work you want to be present, and you want to be available. There are evening things with my job, and basically right now, I don't want to work in the evenings. Fortunately, my job does not call for that very often, but on occasion it does. Right now I've been back here for four weeks since my maternity leave, and I pretty much want to go home right after work.
>
> Q. What was your experience like in terms of making the decision to have a child? At what point in the process, did you seek out or investigate HR policies on maternity leave?
> A. Interviewee 13.
>> I don't mind sharing that we had lost a baby, and I had been on medicine and it just was not happening. I wasn't getting pregnant. I had made a conscious decision to not continue with any type of other fertility treatments, and I had made peace. So in terms of looking at maternity leave, that didn't happen until I would say probably February that I started to kind of plan out what was available to me. I knew I had great insurance, so that really wasn't a concern. My biggest concern was how long I could take off because when you do the things that I do in my job, a lot of different things that don't really connect, it is hard to be away. It was going to take just a lot of planning out how that would be divided. I already did a lot of work at home. I really just contacted human resources to learn about the family and medical leave process, the forms,

what I needed to do with them. It wasn't a bad process, not as bad as I thought it would be.

Q. What professional concerns did you have?

A. Interviewee 13.

I think I'm in a very good place. I feel very fortunate because I've worked in an office, at that time it was eight years, and my coworkers had been with me for a long time. Our boss, my boss, is a father of a middle school student, and a three-year-old, and he's sixty so he's a very family-oriented man, and there is a lot of support there. So I can honestly say that every reaction that I received was positive and happy and supportive. I did not feel concerned about my job or anything other than my personal "how am I going do this, and do I want to do this" question.

Q. What was your experience like in terms of delivery?

A. Interviewee 13.

I was induced in the morning, and everything was going well. Everything was textbook they said in terms of dilating and progressing. He came at 7:14 p.m. But he came out and he wasn't breathing. So our hospital room was flooded with doctors and nurses and they did CPR on him, and he was little. He was six pounds, five ounces. He was taken to the NICU, so we didn't actually get to hold him until the next morning. You know he had an IV, but he was fine though. So that was a Monday, and technically I would have been released from the hospital on Wednesday, but he wasn't going to be. So the nurse called and dealt with the insurance company. I'm not sure how it went, but the insurance granted me one more night in the hospital. So actually Wednesday night, he was released from the NICU, so I got to spend the day with him, and he got to stay with me. That was really the first time, other than me going to the NICU to feed him, that I had really alone time with him. It was very scary.

Q. What was your experience like in terms of utilizing maternity leave?

A. Interviewee 13.

I took ten weeks, and it was paid because I had accrued nine years of sick time, so I had quite a lot in reserve, and still have a little bit left.

Q. You mentioned that you did some work at home before you had the baby. Did you do any work at home while on maternity leave?

A. Interviewee 13.

Yes, because I did a lot of student inquiry responses. If my automatic reply message on e-mail would tell the person "I'm on maternity leave" and then they would contact somebody else, who would then contact me. What do I say to this person? So at the end of the day it was just easier for me to answer the questions directly. Those kinds of things I felt like I had to do. There were a lot of things that coworkers helped out with. Sometimes it's just easier for you to do it than allow somebody else, and then try to figure out how they did it. And it was my choice, and I just felt like it was easier in the long run if I just took care of it, and then it would be done with. I was checking my e-mail a lot, and my mom got mad at me. It was a hard habit to break.

Q. What was your experience like in terms of balancing home and work responsibilities?

A. Interviewee 13.

You know I have to consciously say something's got to give. I'm not a big eater, I don't really cook, and so I've really noticed that the best meal I get is lunch because I bring my lunch. So that's something that I'm going to have to figure out too because I just don't have an appetite. I'm a little concerned because I know I have to eat healthy for my son. So that's something that has been on my mind. My husband has arranged for a cleaning lady and I told her I like to clean my own house, so this is really hard for me. But now I won't have to think "oh gosh, I have to mop the floors or clean the bathrooms." I have to say my husband has been really great, because when I get up with the baby he gets up too. We are getting into a bit of a routine. Personally, the first two weeks I cried all the time. I struggled with life. I felt like I'm the worst person. And I still say I'm falling apart. Every morning now I think okay I guess I just kind of resigned myself, but I've got to figure this out. I've just got to figure out how to do this. I've got to figure out how to be happy, and people have done this many, many more times before me, with multiple children, and I know it will be fine. The one thing is I will always be missing him and the little things. I have never complained about one bottle or diaper I've had to change because I know I am so aware of time. When it's over, it's over. I know each day that goes by he is getting closer and closer to something else. None of that bothers me, not the crying. I just want to experience everything because I didn't think I was going to have a baby at all.

Q. Are you breastfeeding or did you?

A. Interviewee 13.

I did. I nursed and we did great apparently. We were a model breast-feeding team. They said he wasn't gaining weight, and the doctor suggested supplementing. That really bothered me because he was little to begin with. He was hungry, and I just didn't know that was why he was crying. I felt a little bit more at ease. What eventually happened is after my father passed away with the stress of that, it was just, it was all too much. And eventually he just went straight to the bottle, and at his last doctor's appointment he was great in terms of growth. I'm pretty proud of myself that I did nurse for the first six weeks. I think it was because I didn't know if I was going to be comfortable with it. You know at the end it was really special, it was really nice.

Q. Overall, how has having a child affected your commitment to your institution?

A. Interviewee 13.

It's so interesting, working here nine years. I read an article about how being a person who has been employed at a place longer, when you do have a child, has advantages because you have seniority, longevity, and people know you and your reputations speaks for itself. I feel like I have that advantage, so that when my son gets into school and he starts his own life, I will have a good job that will allow me to go to school functions. So I feel good about that. I have no aspirations to advance. I don't know if I'm ever going to be a director of an office or a coordinator of a program. This job has evolved in so many ways that it's kind of ever-changing, so it's not really a stagnant position. So I feel fortunate that I'm here. I feel like I could have longevity here in this position, unless I see something else that looks interesting to apply for. The only way

I'd do that is if it was a job that was comparable in salary, or maybe a little less money, but then a nine-month or ten-month position, so that I would have the summer off.

So I feel like I have longevity here, and I don't think I'll go anywhere else. You know I thought about quitting. The thing about that, with my personal experience with my dad being in manufacturing, working in big business; and watching how he lost his job three times in my lifetime, it was hard to think about quitting. One time was when I was a senior in college and my brother was a senior in high school. My mother had a job. My mother is a teacher, a retired teacher. Then more recently, when they were closer to retirement age, he lost his job maybe about ten years ago, and you know because my mother had a job that of course helped with insurance and stuff. Not that my husband is going to lose his job, but my working, it is security. I'm very aware of insurance and security, and how every little bit counts I guess. So my decision to maintain my job really fell heavily on my life experiences because of my parents. Of course feeling or hoping I could figure out how to do all of this, and manage and do it well, and yet not deny my son his mother, or deny me him. Does that make sense?

Q. Absolutely. So in terms of your commitment to this school is there anything that they could have done to have made it easier for you to want to stay, to return when you did, is there anything institutionally that you would rather see them do differently?

A. Interviewee 13.

You know this is not their responsibility to offer a flexible schedule for people like me, but that sure would have been appreciated. I share with you that I'm trying to get up the confidence to ask about a flexible schedule. My mother and I have talked about it. That would have been a gift. Human resources were wonderful to work with. I can't ask for a better boss or better co-workers here who have really been there for me throughout the past year. So no, other than saying, "Hey, would you be interested in a flexible schedule and working at home a day or two a week?" there is nothing more they could do.

My mother, she wrote down the pros and cons of working. I love working with the students. There are those moments that you have rapport with them, they come in and you're talking with them. They know you, and you know them. I had one of those moments this week, and that's why I work here. I like procedures and processes, and as big of a task as this field placement stuff is, I like organizing it. I have about 500 people I work with that includes students, teachers, principals, and professors. It took me years to establish rapport. I'm a good person to try to make everybody happy, even though that's a terrible role to take on. I'm the oldest daughter, we usually try to make everything okay, and that's how I usually work. Trying to make everybody happy doesn't mean I don't grumble sometimes. I do. A three-quarter-time position, I would love that. I just don't know if that would ever be an option. It's a scary kind of idea to ask, and I'm not a very good negotiator. I'm not an aggressive person I guess. I have to figure it out in my mind. I think I could see how it could work.

Interviewee 3 and I met on campus at her university in a conference room. She is employed as a staff person in a year-round full-time position. She previously worked as a pharmaceutical representative, so she has an understanding of being a private sector employee as well.

> **Q.** What was your experience like in terms of making the decision to have a child? What professional concerns did you have?
> **A.** Interviewee 3.
>> I didn't necessarily have any professional concerns. It wasn't really a professional decision, when I was making the choice to get pregnant. However, I was less than two months pregnant when my current position came open. It was an internal search, and I had kind of been told it was me all along that they had in mind for it. But you never really know when it's a search. So I was very forthcoming with the person that would be my new supervisor. I went to him and just said I am pregnant, and I trust that this will have no affect on the way that this search is going to go. I was very up-front and honest. The search committee did not know that I was expecting, but the supervisor did know that I was expecting.
> **Q.** At what point in the process, did you seek out or investigate HR policies on maternity leave?

A. Interviewee 3.

> I was already pregnant once I looked into the HR policies. I had heard conflicting reports about how the institution was, so I just went straight to the HR office, and asked them how it worked. There were people who had opinions about the use of short-term disability and everybody had horror stories. So I just went straight to the source to find out.
>
> So the stories I heard were of people who paid into short-term disability, for the sole purpose of going on maternity leave, but when they went on maternity leave they could really only use two or three days of that short-term disability. So basically, it was just money paid out every month that they were throwing away, and so it was not a positive experience for them. They felt misinformed by HR. Maybe it is communication. I don't know if they asked the right questions, and I don't even know if I would know the right questions to ask. I do think that maybe just a lack of communication, and not a complete understanding of what short-term disability is, and what it covers here at our school was part of the problem. Even with the way it is set up now, with FMLA, you're using that also, but staff members still have to go online every week and log-in your sick and vacation time into your account. You still have to fill out the FMLA forms, and have forms from your doctor signed. It is not a seamless process. There are several steps that you have to take.
>
> Here there isn't technically a maternity leave. You can take FMLA up to 12 weeks, and if staff members have sick and vacation time accrued you can use that, and then still be paid. I was fortunate enough to have about nine weeks of sick and vacation time built up. So I used that. So I was out for nine weeks on "maternity" leave. I would love to have had the first 12 weeks off, but honestly with the prices of day care and all that stuff, and I know that three weeks doesn't sound like a lot of time to go without pay. We could have survived financially, but it wouldn't have been an ideal situation.

Q. What was your experience like in terms of conceiving a child?

A. Interviewee 3.

> We actually got pregnant within a month, which was a complete shock to us. I had cancer two years ago, and we really thought

that would be a problem because of the treatment that I had. We really thought that could have been a problem, so that was a surprise.

Q. How was working while pregnant?

A. Interviewee 3.

I work in an office that is very understanding about the needs of pregnant women. I think all but two women in my office are mothers, which was nice. In the line of work that I do, I don't necessarily have to be in my office all the time to get my job done. So they were very understanding if I needed to come in a few minutes late because I was twenty pounds heavier than I had been before, and I was moving slower. So, for example, if I was at an event in another city until midnight last night, and seven months pregnant, they would understand if I didn't come in until noon today. They were very nice. I'm back into heels now, but then, they were very understanding and cooperative. It was great.

Q. So in terms of utilizing maternity leave, did you leave all work responsibilities to others?

A. Interviewee 3.

No. I had my out-of-office reply on everything, but I can still see the e-mails. One of the projects that I had been working on was scheduled for the weekend after I came back to work. So there were some things, that as much as I tried to give it back to some other people, and they did the majority of the work, there were still some e-mails and things that I had to check. So I would not say that I took a complete maternity leave. I still worked. I came to an event on campus that I needed to be at, just in the role that I am in. In my area it is who you know, and being seen is important. I do fundraising, and one of my largest fundraising efforts was on a weekend, and that was at the time I was returning to work. I really needed to work on that. So I went to that. I really didn't have a problem with that, and it was nice to get out of the house.

Q. Did your spouse take leave?

A. Interviewee 3.

He took almost a week. He works at a corporation here, and he has a very understanding boss who said take the time that you need, just not excessively. Not all of the managers do that.

I think it is managerial preference, and some give that and some don't. And we are just blessed enough that he works for one of those that does.

Q. What was your experience like in terms of returning to work?

A. Interviewee 3.

My coworkers were very welcoming when I came back to the office. They had pictures of my little boy up on the wall, so I would know they cared, not that I would forget what he looks like. They came and checked on me all of the time. It was very much, so we are glad you had a cute little boy, but you're back. So it was immediately, let's get back in the swing of things. You are a fundraiser. It is time to catch up. Here is where we are on this project. Where are we on this project? Don't forget our 10:00 a.m. meeting. I enjoy being a person on a routine. I enjoyed that, but it's very draining when you are used to being home in your pajamas until 2:00 in the afternoon. I am also a nursing mother so that has been more of a challenge than I realized. He goes to day care, and so I am trying to pump while I am at work. For instance, one day I had an 8:00 a.m. meeting, a 9:30 a.m. meeting, a 10:00 a.m. meeting, and a 2:00 p.m. meeting. So it is hard to find enough time to pump. It creates issues sometimes when you are trying to do that. So that is probably, not a complaint, an issue maybe, a challenge, that's what this is, that's my challenge right now.

Q. What was your experience like in terms of balancing home and work responsibilities?

A. Interviewee 3.

I was talking to a very dear friend, and she said how are things going? I said, I don't know how people do it, you know when I pick him up from child care, he falls asleep on the way home. He is a sleeper in the car, which is great. But I get home and I wash bottles, then we use cloth diapers. I know I'm crazy. I go ahead and start washing those. Then I try to get dinner started because I get off a half hour earlier before my husband. Then just about the time that I am ready to sit down it is time for the baby to eat. I get home at five, and then at eleven I think "oh my gosh where has tonight gone?" I would not change it for the world, but I am tired a lot.

Q. Overall, how has having a child affected your commitment to your institution or employer?

A. Interviewee 3.

It has been a fantastic experience, in terms of my work. We are one of the lowest paid schools in the state, and also in the nation. But we are one of the most successful schools at reaching campaign goals. So we don't get rewarded in actual salary, but we do in those little benefits we talked about before. If I take an hour and fifteen minutes for lunch, and I go down and see my son at day care, there is not somebody with a clock saying, "oh you took fifteen minutes too long, you need to stay after." That is not how we work. There are so many people in my division who if they need to go on a field trip or if they need to go see their child perform in a little play in the afternoon, we are very welcomed to do that. And that is fantastic.

Q. Is there anything else you want to add?

A. Interviewee 3.

I would love to actually have a paid maternity leave. I'm blessed enough to have that time saved up, but what if someone didn't. Or for our part-time employees who maybe only get to take a week or two off when they have a baby, and they aren't paid for that amount of time, then what? After two weeks I still wasn't sure how to handle this little baby, so I can't imagine having to come back to work after that amount of time. So if there was a designated maternity leave, I think that would relieve a lot of stress for some women, but overall I had a great experience with my pregnancy, delivery, and maternity leave.

I think I had the rose-colored glasses on thinking that everybody had maternity leave, and it was just wonderful and glorious, and then you get into it, and you find out it is not that way at all. Having had a child now, I think I understand the importance of paternity leave more. My husband is fantastic, so just to have him around for those first few days at the beginning it helped out so much. So I can see, even if it was only a two-week paternity leave that would be monumentally better than having none at all.

Interviewee 1 and I met in her office on her university's campus. Interviewee 1 is employed in a position that allows her to both teach and perform administrative duties. She works less than full time, and is in a non-tenure-track position. She stopped working full time and negotiated this new arrangement when her children were born. She took a salary reduction in order to this.

> **Q.** What was your experience like in terms of making the decision to have a child? What professional concerns did you have?
> **A.** Interviewee 1.
>> When I first came here, we each negotiated our own maternity leave situation. Now there is a bit more structure to rely on, but at that time it was whatever you could negotiate. Even now, we still we have no sick days, leave days, or vacation days.
>> There were also problems with conceiving, and I had to take medication. I expected it to take about a year for the first pregnancy to occur, and once we figured out what would work, then the second pregnancy was easier. It was just by the grace of God that my children were all born in late spring, which is basically the end of the semester. So I had about three months off with each child. It varied in terms of the amount of pay I received during those three months with each child, but I knew I would have that time off.
>
> **Q.** What was your experience like in terms of utilizing maternity leave?
> **A.** Interviewee 1.
>> I did use FMLA. With my first delivery, we had negotiated that the first two months I think I was going to be working from home ten hours a week. It seemed really complicated, but that would allow me pay through those two months at the end of the semester. And I think maybe the last month I wasn't paid, or I just got half pay. But it all seemed better than what I thought I could get, so I was happy. I thought I might not get paid at all. The second baby I think, there had been more people taking maternity leave in my department, and we were a little bit more rehearsed. I think I had negotiated two and half months of pay, and again he was born in late spring, so it was over the summer period. And I don't teach normally in the summer, so that just kind of worked out well. My main responsibility in the summer is a welcome event for all the incoming freshmen. So I worked with a research assistant who took over those duties.

Q. Overall, how has having a child affected your commitment to your institution?
A. Interviewee 1.
> Your priorities are refocused to the people you just created, but I still like my job. I still want to do a good job. So there are more things and people competing for your time and attention. But I hope I still do a good job.

Q. Looking back on the fact that you didn't have any maternity leave policies here to begin with, what would you like to have seen your employer do differently?
A. Interviewee 1.
> I think it would have been helpful to have done something consistently for everyone who needs a leave of this kind. It really is negotiated, and everyone's situation is different. Had I been assigned a class to teach, which is normal in the summer, what would the school have done? They would have had to pay for someone else to teach my class. That's just how that works. So then how would they have paid me, when they were also paying someone else to teach my class? In other work settings where you accrue leave, you at least know what you have to work with, and you can save up your time. Here, there is no saving up. So it's a problem when you want to take leave.
>
> I remember my friend, who was pregnant at the same time I was. She is from Ethiopia, and she said, "I like everything the American way, except for pregnancy and maternity benefits." She said that in Ethiopia, "I would be able to be paid without a doubt after giving birth." And she said it is so easy to just hire someone really cheaply to stay in your home with you, and help you with the baby.

Q. Is there anything else you want to add?
A. Interviewee 1.
> Being a parent can put you on that "mommy" track and that can definitely impact your career. It's a choice I think everybody has to make.

Interviewee 2 and I met on her university's campus. She took me to a conference room so that we could have more privacy than her office afforded. Interviewee 2 is the mother of four. There are quite a few years difference in age between the first two, and the last two children she had.

Her responses to the questions I asked were mainly thinking back to the births of her last two children, and the respective leaves she took for those two births.

> **Q.** In terms of your last pregnancy, what professional concerns did you have?
>
> **A.** Interviewee 2.
>
>> When I was pregnant the last time, I think I was just bound and determined to have it my way. I think that was actually a luxury afforded to me because I was not a tenure-seeking employee. I think that makes a difference when you are having kids. At that time, we had no HR policies for nonregular faculty, and at that time I was not ranked, so I had no leave time, and no eligibility for paid leave under FMLA. We had staff members who had babies that took six months because they had saved up their vacation, sick leave, and their personal days, everything. That was just simply not available to me as a faculty member.
>
> **Q.** So, why do you think not being in a tenure-track position gave you more freedom?
>
> **A.** Interviewee 2.
>
>> I think I have a little bit more freedom because I was a nonregular faculty member. If I were seeking tenure, and the very people who I felt were judging me for taking time off and for becoming pregnant were the same people who are also going to be judging my tenure application and deciding on my tenure status, then let me tell you, it would have just been very, very difficult. So in terms of the university moving forward, I think that probably it would be helpful to have a policy and expectations where it sets out guidelines. Here is the minimum for what the department can do, and anything beyond this is up to the department head and that faculty member to adjust.
>>
>> You know there is a faculty member here, right now, who might have another child, and she is not ranked, and this director will tell her she is going to get unpaid leave. That is just horrible. And she doesn't want to fight it. She is just up for her three-year review, and she doesn't want anyone to know that she is rocking the boat. She feels she has no power at all. How on earth can a staff person in the same department, who is

making ten bucks an hour, have better maternity leave benefits than a faculty member does, even if she is an unranked faculty member? And that is nothing against that staff member! And then there is another faculty member who is 39, and she now found out she can't have kids, and she is so regretful for waiting. It is really important that we acknowledge that women are delaying childbirth, and the job is the barrier.

Q. Does the university provide for any short-term disability coverage that would apply?

A. Interviewee 2.

We do have a short-term disability policy, but it does not cover pregnancy. I think that it requires you to be out of your job for six months. It is really a long-term leave, you know it is called short-term disability, but it has to be taking you away from your job responsibilities for a long time.

Q. What impact has the decision to have a child had on your employment promotion process?

A. Interviewee 2.

Well, for a nonregular faculty member, there are very limited advancement opportunities. Non-ranked faculty, here, are second-class citizens. It is not like a regular faculty member where you have clear guidelines on what you need to do to advance in rank or to get tenure. So having children has not affected me in that way, but it has affected other people's perspectives of me, those who have power in the school. Absolutely, because I have tried to advocate for change in our maternity leave policies for others and that does ultimately affect any opportunity I might have for promotion in the future. So I wouldn't say it is a direct route, but I think definitely in an indirect route. My boss, the director of this school, encouraged me to become a ranked faculty member, but in order to do this I had to apply and present a colloquium. I didn't get a job change title, and I didn't get a raise. So there was not a tangible financial benefit for me getting this. I did have to go through all the hoops. And it's fine if you are going to reward me, but I think most people if they have a job that values the Ph.D. they get something in exchange. My exchange was the rank, and that only made me eligible for paid FMLA, if I need it in the future.

Q. Overall, how has having a child affected your commitment to your institution or employer?

A. Interviewee 2.

> I see my commitment here as being to my students. And that has never wavered. So I would say my commitment to my work is very firm. It is probably much more of an investment, than I used to see myself as having. I used to think I'm delivering this content, and I think now I take much more ownership over programs, and so that I think has been enhanced. It's the commitment to building relationships within this organization that has just kind of been shot.

> It's just not equitable. So knowing that my director has a lot of power, and that is just ridiculous when it comes to maternity leave. It shouldn't be about how much I like you, how much I think you are a value to the school. It should be about here is the policy, and here is what you need to do to follow it. I think if nothing else, we need equity in how a policy is to be enforced. This is the only way you can truly keep morale up.

Interviewee 12 and I met in a noisy hallway between sessions at a professional conference. Interviewee 12 had an infant and a toddler who were at home, and she was planning to return to her hotel room to Skype with her toddler, as soon as we were finished speaking.

Q. What was your experience like in terms of making the decision to have a child?

A. Interviewee 12.

> I thought about things like could I have a child, and not be sick while pregnant? What if there was not a maternity leave offered, and what that would mean in terms of my tenure clock?

Q. What professional concerns did you have?

A. Interviewee 12.

> I knew that there was no paid maternity leave, period. But I had concerns, I think just in terms of where I was. The department, it was a highly male, older, with no other females of childbearing age, that kind of thing. So when I became pregnant, I didn't know how to act, and I wasn't looking forward to everyone else knowing and giving their advice.

Q. At what point in the process, did you seek out or investigate HR policies on maternity leave?

A. Interviewee 12.

When I was five months pregnant, and I still hadn't told my chair, I contacted HR. I just sort of confirmed what I knew already. I went ahead and told my boss. He's very accommodating, and he has been throughout with my two children, very accommodating. When I had my first child there was no policy, and he was very accommodating. His idea was that I could use a course release that I had available as a new assistant professor on a tenure track. You can use seven over a certain period of time, and you have to use the course releases before you go up for tenure. You can use one per semester. His idea was that I could use some of that course release time for my maternity leave. And my immediate response was no. I need to use that for my research. I did end up using some of my course release. I didn't stop my tenure clock, but that was an option. One of the options, because there's no paid maternity leave, we could stop the tenure clock, but I wasn't going to stop my tenure clock. I didn't want to do that. No one pushed me to do one thing or the other.

By the time I had my first child the policy changed, but no one suggested that I could take paid maternity leave. It was experimental. They wanted to see how it worked, and if they could continue funding it. They were aware it was available. It came up in discussions in meetings, but no one suggested it to me. I had the baby in the summer, so I had that time off.

And part of it was guilt. I felt I was asking too much. Whereas my colleague did take leave. She had a baby in the summer, and she took off that fall. I could have done that, but no one ever suggested it, so I didn't take it. I taught during the summer, too.

I was also putting together my tenure packet. I had the baby at the end of March and the packet was due middle of April, so one night I went into the office when no one was around, and worked on finishing my packet and I submitted it, and that was it.

Q. In terms of returning to work, how about issues with colleagues and supervisors, how are things going?

A. Interviewee 12.

Now, with the second baby, it has been fine. I haven't had any remarks or any comments from anyone because it is the second baby. When I had my first child, that was different. I think it has to do with the fact that there hasn't been someone who has had a baby in 25 years. And they weren't really sure what to say or do.

Q. Why do you think that is?

A. Interviewee 12.

I think it is just the department. It is a great department, but they don't do things like that. Here is the one thing I did. So I have two children, and there was a faculty meeting on a Monday and my husband is not home on Monday, so I'm home with the two kids and I couldn't go to it. And I didn't want to do this huge juggling act to go in for this department meeting for an hour, so I talked to my chair, and she said I'll give you a conference call, and I called in. All this technology … why can't we do it?

If they ever hire another female in the department, and she has a child I would tell her to take maternity leave. I think someone needs to say that to them. No one said that to me, and I didn't take leave. I needed someone to say take maternity leave since we're offering it.

Q. Do you feel that you would have been perceived as less professional if you had taken maternity leave?

A. Interviewee 12.

I don't think I would have been less professional, but I think it may have to do with my comfort level. The institution itself, it's not the message I wanted to send. I didn't want to give the message of who I'm not. So I'm not what you think. I'm not trying to, but I always thought that's what people would have thought of me. If I had another baby, I'm taking maternity leave! I didn't take it. I wish I had been pregnant in October because what would they do with me then? I would have to take a maternity leave right?

Q. So how do we as women send that message to other women?

A. Interviewee 12.

That is exactly what I didn't do. I didn't set an example.

Q. You mentioned the paid maternity leave was experimental. Has it become finalized?
A. Interviewee 12.
   It is not permanent yet. I think it is up for negotiation in our next contract.
Q. Do you earn sick leave, and could you have used that for maternity?
A. Interviewee 12.
   Yes, but I had healthy babies, and in my mind I had them toward the end of the semester, so I didn't want to use sick leave. And one colleague said to me, "well you got April, May, June, July, and August, so that is five months. Why would you want maternity leave?" But, I'm entitled to it though, right? So, when you get a response like that, you think how can I take it when other people are thinking things like that?
Q. Were you asked to sign paperwork for FMLA?
A. Interviewee 12.
   No. There is one person I know of who had to use FMLA before the baby came to stay home for medical reasons. She was perceived as being lazy and not publishing. And she left. She was there a year, and then she just left and went some place else. I am sure there are new fathers. There are men who are penalized too.

Interviewee 15 and I met at her home. At the time of the interview, her son was four months old. He slept most of the time I was there.

Q. At what point in the process, did you seek out or investigate HR policies on maternity leave?
A. Interviewee 15.
   I have to confess that in the spring of 2005, my first year at my university, I attended a gender issues talk that my colleague was kind of instrumental in organizing. I learned at that time from the speaker, the HR director, that our faculty had no benefits regarding leave, they don't accrue leave time, no vacation, no sick, etc. Those decisions were made prior to my arrival by faculty. I understandably agree because we don't want to punch the time clock, or I may only need to be here Tuesday and Thursday or you only on Wednesday and Friday. Nonetheless, the HR director was certainly disturbed that

there was no universal policy, and I can acknowledge that I was new to the situation. So to answer your question, I knew before conceiving that there was no universal coverage based on prior exposure to the issue.

Q. When you were closer to having a baby, did you seek out specific information from HR?

A. Interviewee 15.

I didn't, but I continued to follow my colleague's advocacy work on this issue. She was on faculty senate, and I knew that changes had been suggested, but honestly I didn't know where it stood with regard to the faculty handbook. So, I knew that there was some leave time suggested, and I thought that it was a person-to-person situation to be negotiated, to be negotiated with the immediate supervisor and dean.

Q. So what arrangement did you negotiate?

A. Interviewee 15.

Well, I mean logistically, I spoke with our interim department head the first week of the beginning of the spring semester. At the beginning of the spring semester you get back from the semester break, and that first week they ask what do you want to teach for the next fall? So I said, we're pregnant, we're not telling anyone right because we're really early in the process, but you know that's going to impact my schedule. So, I made a pitch I think to teach one online course, one face-to-face course, and to shift my other face-to-face course to the spring. I have a three-three teaching load normally. He came back, and said that he'd had spoken with the dean, and it was not even an hour after that conversation, and the dean said, "when is she due?" I was due early in the fall semester. The dean said, "why doesn't she teach everything the first bi-term, and forget about shifting anything to the spring?" So, I ended up teaching a section that was capped at 55 online in the first bi-term, and then taught four days a week for an hour and twenty minutes through the first bi-term, that was my face-to-face course. My third "course" was to manage some interns for the whole semester.

Q. Any issues in the classroom in terms of your interaction with students the more your pregnancy advanced?

A. Interviewee 15.

I remember thinking I don't think I could do this with a second child, you know, being on my feet that much, and in the office in front of the computer for five days a week for weeks—teaching during bi-terms. You know I had students come back and say later, "I really enjoyed your class but if you choose to have another baby you should do so during the summer." That was the experience, really, and that student was a female.

Really, I've changed, as we all have, right? We start out one person. I remember my third year teaching, and deciding it's not just how much other people are pleased by your performance, but also "is this a place I want to be, and where I get respect, do I feel valued?" You know, so I kind of developed a tougher skin, developed more definitive expectations regarding students' work, and I really started to contemplate diversity. What does it really mean? It's not just the appearance of diversity, but it is also bringing different things, different approaches, that kind of thing.

Q. What was your experience like in terms of returning to work?
A. Interviewee 15.

I know that during the time I was out, I missed one departmental meeting. Apparently my absence started this whole discussion that was very negative. Most male faculty were saying, "I only took a week when I had a child, and then I came back." In our department, the men in our department, often look around and count the number of women to men and say we're "equal." And they don't understand about the culture, the preference of style among students remains a "male model." They think the students enjoy being lectured to, and that is teaching, you know that is learning. Not to criticize across the board, but you know it's just a different approach of collaboration versus your one-way directional wisdom or whatever. So I think there was that "do as I do" attitude. However, it did result from that conversation that folks were saying we need to have a universal maternity/paternity policy in this department. The only fear expressed by the faculty was, will it be supported if the policy is contradictory or is more liberal than what the college and the university supports?

Q. Overall, how has having a child affected your career goals?
A. Interviewee 15.

I think maybe it's more focused, and people told me that this would happen. I applied for and received a sabbatical for this coming fall, and he will be going to day care then. I've had a number of lingering projects. And I've collected two survey projects, we just met yesterday, about three papers that we want to write from these. So I'm kind of getting more focused, realizing I have to make really good use of my time. And I'd like to have at least one more child. I know that if I really want to set myself up well for getting full professor, I need to finish these projects, but also I feel like I want to get these projects tied up so I can move on to the next thing. And since I'm quantitative, I'd like to do more training in that.

Q. Overall, how has having a child affected your commitment to your institution or employer?

A. Interviewee 15.

I would definitely like to see us put through a universal maternity and paternity leave policy. I think we need coverage or a leave for caregiving of a terminal spouse or family member. My colleague's effort affected the tenure-clock issue only. After the gender issues talk I went to, I became very sensitive to the lack of support by women. For example, I was told by one female retired professor, "but wait, if you're pregnant now, and only twelve weeks along, the baby's not going to come in the summer." I said, you're right, he's due in October. Honestly, our present faculty regent got, if I'm not mistaken, a semester off, and she said I think it works better if you negotiate for yourself, by yourself, almost to say that if we had a universal policy it would be detrimental to those in better positions of negotiation. She was tenured at the time she had her baby though. To not realize the lack of negotiating power of untenured faculty is sad. Why can't we see the benefit of advocating a standard of living and benefits for everyone? Is it because it might take away from our own advantage? I think that the structure is flawed, and I understand that the structure plays off of the culture, but you know I think it's a little bit easier to change cultures if structure is in place.

Q. Looking back, what might you have handled differently? Do you think you should have demanded more formal leave?

A. Interviewee 15.

Probably I would do that now. I felt like, at the time, that maybe I should have. I wondered if I had approached the dean, and requested leave what would have happened. The matter and the impact on our children deserve attention and respect. In the future I will.

Interviewee 16 was busy preparing her tenure application packet when we scheduled her interview. She had one child when she was a graduate student in a master's program. She had that baby over winter break, and went back on schedule to her classes in early January. Several years later, she had her second child shortly before starting a teaching position at a new university.

Q. What was your experience like in terms of making the decision to have your second child? What professional concerns did you have?
A. Interviewee 16.

I didn't have any professional concerns in the beginning, but we knew that my oldest child was getting a little old at that point. She was already five, and we knew that by the time my second child was born the oldest would be six, maybe even closer to seven. And we worried about the age gap. We knew we needed to hurry up and have a second one. When we started planning for the second one I was not the director of the master's program so my biggest concern was just what was I going to be doing in terms of teaching. And I actually found out I was pregnant in May, and about a week later before I told anyone, our department chair asked if I would be willing to be the new program director. So I went from only being concerned about teaching to being concerned about teaching plus the directorship, which was a lot of work. So sort of half willingly and half unwillingly, I accepted the director position because there really wasn't anyone else that could do it. I waited probably about three months before I started talking to our department chair about having a second child and when she was due. So, it morphed into something much bigger than arranging my teaching schedule. There were not a lot of females, and I was the only one of childbearing age too. So I had no one to really talk to about experiences. So that made it a little stressful at that point.

Q. At what point in the process, did you seek out or investigate HR policies on maternity leave?

A. Interviewee 16.

That summer when I was a few weeks pregnant, I started thinking I need to figure out what are my options, and so I started with the broader university websites, and then finally found a little bit of guidance at the college level. And the extent of the policy that I was able to find is that they can give you an extra year on your tenure clock, if you request it and they approve it, and any other accommodations are made just based on negotiations between your department chair, your dean, and yourself. There wasn't any formalized policy on "we'll change your teaching assignments" or "we'll give you six weeks off," it was nothing formal like that. So it was all a negotiation, which I was a little surprised by. I was expecting to find something a little more concrete, but I didn't find that. I probably should have done my due diligence before we decided it was time to have a second kid, but I didn't do that.

Q. Then in terms of utilizing maternity leave, what did you actually negotiate? How did it all work out?

A. Interviewee 16.

I spoke to the department chair around the end of the summer, and said this is where I'm at, and before I ever went to him I had a plan in mind. Actually I drafted a memo that I sent to him twenty-four hours before I met him. I wanted another year on the tenure clock. I thought between being director and having a kid, that was going to be a huge time commitment. It was so apparent that I wasn't going to be able to get enough done for tenure requirements because they are very, very specific about what journals you're supposed to be published in. So that was my first request that I have another year on the tenure clock. My second request was that I can do some of my director work from home as it got closer to my due date. Then post delivery, I would guarantee that I would be in the office every Friday during normal business hours, and I would continue to teach my class on Wednesdays. But outside of those specific times I would be out for the first four weeks after the baby was born. And I also wanted a parking pass outside my building.

So they actually, surprisingly, granted all of those requests, and he had to request from the dean that she give me the extra year on the tenure clock. But the scheduling changes, the chair just took care of that for me. I always kept an open mind for our administrative assistant, as well as the chair, to call me at any point they wanted while I was out. I only missed one class in which I scheduled a guest to lecture to my class. And then it happened to be spring break, following the week I had the guest lecturer. So I actually took two full weeks where I sort of didn't do anything. I eased back into it that third week and made sure I didn't miss any classes after that.

Q. Was your spouse able to take any time off?
   A. Interviewee 16.

He was actually in a master's program, and he was working for a school district as an at-risk coordinator so his schedule was extraordinarily flexible. So in terms of his school work, the first week she was born the professors were very accommodating with him needing to leave early or needing to miss a little bit. He was working for a middle school, and they were very accommodating about shifting his schedule around. So that was part of what enabled me to take so little time off is that he was flexible enough that when I left he stayed home. We didn't put her in day care until actually this year. This is the first year she's been in preschool and she is three. It has been one of the best things I think we've done for both of our children is they stay home when they are young. Without that flexibility of both my schedule and his schedule, we would never have been able to do that.

Q. Were you ready to go back to work two weeks after delivery?
   A. Interviewee 16.

At that point I was lucky enough that I looked fairly normal pretty shortly after the delivery. So my immediate faculty members that I share that little wing with, they all were very aware that I'd had a baby and were very much in tune with what was going on. They were all excited and they got together and gave me some baby gifts. And at that point they were very supportive. Those that I believed would not be supportive, well they pretty much were not part of any of that. At that point I didn't have any concerns, and I was able to hit the ground running. I looked pretty much like I always looked, and if anyone wanted to talk about it, I tended to not want to talk about it with people.

I wanted to keep everything professional, very much so. That was a very male-dominated department, unlike here. There, no one brought their children in. Occasionally, you would see one colleague's son or daughter in there, and everybody would sort of give him a look. So it was very clear that it was not a family-friendly place. Spouses didn't come in and have lunch. Children never came in on Friday afternoon to have cookies in the conference room or anything. So I had been there long enough to realize it was not a particularly family-friendly place, and only two or three faculty members I think even had children that were school age. So it was just not something that you mixed with work very well.

Q. What was your experience like in terms of balancing home and work responsibilities?

A. Interviewee 16.

I was very tired all the time. I'm certain my teaching, the rest of that semester, was less than it would have been otherwise. My evaluations were fine. I just felt like I didn't give it as much as I would have otherwise given it. I was so tired. Going from one kid to two kids is far more than double. It's doubly difficult. My oldest child was still having her school plays and school musicals, and we were still going to things with her at her school, and we had this baby that's not sleeping at night. So I was in a fog from February until probably June. My husband was wonderful. We had been rotating night duty, I would do it one night, and then he would do it one night. And then he was at the point that he had passed his comprehensive exams for his master's degree and he just took the rest of the nights from that point on. So that way I could finish teaching, and grading, and doing what I needed to do. So probably looking back, it would have been helpful not to have taught that semester at all, but I got through it, and I think the students were doing okay at that point. I hope.

Q. Recognizing that you changed schools since you had the second baby, and that you are now going up for tenure, how do you think having a child has impacted your career?

A. Interviewee 16.

Well, had I stayed at my other school, I think it would have had a huge impact. Just because of that arbitrary list that faculty had put together for acceptable publications, and trying to gear my research for very specific journals. I knew I was always going to have a hard time with that. It was even going to be a harder time having very small children at home.

Here, having come here, this new department actually is 50% female, which is totally unheard of in my field. And everyone around, all the females around here have school-aged children. Even the oldest ones of us around here have school-aged children. Our department chair has been phenomenal in making sure that all classes are scheduled between nine and three. So you can drop off and pick up children, and if you want to bring your kid in, and let them draw on the white board in the classroom there's no problem with that.

And they've been very, very flexible with the tenure and promotion requirements. We all do something a little bit different, so we have no set journals, and practitioner-based research is just as important as more traditional academic-based research. So here I couldn't have asked for a better fit in terms of school, having children at home, and having a family. Actually one of the things the department chair told me when I first got here was that we actually want people to have a life and enjoy a life, not be worried about making some arbitrary list at the end of the day.

So here I don't believe it has had any impact. My daughter who is nine, sometimes she'll come in. My husband will pick her up from school and drop her off here, and she'll do her homework on my other desk, then go down to the computer lab. She knows all the graduate students, and it certainly has made it a much happier place to work because they actually value family and children, as opposed to my last job where someone would give you a funny look if you brought your child to the office. Here I don't think it has been at all negative, it has been very positive.

Interviewee 17 and I began the interview with a discussion of her decision about when to have a child.

Q. Did you have any professional concerns at the time you decided to start a family?

A. Interviewee 17.

Certainly, my first child was born during the fall semester of my second year at this university. I definitely had concerns. I remember being apprehensive about whether or not to start a family then or to wait, because I was so new to my job. I knew there were risks. I was definitely nervous and fearful, but I knew that I wanted a family, and I also knew I was not getting any younger. I did not want to be starting a family in my late 30s, as opposed to my early 30s. I certainly remember being very nervous going in to tell my department chair that I was pregnant. I remember I waited as long as realistically possible to have that conversation. I was especially nervous because no one in my department, no female faculty members were having children in my department. Male faculty members and their spouses had children, and some fairly recently, but nobody could remember a woman in the department actually being pregnant and giving birth while working in the department. This was sort of unprecedented, and I did not know how they would be able to accommodate the birth, or if they would be able to accommodate it.

Q. What was your supervisor's reaction?

A. Interviewee 17.

It was positive. I felt my supervisor was very proactive about finding out how we would accommodate my leave because I was due early in the spring semester. I think I benefited from the fact that a few weeks before I told my supervisor that I was pregnant, the college had implemented a maternity leave policy. It was short-lived, but was passed, and had been disseminated just a few weeks before. So there was a framework to operate within, as opposed to sort of an announcement that I was pregnant, and then trying to figure out what was next. We were able to pull up this memo online that outlined the policy from the dean to help decide what would happen next.

Q. Why do you say the policy was short-lived?

A. Interviewee 17.

It was short-lived because it was determined that the college could not implement that type of policy on its own. That type of policy had to take place at the university level. This was a college-specific policy. I believe it was in place for literally one year, before it was rescinded. After the college rescinded the policy, it was directed to each department to figure out how they would accommodate leave, which you can imagine how it is. It is really uncomfortable. To have to negotiate, that was a very negative and uncomfortable environment.

Q. Did the human resources department play a role at all in the leave that you actually took?

A. Interviewee 17.

Actually that was the thing that was shocking to me. It was the one thing that really surprised me. I familiarized myself with the college policy, and then went to HR, and talked to them about the Family and Medical Leave Act, and how that would sort of be in play. I did not understand this at the time. I didn't understand that we were entitled to six weeks short-term disability at full pay, presuming that your doctor submitted a note saying that you should have six weeks leave, and that was for a vaginal delivery. I think it was eight weeks for a cesarean. I did not realize that the Family and Medical Leave Act ran concurrently with paid leave, so I had been operating on the assumption that worst-case scenario, I would have six weeks paid leave under my short-term disability insurance, and then if I had to, I could take 12 weeks unpaid leave after that under FMLA, and that total of 18 weeks would get me through the semester. So it was kind of a shock to me to learn that the Family and Medical Leave Act clock started from the moment of delivery. So, that would only give me six weeks then of unpaid leave, after my six weeks of paid short-term disability leave. Both of my children were born at the end of the fall semester, so that would not give me enough weeks to get me through the end of the spring semester.

That is another thing, I totally forgot. I think I had to use my sick leave at the same time. After the birth of each child I had no sick leave left. I don't even know how that worked. I think sick leave ran concurrently with my disability leave. I remember thinking I could use my disability, and then use my sick leave after that, but I could not do that. It was not allowed. I thought I could string all of these things together. I could not exhaust one and then use another. I remember being really irritated, because I was on winter break and I still had to use my sick leave. I forgot all about that. I remember saying if I had the stomach flu nobody would have been the wiser. I would not have had to call in on New Year's Eve and say I'm using my sick leave today. They took my sick leave over the breaks. As soon as I called it in, and said "I'm in the hospital, I just had the baby," my sick leave started. My FMLA started. I remember I got notarized letters in the mail that I had to sign for, acknowledging that the FMLA clock had started ticking immediately.

Q. Did you ask for reduced or modified teaching duties when you returned to work?

A. Interviewee 17.

Under the college policy during my first pregnancy, you were relieved of teaching one course. So the understanding was that I would teach one course in the spring semester, the semester during which I would give birth. And the college policy was that they would be very accommodating in terms of what that course would be and allow me to select when. So I chose to teach a graduate seminar one night a week. So that meant I would be paid for the whole semester, because I realized I was not going to be able to take six weeks leave. And this was logistically because I couldn't figure out how I could be out 12 weeks, and then would come back into a semester to teach with only four weeks left until the end of the semester. So, I received disability leave, but my paycheck looked the same the whole semester. I think the department was reimbursed for my disability leave. I didn't have any service or advising responsibilities that semester. So, because of the timing of the birth, I actually only missed the first two weeks of class, and then came back and taught for 14 weeks.

Q. When you returned to work, what professional concerns did you have in terms of reactions of colleagues or supervisors?

A. Interviewee 17.

Honestly, none. The benefit of teaching at night was that nobody else was around, so I did not interact with my colleagues at all. I don't remember hearing any concerns about that at the time. I think I was just so fixated on my first child, and it being my second year in a new job, that I was just fixated on getting by day-to-day, that I didn't really think about that. Had I been exposed to my colleagues on a daily basis that might have been different, but I was really only going onto campus that one night a week to teach, and nobody else was there, so I was able to block that out.

Q. What was your experience like in terms of balancing home and work responsibilities?

A. Interviewee 17.

I give my department incredible credit for really abiding by the policy that was in effect at that time, and really staying true to their word that I would have no service commitment. I must give credit to my colleagues who picked up the slack to cover my service commitments, and to advise my students. There was no pressure to come in and attend meetings, even though I was not supposed to have those responsibilities. I have to say I felt very well supported by my department, and I felt as best as I could, I was able to strike a balance. I certainly was not doing as much research as I would have liked, given the fact that I was only teaching one course. Personally I felt I had the support of the department to do what I needed to do. Colleagues would come over to see the baby, and would affirm my sense about what was the appropriate use of my time that semester.

Q. Overall, how has having a child affected your commitment to your institution?

A. Interviewee 17.

Not loyalty toward my institution, but to my department, yes. In hindsight, the more I think about it and the more I talked to women in other schools, I feel incredibly lucky to have been in the department that I was in. I felt incredibly well supported. I don't think I could have asked for more, to be honest, from my department, in terms of what I got. To be honest, it has forced me to reevaluate my priorities about my professional trajectory, in terms of do I want to spend more time with my children? Or do I want them to be in child care in the summer, so that I can do research? I have chosen to be at home with them in the summer. We are paid on a nine-month contract. I may not go as far as I used to think that I would in my field because of these choices. I just had a conversation with somebody, and I said I never would have thought these would be the choices that I would be making, but I am very happy with them. There are definitely differences in the priorities that I have now compared to before I had kids.

I think before I might have thought about this school being the first stop in my career, publishing more in different venues, producing more work, more research, in the interest of going somewhere else someday. Now, I realize it is a very accommodating supportive department, in a place where now there are several women, who all gave birth to or had young children prior to getting to our department. Two of my male colleagues have young children. It is a department with a lot of people who have families, who are very understanding of the competing demands, so I have come to sort of appreciate that, and I feel less pressure to publish my way out of here.

Interviewee 18 and I began the interview by talking about the international perspective she brings to this research project. Interviewee 18 is from another country, and the culture there is quite different with regard to childbirth and time off for maternity leave.

Q. What was your experience like in terms of making the decision to have a child? What professional concerns did you have?
A. Interviewee 18.
Absolutely, yes, I had concerns because there is no opportunity to have leave in my school. There is no other leave than some sick leave. So, as a non-tenured faculty member, I was very much concerned. Because you just want to publish and publish, and I knew I wasn't going to be able to do that if I had a child. Besides I was also commuting to work from another city.
Q. Did you seek out or investigate HR policies on maternity leave?
A. Interviewee 18.
I have so many female colleagues that had kids. And they were sharing this information with me, that one could only take six weeks total of sick leave. So if the birth is in the middle of the semester that doesn't cover the entire semester. I was very much aware of those kinds of issues.

Q. How about FMLA?

A. Interviewee 18.

Oh, unpaid time off, I wasn't interested in that. My chair talked to me about it. I knew I had the right to take some unpaid leave, but I considered that honestly, a punishment. I really don't think that should be part of the maternity policy. That should be something additional to the maternity policy if a woman wants to take time off, then yes, she should be able to do that. To me, I mean that's a punishment because that's when you need money the most when you have a new baby. So I said absolutely not, I was not going to take FMLA.

Q. Did your spouse take leave?

A. Interviewee 18.

He took an entire semester off. He teaches, but he is at another university.

Q. What was your experience like in terms of returning to work? Colleagues? Supervisors?

A. Interviewee 18.

I didn't have any concerns about that, I mean they were all just extremely helpful, but I had other concerns. My child was sick and I was commuting. And there was a mistake, totally an honest and unintentional mistake. My husband and I tried to schedule our courses on different days, so that one of us was always to be at home. But there was a mistake, so the two different schools both scheduled our courses, both of our courses, on a Tuesday and Thursday teaching schedule. And he had to commute too, so we had to leave the child in the town where we lived, and then we both go to other places to work. Our child was very sick so he couldn't go to day care. So I called my parents. I just called my parents and said, you just have to come here, there is no other way. They stayed for the entire semester. Even with my colleagues, almost everyone gets help from their families. What I have seen with my colleagues, they are willing to sacrifice so much for their families. Their parents are close by, and I didn't know that American families could be so close.

Q. When you had health concerns with your child, did anyone at work approach you about taking FMLA leave at that point?

A. Interviewee 18.

My chair always told me you know we can talk if you want to, but we just could not afford for me to take unpaid leave. I mean I was extremely stressed out because of trying to deal with a sick child, and we were trying to nurse, and I was trying to prepare for a new class. So you can never concentrate on anything. I was extremely stressed out. I gained more weight after my child was born than during pregnancy because of stress.

Q. What impact has the decision to have a child had on your tenure and promotion? Have your professional goals changed any?

A. Interviewee 18.

It does impact my goals. I have to do fieldwork because of my area of specialty. I have to study in other countries. So fieldwork is fundamental. Right now even with one child, leaving the country for three months, and having an academic husband, that's just not an option. I have to find topics that will not require me to do such excessive fieldwork. So having a child has had a significant impact on my career. So, I have to decide: Do I concentrate on articles instead of books because articles do not require that much fieldwork? Or do I write a book because it may have a more significant impact? Sometimes I feel like without a book nobody knows who you are, so maybe I lost an opportunity by not doing a book earlier. I had to do a lot of planning before I got pregnant. I was trying to get published as much as possible so when the child was born I could back off. I knew it would be too much, and it was, and I didn't do anything major for two years, during my pregnancy, and then until he turned one.

Q. Overall, how has having a child affected your commitment to your institution or employer?

A. Interviewee 18.

I think I have a much more balanced life right now. I think I would have been more of a workaholic if I didn't have a kid. No question about it because what else are you going to do with your time? We are already kind of a workaholic people. I think I have a much more balanced life right now.

Q. Looking back on your experiences, are you thinking that you need to help your university resolve the maternity leave issue for others?

A. Interviewee 18.

Actually, I am fighting that battle because I've been serving on the benefits committee of the university, and we prepared maternity policy proposals for consideration. The United States is just dragging behind on so many fronts that we can only do so much. There has to be a national struggle because little by little incremental changes at the university level won't help without a national policy.

One more thing that I would like to say is that having a maternity leave or parental leave policy, and having a national parental leave policy or not, that decision has nothing to do with money. What I mean is it has nothing to do with money, because these issues are usually presented to us as budget problems. So the response is we don't have the money. This is the richest country in the world, if my country could do this, if a third-world country could do this, anyone could. It is just about how much we are willing to allocate the resources to it. It is about whether we are really valuing this policy area or not. It is just all about that. People always talk about family values. This is the ultimate in family values.

EMPLOYEES OF PRIVATE UNIVERSITIES

Interviewee 4 and I met in her office on the campus of a small, private university. She showed me pictures of her two daughters. Interviewee 4 first explained how she became a mother through an adoption process.

> **Q.** What was your experience like in terms of making the decision to have a child and then ultimately adopting two children?
> **A.** Interviewee 4.
>> Well, fertility issues, that was the actual prompt in a nutshell. It was quite a pathway to get there. Then, when we decided we would adopt, we were told that my husband was too old to adopt by several agencies. My husband is older than I am, and so some adoption agencies really wouldn't take us because of his age, which at the time was mid-forties. A lot of agencies won't take you if you are over forty. In international adoptions if you are over forty forget it, but in any case, we got turned

down by several agencies. Then we started looking at adopting older children because the policies are different. So we adopted an older child the first time, and then as a result of that we joined a support group to help other parents. We like to support other people through some of the difficulties, but anyway there was a homeless girl that contacted our support group, and they contacted us to see if we were interested in adopting her baby, and that is how we got the baby. The birth mom lived with us for six months prior to the baby's birth.

Q. When you started this adoption process, did you have any professional concerns when it came to your career?

A. Interviewee 4.

With my first child, I was very nervous about starting back to school five weeks after the adoption. I had no inkling of taking time off. I had no maternity leave with her. When she arrived, I was teaching a summer course here, and I did have somebody cover four days of that course. Since that time, I have never been asked by the person who is in charge of summer courses to teach summer courses again. I know it is due to that, having a substitute cover for the four days. It is a three-week session, and I missed four days of it and this person was not happy with me about this. She is in charge of recruiting for this particular summer program, and she has never asked me to participate again. My absences were covered by a competent individual. I gave her an appropriate fee to cover that time, an amount of money that I would have received. I paid her to do it for me.

Q. When you were going through that process, and then more recently with the adoption of the baby, did you seek out information about the actual maternity benefits available under the university's policies?

A. Interviewee 4.

I did, I went to our HR person and talked to her about what my options were. The institution did not want me to teach that semester, and this made sense to me. I had no complaint. But if it weren't for my husband's income, I would have had a complaint. But basically it was not good for me to come into the classroom the semester the baby was born. She was born right before the fall semester started. So if I were to take six weeks off, and come into a classroom six weeks after it started that would not be a good option, so I took the semester off. I was able to cash-out my accumulated sick days, but there were several months during that semester that I received no pay.

Q. What was your experience like in terms of returning to work in January?
A. Interviewee 4.

It was hard. The only thing that made it bearable for me was that my mother takes care of the baby. If that ever ceases I would probably go home and stay. I am not for putting my baby in a day care. Many women do very well with it, but I'm not one of those women.

Q. What professional concerns did you have?
A. Interviewee 4.

I have been full time here for five years. So I was eligible for a promotion to associate professor. The year before I became eligible I talked to my department chair and said, "what do I need to do in the coming year to prepare to be up for promotion to associate?" And I was told, "nothing, you're on track, you are right where you should be, go ahead and apply." Because we have a policy here, it is a spoken policy that if the chair can't support you seeking a promotion, then they will guide you against it, they will discourage you. So that did not happen.

Further identifying details are omitted here to protect the privacy of Interviewee 4, but basically she was asked to withdraw her application. She was told she was "short" on years of teaching required for a promotion due to taking a semester off for maternity leave. Tenure and promotion are handled at different times, and through a different process. At this particular university you must be at the level of associate professor before you may apply for tenure. (More details related to this issue are presented in Chapter 7.)

Q. What happened after you were asked to withdraw your application for promotion?
A. Interviewee 4.

I explained to the dean that this was "maternity leave" and that I have a legal protection. She said our HR person said FMLA is basically just to protect you. FMLA says you still have a job. It does not guarantee you will get a promotion. So basically the school is sending the message that if you have a baby you could be professionally harmed. And I have been. All that

FMLA law says is that we have to hold your job. My dean said, "you took a semester off, and we only had to hold your job for a few weeks, but we let you have the semester off, so you should count your blessings."

Q. Have you consulted legal advice, or asked for a Department of Labor clarification?

A. Interviewee 4.

No. I would be fired if I did that.

Q. Given this turmoil, do you feel like you have kept your work and home life in balance, has it been a struggle? What has been the most challenging thing?

A. Interviewee 4.

It has been a struggle. Probably the amount of time I am home following up on e-mails while trying to take care of the baby, that has been a struggle. I am very nervous about being asked to do things after hours or on the weekend because I want to be with the baby.

Q. What impact has the decision to have a child had on your career?

A. Interviewee 4.

It has cost me a promotion, a timely promotion. It could potentially cost me tenure in the future. I was very bitter at the beginning of the semester, but there is nothing I can do, so I am trying to make peace with it. Still trying.

Interviewee 11 works for a private university in a unique position. She is a full-time administrative assistant to a professor. In her position, she works primarily from home, which is a great geographical distance from her employer and her supervisor. This is also a unique position in that she followed this professor from one institution on the East Coast to one on the West Coast. Her position was a condition of his move to the new institution. However, she is not a resident of the state in which she is employed, so there have been some difficulties with employee benefits. Further, she had one child while an employee of one school and the second child while an employee of the second school. Her youngest was an infant at the time of the interview.

Q. At what point in the process, did you seek out or investigate HR policies on maternity leave?

A. Interviewee 11.

That gets a little tricky. My first employer did not allow people to work from home, so in order to keep my job they had to switch me to a temporary agency, and I kept my same salary and everything, but lost all benefits. We decided we would just work things out. They would give me vacation days and such. Then with my second employer, the school, they did not do that to me. They hired me as a university employee, but communication wasn't great about benefits. Because I wasn't on-site, they had no one to really keep track, and the laws are so different in all of these three different states, it was really complicated. I worked in two different states, but lived and paid taxes in another state.

So, with the first baby, in terms of maternity leave, we just worked it out. The second time, when we discovered we were pregnant I jumped online and I found a few paragraphs about maternity leave at the university. And it indicated to me that you only got leave if you were paying into their short-term disability insurance, which is a state requirement, and which I wasn't. We had looked it over, but we really couldn't figure it out. We weren't ready to take it to HR, and I wasn't ready to talk to my HR person because it was so early on in my pregnancy. My husband said surely that's not the case, that this is the only way you can take time off, so we really didn't think about it again until I brought it up with my boss in January. So, everyone was happy for me in terms of the pregnancy, but then they said since you are not paying into the short-term disability, you can only take unpaid FMLA.

Q. Did you have any other type of leave accumulated, so that part of FMLA leave might be paid?

A. Interviewee 11.

That would have taken all of my vacation and sick leave first, and I had already taken some vacation days that year, so I think it amounted to about four and a half weeks of leave. I called my boss and I was very upset, and I said I can't believe this is happening. This was never communicated to me that I should pay into this short-term disability. He said to basically just keep turning in my time sheets even when I couldn't work.

Q. Were you satisfied with that arrangement?

A. Interviewee 11.

No. I've been through sexual harassment training. I've been through that and other training online, and it was irritating to me because my health insurance benefits should be important too. Later, I found out I had signed a waiver on the short-term disability, but I didn't know. And I could have signed up for it at open enrollment time for benefits the next year, but I had no idea that I should do this when we got ready to have a baby.

Q. So, back to the first employer, and your first baby. When you did become pregnant then, did you have any professional concerns from a colleague or work responsibility issue since you worked from home?
A. Interviewee 11.

I certainly got some pushback, probably the strongest pushback I received was when I told the office at my first school, nothing at my current school, but at my first school the office manager said, 'Oh well you're going to quit your job, there's no way you can work with a kid.'

Q. Was that a male manager?
A. Interviewee 11.

No, interestingly enough, she was a woman who had just had a child.

Q. Was she frazzled at the time or anything? Did it feel to you that it was a statement of "I'm a super woman, and you're not," or that it was "you just can't manage?"
A. Interviewee 11.

I think it was that she thought when people work from home you're not "really" going to work.

Q. So, what did you work out in terms of time off at your first employer when you had your first baby?
A. Interviewee 11.

They gave me eight weeks off, paid. With the second child, I ended up having five weeks accrued leave, so I had five weeks paid, and then I took two more weeks off that my boss gave me. And that was paid too.

Q. But an informal arrangement?
A. Interviewee 11.

Yes.

Q. Did HR talk to you about FMLA too?
A. Interviewee 11.

Yes, I had signed all of the paperwork and turned everything in, just in case something went wrong and I would need more time off. But that would have been unpaid. The e-mails from my HR person said that I'm going to put this FMLA paperwork on file should you choose to use it, but it was all very vague. And that is what is scary. I felt like I wanted to become an advocate for women after this happened to me. I was shocked. I was at this great school, in a state that has some really great laws for maternity leave, but I still had no maternity leave coverage.

Q. Did your spouse take leave?
  A. Interviewee 11.
    He took two weeks paid vacation leave.
Q. So, since you work at home, what was the leave like? Did you answer e-mails while on leave?
  A. Interviewee 11.
    There were some things that no one else could handle. But every day I had four or five e-mails, and I would handle those because someone needed something.
Q. Were people apologetic about bothering you?
  A. Interviewee 11.
    Yes, some of them apologized, but they still e-mailed me. So okay, I'm turning in my time sheet, but I never thought with all my vacation and my sick leave accrued that I would still be answering my phone, or still writing e-mails. Definitely, an infant is much easier to take care of, because they sleep and they eat, than my two-year-old. I was still worried about taking care of her. Taking care of the baby, taking care of her, it is pretty much we're up from 5 a.m. to 1 a.m. and we get some sleep, and then it starts all over again.
Q. What was your experience like in terms of returning to work?
  A. Interviewee 11.
    I've been back two weeks. This has been my second week. It's all very brand new. I would say my biggest concern is the fact that I have to be on my phone, and I knew I would be. There is a time difference. Time actually plays an important role for me because that means that I don't actually have to be on the phone until 10 a.m. and then my husband gets off work fairly early, so 4:30 p.m. to 7 p.m. I can be totally by myself if I need to.

Q. What has your child-care experience been like?
A. Interviewee 11.
   Sometimes we will have my husband's mother come, but we don't hire anybody at this point.
Q. How is breast-feeding going?
A. Interviewee 11.
   It is going fine actually. My husband and I were joking last night that we don't know how women who don't breast-feed do it, because it is so hard sometimes to keep the baby quiet. It is hard. I'm tired, I'm hungry, and I'm thirsty all the time. I'm in a unique situation since I'm at home, but honestly if I had to be on-site, I don't think I could keep up with breast-feeding. I know that no one is going to want to give you a break to do that. In fact, my aunt that is a teacher, when she had her son four or five years ago, she had a big problem. The principal would not let her pump in her room, after the kids were gone of course. But, during her break, he insisted that she pump in the bathroom, in an elementary school. I always felt more comfortable breast-feeding in the car when we would come to visit here. You know on the East Coast, I had no problem getting my nursing cover out in whatever restaurant I was in, but here I feel a little self-conscious.
Q. Overall, how has having a child affected your commitment to your institution and to your immediate supervisor? Looking back, what might you have handled differently? Looking back, what might you have wanted to see your employer do differently?
A. Interviewee 11.
   Yeah, for the institution, I was ready to quit. I was very upset. I was beside myself because it wasn't even about the leave itself. I kind of knew in the back of mind that my boss would protect me, but it really upset me that my husband was going to get paid time off that was short, but I wasn't entitled to it because I didn't read between the lines and know the language. I didn't know they called pregnancy a disability, and that vocabulary really bothered me. And when I had read about disability leave online, it was talking about that you would only be able to take out what you paid in, and it wouldn't cover 100% of your salary anyway. In most cases it

was just 50% of your base salary, so when I read that, I never thought about maternity leave.

So in terms of changes, at the lowest level, I would like to see more communication. Something that clearly says this is the policy. When I joined the university I had just had my first daughter, so to me this was an obvious sign to an employer that maybe this new employee, she might like to have another daughter or a son. The employer should educate this new employee. Tell the employee how you go through the process every time. I did a significant amount of research and still didn't find clear answers on how maternity leave works.

As for my boss, he's amazing. He was born and raised in Georgia. He's Southern. He was on the East Coast, and now he's on the West Coast. He's a friend too, but he's like this with everyone that works under him. So I don't think this just applies to me. But I think he doesn't have the idea that you have to work 9 to 5. If you're getting your work done, and if you're getting more than your work done, then he really doesn't care when you do it.

Interviewee 5 and I met in her office on the campus of a small private university. Her children are a little older than those of most of the mothers I interviewed, but she was willing to talk about her experience with her youngest child. At the time of that birth, she worked at a large public university.

> Q. What was your experience like in terms of making the decision to have a child? What professional concerns did you have?
> A. Interviewee 5.
>> Well, my first two children were born when I was in the private sector. So, that did not have any impact on my career in academics, but my youngest son was born when I was in a clinical teaching faculty position, and there was no maternity leave policy. In my department, that year my son was born, there were also two other children born to faculty, and those were the first children born in about thirty years to teaching faculty members. So nobody knew what to do. There was no policy, and I was really fortunate because my son was born in July. So we really didn't know what to do, and we were scrambling. I was willing to negotiate a contract with my boss at the

time. I wrote it out, what I wanted. I was teaching summer classes, and I wrote out what I would be able to do with those. He was very informal about it all, and he didn't really want to sign it, but I really wanted the formality of it and the security of a written agreement. So I asked him to sign it. At the time it sure was scary, thinking, I don't have any sick leave. As faculty we didn't have sick leave, or vacation, and we had an eleven-month contract, and with that no one knew where that one month of time off actually was. So it was very ambiguous. At the time I felt it would give me a little bit more security, and you know I was really worried about not coming into the office even though it was summer, and faculty were all gone. Being the lowest-ranking person in the teaching profession, I didn't want people to think I wasn't doing my job even though I just had a child. So I was very worried about that. So, I still continued to work, but I was working from home. I still had responsibilities of grading, online work, and correspondence with students and things like that all summer.

Q. Did they subsequently come up with some new policies?

A. Interviewee 5.

Yes, I was actually appointed to a committee, and we looked at maternity leave policies from other schools around the country, talked to other faculty at the schools within the university, and found out that there was no consistency in maternity policies. I don't know if there is now. But at the time, we came up with recommendations. The way the university dealt with it at the time was each school or college within the university could come up with their own policies. We looked at options such as six weeks leave, a half of the semester off, a whole semester off, but then we thought what if the baby is born at a time in the middle of the semester? When I left the university there still was no maternity policy.

Q. What professional concerns did you have about negotiating your own maternity leave?

A. Interviewee 5.

Well, I had only been there a year, so I thought that they probably wouldn't take me seriously. And he was my third child, so thinking back there was just a lot of judgment I think, being a teaching faculty, already having two other kids. I felt pressure or paranoia about them thinking I wasn't going to return after the baby, or maybe I didn't take my job seriously enough, or that I should put academics first.

Q. So when you were negotiating the time off, was your direct supervisor a male or female?

A. Interviewee 5.

Male, and he was very supportive. He was a grandparent. He was wonderful, very supportive, I never had a problem. He was so happy when I told him I was pregnant. I was so scared to tell him. He said things like, "congratulations, this is what life is about." I was so scared, but no, he was fine. It was the female faculty who said less than supportive things, and said things like, "they didn't get this benefit, so why should you?"

Q. So, how does the maternity leave policy here at a private university compare to your previous public university?

A. Interviewee 5.

That place is so different from here. There, it was not clear what my teaching load would be, and it would change. My responsibilities would change just on a whim. Here everything is very laid out. I've never looked at the maternity policy here, but I know one woman took the whole semester off, and then she went back to her job, so I know there must be something here.

Q. Upon returning to work, what was your child-care decision like?

A. Interviewee 5.

It was fine. I actually was very fortunate, and got him into the day care on campus. So the preschool, first he was in a home day care, and then he went to the preschool program on campus. The waiting list is crazy. He was on the waiting list while I was pregnant. The fact that he got chosen was probably a fluke. They try to have a balance, and they consider diversity, and he is a healthy, white boy, so we really got lucky, and it worked out very well.

Q. Obviously, you changed where you worked since you had your last child, but looking back, what might you have wanted to see your employer then do differently?

A. Interviewee 5.

I think that this environment here, because it is smaller and because it is more family friendly, the faculty who are here are more open to hearing about my kids and accepting of the fact that I am also a mom and working. I really didn't feel like I could talk about my kids at my other school. I really thought they didn't take me seriously if I did. That definitely should change there. Here is definitely a different feel as far as this university is concerned.

Q. Is there any advice you would offer a new young female faculty member if she accepted a job at your former university?

A. Interviewee 5.

I would say find out what the policy is now before accepting a position. Part of our committee's recommendations included that the tenure clock should stop. The tenure process should stop when she goes on maternity leave, and we suggested that the person negotiate leave ahead of time. If I was a new, young graduate looking for a teaching job I would want to know that and how much time they would allow. You know I've got mixed feelings about coming back full time versus part time. Do you get a course reduction, or something? Maybe there could be a series of options she could choose from, a whole semester off, and you come back full time ready to go with a full course load, or you teach online during that time, and you come back for a reduced amount of teaching for the year. But I think there should be some flexibility because not every situation is going to be the same. If you have a baby in October and you come back and teach full time in January that seems okay. But what if your child was born in December? So there has to be some kind of flexibility that they can negotiate, but I think having it in writing is going to be the key. I do think that the tenure clock should stop. I would say twelve weeks. I would say the Family and Medical Leave Act was what we were using to gauge the amount of leave a person should have off, but the semester is longer than that. You can't really come back and teach for just four weeks or six weeks then. When I was on the committee, I just didn't know all of these things to think about at the time because it was my first teaching experience. Generally, most of the time faculty could kind of do your own thing, do your job, and nobody really paid attention to you, but when something like maternity leave came up you really wanted the uniformity of a policy and the ability to plan ahead of time. As far as policy and planning, here at a private university, I was shocked when I came here and found out I have a sick leave. I didn't know how that worked. What do you mean I have a sick leave? And then I thought I've never really taken a sick day when I didn't have it, and not now either when I did have the leave. But it is nice to have sick leave available if I need it.

Interviewee 8 and I met for the interview in a coffee shop in her hometown. She had driven hours to get there to spend time with her family, so her mother kept the baby while we talked. I had driven a few hours to meet her there. In her position at a private university, Interviewee 8 is not in a tenure-track position, but she is in a position where she can receive promotions. She works on a three-year contract basis, and her position requires teaching and service, but not research. This arrangement and the expectations are a little unique. Research is looked upon favorably by her institution, however, and is rewarded monetarily in addition to her base salary if she is published. Interviewee 8 is one of only a few women in a very male-dominated department in a very male-dominated field. As a result, Interviewee 8 spent considerable time before getting pregnant deciding when and if to have a child. Her story is even more compelling because she gave birth to twins, and one of them did not survive. Part of her story is presented in Chapter 7, but some of what she confided is omitted out of respect for her privacy and to protect her anonymity. Her story of joy is also one of sorrow.

> Q. At what point in the process, did you seek out or investigate HR policies on maternity leave?
> A. Interviewee 8.
>> I did go ahead early on, and ask HR about maternity leave. Our HR department has an anonymous information line where you can just call and ask questions, so I wasn't worried about the signal I may have been sending because it was anonymous. And the only thing about that was that for faculty, maternity leave just depends on your situation. So, I didn't get a whole lot of information from them except to check out the Family and Medical Leave Act, and that applies to you, and then whatever your department wants to do, that's up to them.
> Q. What was your experience like in terms of conceiving a child?
> A. Interviewee 8.

So based on all my conversations with other women, I wanted to have a "summer" baby. We decided that we would try through the fall, so that I could have the baby in the summer. I wanted to be able to have the baby at a time where I wasn't feeling guilty about pushing my teaching off to someone else, because the thing about my job is I'm primarily a teaching professor, and I have a lot of students. I have four sections. I have over two hundred students a semester so pushing my teaching off on someone else during the regular semester would be a big deal. So I wanted to have a pregnancy that was guilt-free in that sense. It ended up being pretty easy to get pregnant. We got pregnant three months later.

Q. So in terms of the delivery and the time frame, you were seven weeks early?

A. Interviewee 8.

I delivered seven weeks early. The summer class I was supposed to teach hadn't even started yet when I gave birth. And my semester had ended and I was able to finish the spring semester completely normal. I was actually working on research that I was due to present to the department. In fact, this research project has been hard for me to return to because of the emotional connection to working on it the day I lost one baby.

Q. What was your experience like in terms of utilizing maternity leave?

A. Interviewee 8.

So it was kind of weird at first, and it was hard to get answers from my human resources department because I was due in the summer. So I didn't have any duties for my contract. So because of that, I didn't necessarily feel like I needed to request leave, but according to FMLA I should. So I wasn't sure what to do, and so what HR decided was that just to have everything on the books, and in case something happened that I needed to take extra leave later, they wanted me to still apply for the six weeks off in the summer. They wanted me to apply for FMLA based on my due date, six weeks out from then. Even though the six weeks would have ended before the fall semester even started, that was when I was next scheduled to teach, and yet they still wanted me to apply for it.

Q. Did you ask for reduced or modified teaching duties for the semester when you returned to teaching?

A. Interviewee 8.

When I told my chair I was pregnant, I said the only thing I would ask for is that maybe my schedule could be arranged so that I was only teaching two times a week, or I could lump my teaching all in the morning, or space it in a way that I could breast feed and have time for stuff that like that. And he said we'll do what we can, and he came back to me shortly after, and said that the university wanted me to be able to spend time with my babies, so they gave me a half-load for teaching in the fall. So, eventually as it turned out, they gave me a half-load, so two sections instead of four sections, with no reduction in pay. They gave me the first two morning classes, so two days a week, on Tuesday/Thursday, lumped together in the morning. So I was there two days a week, and I stayed home the other three days.

Q. Did your spouse take leave?

A. Interviewee 8.

He works for a really small company, five employees, and so he is not eligible for FMLA. So, I gave birth on Tuesday, and he maybe didn't go back into the office until Friday, just part time. Then the following week he went back, and he would go in a couple hours some days. He was able to take the day of my other daughter's funeral off, and the day after, and then he would intermittently go in. The other days we were in the NICU with our other daughter, he would take time off, but it was all completely unpaid. He would work from home. I guess it probably wasn't until three weeks after our daughter was born that he finally went back full time, and then he took a week of paid vacation once we got settled.

It was really generous of his boss to let him off. But it was also very hard. I was mad about the treatment he got because, although I understood it was a small company and they didn't really owe him anything, he felt guilty taking off to go to the NICU, and he felt guilty about not being at work. There were other days that he couldn't go to work because we were so overcome with grief, and he didn't have any bereavement leave. He didn't have any paternity leave. It was somewhat of an economic strain to both be out of work. My pay wasn't affected, but with him not being at work and being unpaid, and then coming home with a baby, and all the extra expenses that was kind of stressful. But we chose that because it was important for him to be home.

Q. What impact has the decision to have a child and also losing a child had on your career goals in the future?

A. Interviewee 8.

So one thing it has done, it has made me very grateful for a teaching professor position. I without a doubt love teaching more than research. But there is a part of me, you know I was valedictorian of all of my classes, a part of me, there's a part of me that says I can do better than just that. And there is pressure by my husband. For example, he believes that I could thrive in a tenure-track position. And there is a part of me that thinks you know that is something I could do, and I could do well at it. I don't think that I would be able to have the family life that I have now if I had a tenure-track position. And although before having a baby, I wasn't okay with it, now that I have her, I'm fine with that. My university pays us well enough that I don't feel like I'm constantly trying to do better just for the economic benefit. So I'm financially doing well. I still get the respect of my department even though I'm not tenure track, and I get to have the family that I wanted to. I don't want to never see my child. That is not me. So I think now professionally my outlook is different.

Q. Looking back, what might you have wanted to see your employer do differently?

A. Interviewee 8.

I think the university as a whole is not very organized about the whole maternity leave process, so I went through a couple of seminars on family-friendly benefits to learn more. The university presents itself as very family based, which is appreciated. But why they say they're family based is not something to brag about. They say we have this day-care program, but it has a waiting list, and you're probably not going to get into it. And then they have family days at the gym, which is great. But what I learned at some of these seminars is that it all depends on how your college feels about maternity leave, not the university as a whole. So we know somebody from another college, and she was afraid to take maternity leave because she was new. She had just started with the university, and they really didn't come out and say we want you to enjoy your family like the way my department chair did. So she didn't take it, and she was open at this meeting about telling the university, "you have this wrong, you claim you're a family-oriented university and I believe that you are, but this is not the way to show it." I heard that complaint, and that really scared me. I mean looking at that example, and at first I thought well this is not her first child so maybe she felt like she didn't need leave, so she didn't request it. But that was not really what she wanted. I still don't know how she did it, given my experience, so I think that the university probably could be better at communicating about maternity leave.

However, I think that my college and my department, their reaction to and their involvement in what happened to me completely boosted my dedication to the university. I think that the people in my department are just kind in general and they were very supportive. You know looking back, I think that any issue that I have in terms of feeling guilty or feeling that I should work more, and stay home less, I think that is all completely self-imposed. It is not from them, it is just something I imposed on myself because of other people's experiences, but not from anyone in my department.

EMPLOYEES OF THE PHARMACEUTICAL INDUSTRY

Interviewee 9 and I met at 8:00 a.m. at a Starbucks. One of the initial questions asked of Interviewee 9 was whether she had worked in any other field prior to becoming a pharmaceutical representative. Her reply was surprising and humorous, and set the tone for the interview. Interviewee 9 replied, "I was a marketing coordinator and project coordinator for a plumbing company actually, and yes, I know how to fix my own toilet."

> **Q.** What was your experience like in terms of making the decision to have a child? What professional concerns did you have?

A. Interviewee 9.

Unlike the other people you may have talked to, I had no hesitation about having children. I honestly didn't really think of the impact that it would have on my job. I think because I had seen other people before me have children with my company, I didn't think that they were in any way punished or not promoted later on, so really it was just the right timing for my husband and me. We waited for about five years. We wanted to make sure that we had a house, and were somewhat established so we could afford children and that was it.

Q. At what point in the process, did you seek out or investigate HR policies on maternity leave? What professional concerns did you have?

A. Interviewee 9.

No concerns at all. You call HR and they put you through to a person who actually deals with maternity and everything is pretty comprehensive. They tell you really not to call them again until you are about to go out on leave, and then you fill out paperwork. There is also paperwork to fill out once you have the child too.

Q. What was your experience like in terms of utilizing maternity leave?

A. Interviewee 9.

I have had the same boss the whole time through all pregnancies. He is very strict with all of the rules. He is very "by the book." I actually reached out to him, probably a week or two weeks before I came back with my first child, just to see where things stood. I was trying to get ready and plan what I needed to have prepared to return to work. And he said, "you don't need to really be calling me right now," and I said okay.

Q. So he thought you were jumping the gun? Was he concerned that he might be infringing on your time off?

A. Interviewee 9.

Yes, he didn't want to hear from me until I was officially back at work. I never felt forced to have to get online and check my e-mail. I would periodically go through that during the week, but I never felt like I had to do anything, or that I was penalized for not doing anything. With the second child I didn't look at e-mail at all. But the funny thing is and this is a different situation, when I was pregnant the first time, the actual benefits that the company gave were only six weeks.

Six weeks for natural delivery, eight weeks for C-section, and both of mine were natural. So I was out on leave, and I think I had a week left of my six weeks, and I was thinking that I was having to come back, and HR called me and said that they had changed their maternity policy, and because I was still on maternity leave when they changed their policy that I could still have an additional six weeks. So I thought it was pretty nice.

I took the leave. At first I felt a little guilty because I knew I was supposed to come back, and I'm sure that my boss was excited that I was coming back, but at the same time knowing that I was having to go back at six weeks, and seeing where I was at that point, specifically with my first child. I really do see the benefit of the 12 weeks. Because I think at six weeks you are just, especially with your first child, you are just getting the hang of things, you just got your routine down, they probably have their sleeping routine down, but you haven't gotten to know them as much yet. So I think that extra six weeks is really important, just feeling that connection, and for the baby it is good for them that you are just not leaving them so soon.

Q. Did your spouse take leave?

A. Interviewee 9.

He works for a company that doesn't offer paternity leave. He told them when I was due, so the day that I went into labor they let him have off, and he took vacation for a week.

Q. What was your experience like in terms of returning to work?

A. Interviewee 9.

It was an option to go back part time under flextime, and they told me about it. They actually verbalized it when I called human resources about returning. You don't get paid your full salary obviously. We just couldn't take the pay cut. We were actually, with the first baby, we had a person who we knew really well from church, coming to take care of her. So I think the anxiety of leaving the baby wasn't as bad because I knew the girl really well. I mean you are still a little worried, it's not you. But it wasn't that bad. The thing was I wanted to breast-feed. I breast-fed both my girls, actually. So a lot of it was trying to figure out how to breast-feed on the road, in between what I'm supposed to do, and when to do it if I'm riding in the field with my boss, or at meetings. I never felt like I shouldn't do it or couldn't do it. In fact I would actually do it about four times during the workday, and I actually did it for six months with my first, and I did it for nine months with my second.

Q. Are you saying you were pumping on the road?

A. Interviewee 9.

Yes. Granted, on the second baby, I got a new breast pump, which is awesome because I could pump while I drove. It only took ten minutes; my other pump took thirty minutes. It was hands-free though. The law in our state should be no cell phones, and no pumping!

Q. Any modified duties in any way during that initial time when you were going back to work?

A. Interviewee 9.

No, I know that in dealing with my boss, I know that when a person has a baby and specifically if they don't have family in the area, which I didn't have, he tries to make accommodations. If we have overnight meetings he will schedule the location close to the person who has a new baby, so they can go home if they need to. During the meeting I didn't even have to let them know if I had to leave for pumping, I would just leave and come back. I think during that transition back for me, that first two days, my boss actually kept me out of the field and just let me get caught up on what was going on, which is kind of nice. You just were not thrown back in.

Q. After you had a child, what was your experience like in terms of balancing home and work responsibilities?

A. Interviewee 9.

I definitely do my work differently. Whereas before I had children I would do a lot of work at night as well, I almost let it consume me, probably too much. Now what I try to do is leave a little early, try to get to where I'm going, and then do any kind of paperwork or answer any e-mails before that. I try to get everything done that I have to do during the day because I leave my cell phone in my car, my business cell phone. I will not take it inside the house because I don't want to constantly hear beeps. Also, once I sync my computer on Friday night, I don't look at it until Monday morning. I sync again Sunday, but I don't look until Monday. I also don't take it with me on vacation.

Q. What has your child-care experience been like?

A. Interviewee 9.

It was good. The first one went to day care at about sixteen months, and with the second one, we had the same girl come and take care of her at our home. The oldest was still going to day care, but we transitioned her sister into day care earlier, and the reason was a conflict with the sitter's schedule. She couldn't do it anymore. So we went to day care earlier. It was actually okay. I was a little worried at first because I really liked the one-on-one attention that my oldest received, but at the same time, I see such a difference in their personalities. I think that if I had it to do over with my first one I probably would have put her in day care earlier, probably nine months to a year old. I would have felt okay with that. Because I think that socially my youngest wanted to talk earlier just because of being around other kids. She learned how to share better. She learned those things I see a benefit in, and I also feel she hasn't lacked any in love or in one-on-one attention.

Q. So they are at the same place then, do they get to interact?

A. Interviewee 9.

Well, the oldest is upstairs now and the youngest is downstairs. They were together, and they overlapped for a few months. And I told my oldest that if anything happened to her sister to come and tell me. Then, when she turned three, she went upstairs, which is more like a preschool.

Q. Overall, how has having a child affected your commitment to your employer? Looking back, what might you have handled differently and what might you have wanted to see your employer do differently?

A. Interviewee 9.

We had changes in my organization when I was six months pregnant. What I have to say for my company and my current boss is this, two years ago my whole territory was eliminated and I was six months pregnant. My territory was broken up into pieces and merged into other territories. So I didn't know what I was going to do, because at that point I was showing obviously, and so no one is going to hire me at a certain point. Why would they hire somebody pregnant when they could hire somebody else who wouldn't be out of the field for maternity leave? So, I re-interviewed with my company and my new manager actually hired me back, fully aware that I was pregnant, and knowing that I would be out for three months.

Q. Were you ever during that time unemployed?

A. Interviewee 9.

I never was completely severed by my company. I was at the point that I was not going to have a job after the end of that month. I would have collected severance, but I was hired back within three weeks, so it didn't affect my tenure or my standing with the company. So it was really weird. I had three weeks of a very stressful vacation. I was actually paid at that time. They give you a thirty-day notice basically, so within that thirty day time I was paid. I was just grateful to have a job at that point. I did get my raise from the previous year though. They let us all go on January 31st, and I was rehired the last week of February, and then I actually got my scheduled raise in March.

Q. And did this solidify your loyalty and commitment to your company?

A. Interviewee 9.

I am a motivated person. At the same time if I had enough money to stay at home and be a stay-at-home mom, I would. When I am doing a job I like to do it well, and I won't sacrifice that. However, I do believe there should be a separation between your home life and your work life, and if push comes to shove my family will always come before my work. I would like to see less layoffs, but I think that is because in the years I have been with them we have had four reorganizations and layoffs during that time period. But as far as my loyalty, in terms of what they have given us in benefits, it is really an eye-opening experience when you feel like you are about to lose your job and then you look at all these benefits that I get. It's wow! It does add up. So we are very fortunate. Oh, and as far as goals go, I would like to get promoted probably to a specialty position, but I don't feel like I could be able to be the best employee at a higher level than that because I wouldn't want it to consume me. I would feel like it could consume me. I don't want that. But I think if you don't know what other people are normally given in benefits, then you are not aware of how blessed you've been. I think it would definitely heighten loyalty, that if a company has a good employee they recognize that employees shouldn't be penalized just due to the fact they can have children.

Interviewee 6 and I met for lunch in a sandwich shop on her "sales route." In response to the first question about starting a family, she brought up day care almost immediately.

Q. What was your experience like in terms of making the decision to have a child?
A. Interviewee 6.
Oh well, my husband and I decided to start a family, and it was first the question of my career, and then his career came up in the conversation probably last because we knew we would be able to work it out. We always knew that we would weave children into our lives, it was more like, "okay, well where would be a good day care?"

Q. What was your experience like in terms of utilizing maternity leave?
A. Interviewee 6.
Before I had my last baby, in my last pregnancy when I was probably six, or seven months along, the doctor said we want you to stop working and go to half day, so I had a note to be out half of the day. I never had a problem with it, and my manager at the time said whatever time you need, you take, so it was a great support system.

Q. So did you work in the field but closer to home?
A. Interviewee 6.
I was still going where I needed to go in my sales territory, and I would work until lunchtime, and then I would go home.

Q. How many weeks of maternity leave did you take?
A. Interviewee 6.
Well I ended up having eight weeks off because all three of them were C-sections. And then, I had at the time three weeks' vacation, so I just added it all on. So, I never took any additional FMLA or anything like that. So, eleven weeks.

Q. During that time, before you went back to work, were you tempted to check your e-mail?

A. Interviewee 6.

Absolutely. I did. I did check it, and I would get the response back, "get off of your e-mail."

Q. What was your experience like in terms of returning to work?

A. Interviewee 6.

The two oldest, they started out at the day-care facility that was affiliated with work. And the care was wonderful. It was a brand-new facility, and then we moved, so we had a new day care. The transition was wonderful. It was nice there, too. Each of them was 13 weeks old when they started at day care.

Q. How was the breast-feeding and return to work?

A. Interviewee 6.

It was fine because so many people do it now. I would eat my lunch in my car, and I would just bring a blanket and sit in my car and pump. And, at that point I was kind of weaning them off of it, so I would pump maybe twice a day. And then during the weekends, I would just breast-feed them all of the time. So it is amazing how your body can do that, you know?

Q. Is there anything else about child care you want to add?

A. Interviewee 6.

What the company could offer is more subsidized day care. If you live near a company-sponsored facility they would subsidize your day care because they have on-site day care there, but they don't give it to the rest of the employees. Another thing that concerns me is sick leave. When your child is sick, or your child has a fever or your child has thrown up, you can't send them to day care for twenty-four hours, so one of the parents needs to stay home with their child. There are plenty of females who say, "I can't take any more time off, or I'm going to lose my job." So they send sick kids to day care. And then that makes my kids get sick. So that's another thing because these women don't have enough time to take off, or because you were late two days this week, they are told "we're going to dock your pay." That happens a lot. That doesn't happen at my company, but we don't accumulate sick leave, and we can't take it for someone else's sickness. A manager can use his discretion to let you use it if you have a sick child, but it is not the policy. Women who work for an hourly wage can't do that.

After she put her children to bed, Interviewee 7 and I met for coffee late at night at Dunkin Donuts. Interviewee 7's pregnancy story begins with her husband returning from Iraq. She and her husband had recently relocated, and she had started a new job with a new pharmaceutical company when she found out she was pregnant.

> **Q.** At what point in the process, did you seek out or investigate HR policies on maternity leave?
> **A.** Interviewee 7.
>> I did my own research until I had confirmation that I was pregnant, and I contacted human resources when I was a few months in. I was very hesitant to tell my manager because I had just been hired. I was three months along before I told.
>
> **Q.** Were you eligible for maternity leave?
> **A.** Interviewee 7.
>> I feel very fortunate because a lot of times when you are with a company for less than a year they are not required to pay you anything. I have a friend who works for Enterprise car rentals, and she and her husband waited a year to have a baby, because they would not pay unless you had been employed there a year. So my company paid me for six weeks' leave, and then I could go on FMLA for up to 16 weeks in our state. So you could do unpaid time too. I took all the time available. They have a really great program where you can go back part time. I stayed home right up until the end of my leave, and then went back full time. But I mean it's great to have the opportunity to do a few days a week to get back in.
>
> **Q.** What was your experience like in terms of utilizing maternity leave? Any professional concerns?
> **A.** Interviewee 7.
>> I mean everybody was very supportive and my manager had seven children. He was 100% supportive, and I wouldn't feel like it would have held me back at all professionally. I just felt, I felt more guilty that I was going to be out when they just hired somebody, and that somebody will be out of the field. But I wasn't nervous of whether having a baby would hold

me back. I just didn't want to disappoint him, I guess. I do remember before I delivered at my company you work right up until you deliver, and having your first child is extremely stressful because I'm traveling far from the hospital. I've never had a baby, and I don't know what to expect. What if I'm really far away? So I specifically requested a note from my physician to stay within a certain range of the hospital. My company allowed that, but I don't know if many people do that or not.

Q. Did your spouse take leave?

A. Interviewee 7.

He works for the state, and I think he was able to take three weeks at home. It was paid. Granted he saved up all of his vacation time, everything he had, in order to do it. I mean mine was considered short-term disability leave, and he didn't take anything like that. He was at home a considerable time because he saved his vacation time, which was nice. And he did this for our second child too.

Q. How about your leave for the second child?

A. Interviewee 7.

So when my second child was born, my daughter, we just decided I wanted to be home with her. The reason is because you know for pharmaceuticals a lot of time your work doesn't stop when you come home. You still have a lot of work to do as with any other profession I'm sure. There is a lot of traveling involved, and my priority was my family. I literally went back for one week, and then put in my notice. We are just fortunate. I didn't know if I would like it. It's great to be in with a good company, have security. I actually, honestly, was not sure if I would enjoy being home, because having a professional career is something to be proud of. Ultimately, it was the best decision for us, and I do love staying home. I feel like it is a professional career, it's different, but I enjoy it.

Q. Upon returning to work, what was your child-care decision like?

A. Interviewee 7.

So we got a nanny, which we were excited about. She came in daily. We thought she was great. At first she was, but I ran into challenges all the time. It was just extremely frustrating. I really didn't like the day-care centers around us. If there was a scheduling issue with the nanny, it was always me that had to come home or miss appointments, and that hurts your reputation. I mean I never missed a lunch appointment with doctors, but it was just frustrating. I just felt like I was stressed. I like being prepared and I felt like I was passed over a lot, because I was relying on somebody who was unreliable.

Q. Did this affect how you felt about balancing home and work responsibilities?

A. Interviewee 7.

Yes, because then I had to work late at home to catch up, and then I just felt like my son wasn't getting the time that I wanted him to have with me, and it wasn't fair. Because I was always pulled to do stuff that I couldn't do during the day, and during the day I would have to rush home, and it was frustrating. We had the nanny reduce down to part time, and then I got a friend of mine to help us with day care. My son was 18 months old when I stopped working, but although our nanny was late and unreliable at times, there was no question that our son was safe, and that she was someone that we were very comfortable with. She was really good with him.

Q. Overall, how did having a child affect your commitment to your employer? Was there anything that they might have done to outweigh your decision to ultimately quit and stay home?

A. Interviewee 7.

No, I don't think that, but again, I mean my perspective toward life in general completely changed when my husband got shipped to Iraq, so I mean it just put things in perspective. I can always get a job. Jobs are always going to be there. I can always work hard and work my way up, and I know that the company I worked for has a good reputation. But I just knew that I couldn't get this time back.

One other thing, I think that HR should have had a little bit better training, going back to that whole nursing and breastfeeding situation. And I remember HR at some point had messed up something and I was supposed to get paid up until six weeks. It ended up getting stopped before the six weeks were over, and we were depending on the money. The problem was because the HR representative had gone on vacation and he had forgotten to do something. It totally messed us up financially, but it was eventually taken care of.

Q. Is there anything you want to add?

A. Interviewee 7.

I mean I would not regret staying home even for a second. There are frustrating days, but I would never change it. I just feel very fortunate for the opportunity to be able to do it. Especially because I think nursing is not easy when you are first starting out. It's frustrating to have to pump in a car, and getting your manager to leave if he is with you. I know other people in other professions have it just as difficult, but I mean it's just not comfortable, or easy, and you know that it is the best thing for the child. I just can't imagine why they don't make it a little bit easier for nursing moms. So, when I went back to work, I nursed my son for six months, and six months was a long time for me, because it was hard nursing and working at the same time. With my daughter, when I was home, I nursed her for over a year. It was like I didn't even notice, it wasn't challenging at all. I didn't have to worry about anything and doing all of that pumping stuff. And it was what was best for my child. When I have a third child, I will do it as long as I can because that is what is best for the child.

Interviewee 19 and I first met quite some time before the interview, so we had an easy conversational rapport that set the tone for the interview. I asked, "How is the little guy?" referring to her young son. She replied, "He is doing excellent, he is growing and big. It is a lot less scary now."

Q. At what point in the process, did you seek out or investigate HR policies on maternity leave?

A. Interviewee 19.

I would say about two months, when I was two months along. I think I found what I needed, but I don't think it becomes relevant until you actually go out on leave. I say that because when I contacted my human resources department, they gave me some information, but nothing in writing. They basically referred me to my insurance company. I told my boss at the time when I was eleven weeks along. I was expected to work up until my due date, except I actually didn't work up until my due date. We don't have maternity leave. It is short-term disability leave only. And there is no paternity leave.

Q. So you had the baby later than your due date, but you took leave earlier?
A. Interviewee 19.

Yes, I ended up going out two weeks before my due date because I was so uncomfortable. I did that with short-term disability, and I had to have a doctor's order.

Q. What was your experience like in terms of delivery?
A. Interviewee 19.

I had a C-section, but no issues out of the norm.

Q. What was your experience like in terms of utilizing maternity leave?
A. Interviewee 19.

Actually I think what concerned me leading up to the leave was that I didn't have all the information. It seemed too easy. I went to HR, and they said you just contact your insurance company, and let them know within the week that you have the baby, and they will send your physician paperwork to complete. So that accounted for my eight weeks of maternity leave that I got. It was paid, fully paid. So I had eight weeks' leave because I had a C-section. If I had not, it would have been six weeks. In my state, you are entitled to 16 weeks of FMLA time; however, that 16 weeks runs concurrent with the 8 weeks. So I had my eight weeks paid, and then I had essentially another 8 weeks I could take FMLA, which would be unpaid time.

Q. Did you take that entire leave as allowed?
A. Interviewee 19.

I did. I was home, and what happened was, I took a couple of unpaid FMLA weeks when my eight weeks expired, then for two and a half months after I worked three days a week.

Q. And did your spouse take any leave?
A. Interviewee 19.

My husband took the first week after our son was born, but it wasn't paternity leave, it was vacation time.

Q. What was your experience like in terms of returning to work?
A. Interviewee 19.

It was overwhelming at first.... I would say primarily because of the anxiety of bringing him to day care.... I mean other than that you know it was tiring to come home after working and take care of a baby. But other than that it was okay. No, honestly it would still to be nice now if I had the option to work part time. I definitely would do it. However, I had a great manager. I couldn't have had a better boss throughout my entire pregnancy, and after my pregnancy, she was totally supportive and understanding.

Q. Looking back, what might you have wanted to see your employer do differently?

A. Interviewee 19.

Maybe having some time off before delivery. That's a big one. Just because of the nature of what we do, in and out of the car, and I mean it was sweltering hot. There were days that it was 95 degrees and humid out, and having to be dressed in nice clothes, and getting out of a hot car, and standing for long periods of time in offices. I think having that month off prior is important. I think that more time afterwards or flextime would be great. Or the option to work part time would be great. Even more important than that is maternity leave, and I can't even call it maternity leave because for my company it is called short-term disability. The short-term disability time off should be longer.

My conversation with Interviewee 10 was held at her home in hushed tones while her baby was sleeping.

Q. What was your experience like in terms of making the decision to have a child? What professional concerns did you have?

A. Interviewee 10.

Around the time when we wanted to start trying for a baby, my company had announced the threat of layoffs in early 2009. So we wanted to make sure that we got through that before we tried. When I had survived the layoffs, then of course we knew it was okay to try at that point.

Q. At what point in the process, did you seek out or investigate HR policies on maternity leave?

A. Interviewee 10.

Probably the day that I found out I was pregnant. I called HR, and talked to someone live about it, and they spelled out the plan. So for my company at least, I was granted 12 weeks paid leave, and if my baby had come on time I would have been granted three weeks prior to my due date to stop work, and just stay at home until my due date. So then after the 12 weeks expired I was then given the opportunity to do eight weeks' flextime. During those eight weeks flextime, I had a minimum requirement of two days per week. And that is what I chose to do for eight weeks.

Q. Did you have any other questions for HR with regard to health insurance and other benefits that your company offered that you checked into?
A. Interviewee 10.

After my baby came early, I checked in with the company to see if there were extra days or extra time allotted for an early or pre-term baby, and there were not. So my maternity leave started as soon as she came. So I lost out on the three weeks prior, and of course my 12 weeks started sooner. But my company covered everything at the hospital, so I still only had to pay a small deductible or co-pay. So out of a $75,000 bill for all the time she spent in the NICU, we only paid maybe $500 out-of-pocket.

Q. Prior to the early delivery, did you have any professional concerns?
A. Interviewee 10.

I had just gotten a new boss that same year because of the lay-offs, and I lost my old manager and acquired a new one. He wasn't new to the company, just new to me. So April 1st, I was assigned this manager, and April is when we started trying to have a baby. I remember casually over dinner one night with the team, I mentioned to my boss because he was sitting next to me, and we were talking about children, and I said, "oh by the way, my husband and I are trying." He said he didn't want to hear about those things. He said, "Great, enough said" and I said, "Oh what's wrong?" He said, "There is a difference between trying and being pregnant, and I don't want to hear about the trying business." He said it in the nicest way possible, but I think it was "too much information" for him. I was just trying to be up-front about my plans for starting a family, and how that might impact my team.

Q. What was your experience like in terms of returning to work?
A. Interviewee 10.

I should say that during this time period I was trying to get a transfer and relocate for my husband's job. When I was on maternity leave, I just remembered this, I applied for and interviewed for a position with my company in another state, and I didn't get the job unfortunately.

Q. Did you feel at a disadvantage because you were on maternity leave?

A. Interviewee 10.

Maybe my skills were a little rusty. I remember I had to talk about reports and things. I had to take a lot of time that morning before the afternoon interview to look it all over and remember where I was again in my sales, as far as quota and things like that. Maybe I was at a disadvantage because I was out of practice. Of course, the interviewer didn't ask if I was on maternity leave, and he didn't know that until I offered it up, which I did because it affected when I would be able to start if I got the transfer.

Q. So when you returned to work part time, any concerns?

A. Interviewee 10.

No. I was one of the first people in my district to take flextime and people were very supportive of it.... I was in a place that I could financially take it. I think that other women couldn't because they obviously didn't get the full paycheck. It was slightly overwhelming because I had to take care of responsibilities that are normally done Monday through Friday, and it had to be condensed to Tuesday and Thursday.

Q. What about your immediate supervisor, do you think there are things he could have done to make that transition back to work easier?

A. Interviewee 10.

Maybe he could have just recognized that I was on part time, and he could have just said, "Hey listen go to work Tuesdays and Thursdays, give one hundred percent, but I don't want to see anything coming in on Mondays, Wednesdays, and Fridays." That would have been nice to hear.

Q. How did breast-feeding work since the return to work?

A. Interviewee 10.

So I breast-fed my baby until she was ten months old, and so the part-time stuff was easy because I could pump while she was napping or pump on the weekends and store up. Of course, I would only have to bring my pump to work twice a week because of the part-time status, but when I went back full time I was pumping two times a day. So I would pump at 10:00 a.m. and 3:00 p.m. Well, obviously I don't have an office space to go to at work every day. So there is no electrical outlet. No private places, so I had to have a car adapter. I would have to drive around and look for spots where I wouldn't be seen. A lot of the times it would be in a town and I would have to drive on a residential street and find something behind a tree, behind a fence, that kind of thing. There were several times that I would pull up and think that everything was great, and as soon as I would get started there would be construction crews pull up, and four or five men would jump out and start working on a house. So, I would have to drive away or pretend I was working or something.

It got really stressful though because of appointments with doctors. So, for instance, if I had a lunch appointment at noon and I was responsible for picking up the food at eleven, and I was pumping at ten, and I had an hour's drive to where the food was going, then sometimes I would have to pump and drive. Or sometimes I wouldn't be able to pump until after lunch, and during lunch I would be so engorged that it would hurt so much. I remember too, pulling over sometimes at 4:30 in the afternoon to do my second pumping, sitting there pumping until five. Then I had an hour or more to drive home. It really took a lot of time out of the day. I was able to then graduate to once a day, and that became easier, but again pumping through the summertime was hard because I would have to ask staff at a doctor's office to let me use their fridge to get my ice pack re-refrigerated, or if I was going to be in an office for a couple of hours I would bring it in from the car and put it in their fridge. It was hard to find that accommodation. It was hard to find that on a regular basis at least. Then as the weather got cooler it was easier.

Q. Upon returning to work, what was your child-care decision like? Problems, issues, concerns?

A. Interviewee 10.

I always thought that when she was in my belly, and then even up to when she was three or four months old I thought it would be easy to do day care. But as she got older and knew who we were, and we had the opportunity to go look at some daycare centers that I was not impressed with, I just couldn't do it. Because I wanted the care to be personal and I wanted her to have all of the attention. So we were fortunate enough to have someone that lives in our building to watch her. It is sort of an in-home nanny kind of child care because my husband works at home sometimes. So he can sort of help out when the caregiver can't or at least oversee what is going on. And it makes me feel better going out the door knowing that she is in good hands. We've had a nice nanny experience.

This particular interviewee also sent me an e-mail later on after we met in response to the following question, which she felt she had not fully answered during the face-to-face interview. The e-mail subject line read: The Tests. Her interview and this chapter would not be complete without including this correspondence (see Figure 6.1).

> **Q.** What was your experience like in terms of conceiving a child?
> **A.** Interviewee 10.
>   My husband and I had been trying to conceive for at least six months when I finally missed that first period early one August morning. Well, let me back up for a second and be clear about one thing. I hadn't technically missed it yet at

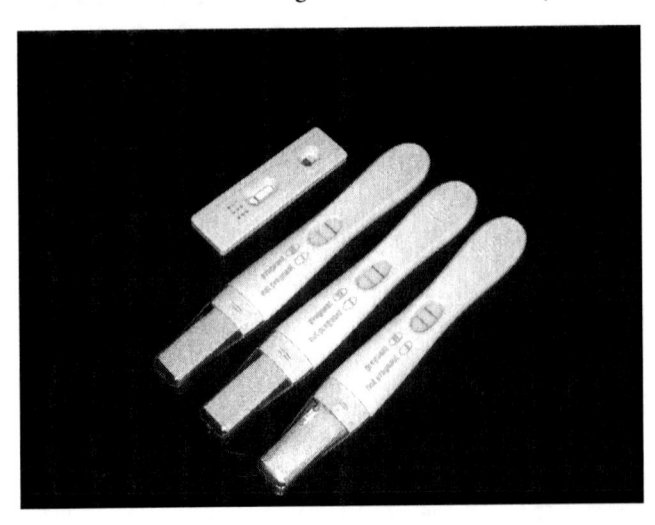

FIGURE 6.1
Pregnancy tests.

this point, but because of modern-day medical advances, the more expensive over-the-counter kits could detect pregnancies several days before a missed period. So after six months of tirelessly trying and testing, I was sure this time I had seen the faintest of pink lines! Or did I? I had to be sure!

I ran to the kitchen, chugged a glass of water, and sprinted even faster back to the bathroom. Remember, with every test comes a trip to the toilet and my bladder was on empty. I reached under the sink for another box of kits—empty! The drawer—empty again! You'd think after six months of this I would have stockpiled them in my sock drawer, but my stash was gone ... and so was that pink line! Was I pregnant or not? I frantically showered, kissed my husband good-bye, and was out the door in no time. I couldn't tell him any of this just yet. What if it were a false alarm again? I couldn't do that to him.

Because of my flexible work schedule as a pharmaceutical representative, I headed straight to a doctor friend's office, and begged him for an in-office kit. His nurse took me in the back, and within a few minutes I had another pink line. I was pregnant! Just to be sure, I peed on another one. What? The first pink line disappeared, so at this point it didn't count. It had to be two out of two lines. The kind nurse reassured me that I was pregnant! I was going to be a mother! I couldn't wait to surprise my husband when he came home from work.

As soon as I got back to the car, I phoned my ob/gyn and asked to be seen right away as I had just "scored two pink lines—twice!" What came next was a devastating blow to my excitement. The doctor's policy states that a pink line is satisfactory enough for a pregnancy confirmation, so he would be fine with seeing me at eight weeks. Eight weeks? I couldn't wait that long. What if there had been a mistake? For anyone that knows me, I am a planner, an organizer, and a perfectionist. I am an "I can't-wait-4-more-weeks-to-know-for-sure-that-I'm-pregnant kinda gal!" I reluctantly scheduled my first visit for the end of September, but just to be sure I raced to the drug store. I needed more pink lines for absolute proof of life.

Finally, three more pregnancy kits and four juice boxes later, I had the proof that I needed. I was going to be a mom!

REFERENCES

Sandelowski, M. 1998. Writing a good read: Strategies for re-presenting qualitative data. *Research in Nursing and Health* 21: 375–382.

7

The Themes: How Women Cope with the Myths and Realities of Maternity Leave

This chapter summarizes the commonalities from among the interviews of the women profiled in Chapter 6. The themes and patterns that developed from the interviews are inconsistencies in administration of maternity leave policies, timing, transition back to work, child-care, breast-feeding and pumping, and unmet needs and professional concerns.

Included in this chapter are photographs documenting the "realities" of having a newborn. See Figures 7.1 through 7.13.

INCONSISTENCIES IN ADMINISTRATION OF MATERNITY LEAVE POLICIES

The theme of how much maternity leave is available and utilized can be summed up in one word—inconsistent. Among the women interviewed, the amount of time they took for maternity leave ranged from none to about 20 weeks (including a return to part time). Some interviewees had to negotiate for time off or a reduced workload. Interviewee 1 said, "I knew HR couldn't help. I knew I would have to negotiate time off." Interviewee 5 negotiated to work at home and finish her summer teaching online. Some were in departments in which the nonacademic staff had paid maternity leave, sick leave, and personal leave, but the interviewees did not have access to those benefits. Others had only minimal leave accrued, so they had to return to work in a short time. Most were hesitant to ask for too much time off, and some felt guilty about being away from work responsibilities.

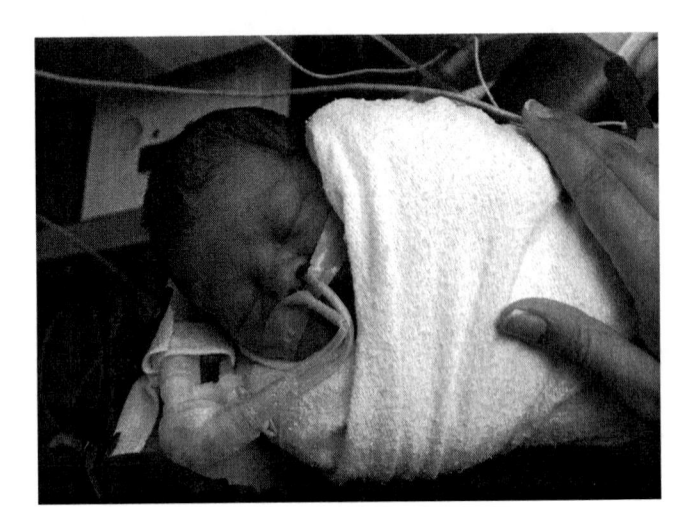

FIGURE 7.1
Baby in hospital.

Interviewee 8 had a half course load for the fall semester following a summer birth, but felt she should attend an open house in the department early in that fall semester. Her colleague told her it was not necessary, and that she should go home. She also felt that she should be in the office for formal student office hours during this semester. Interviewee 3 had sick and vacation leave accrued for 9 weeks of leave, so her leave was paid, but it was not maternity leave. She was required to utilize FMLA, and was eligible to take an additional 3 weeks unpaid, but she could not afford to do so. She reported having to have her doctor recertify every 30 days her need to be away from work for her organization's FMLA requirements. This was an unanticipated detail no one in human resources had told her about. Interviewee 2 at the time she last gave birth was a nonregular faculty member with no benefits. She negotiated to get time off by working a course overload before delivery.

Interviewee 16 was changing jobs while pregnant. She said:

> I actually discovered that we don't have a maternity leave policy....Although we are super family-friendly, it's still a negotiation-based policy.... I wanted something a little more formalized that doesn't put the newly hired female faculty member in a bad position to have to negotiate with someone who may or not be understanding or willing to negotiate.

Interviewee 17 was also frustrated by the lack of certainty about what length of maternity leave she could take. She said:

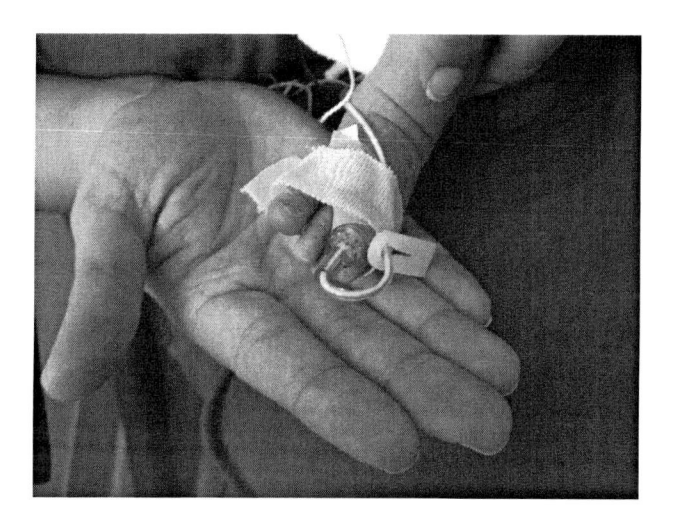

FIGURE 7.2
Premature baby.

> I don't feel that as an individual woman about to give birth, that I should be e-mailing and trying to negotiate with the department chair.... While it worked out very well for me, I think there are other people who it worked out better for, and others who clearly it did not work out well for. I think it was really shocking to me that this was the expectation, sort of like every woman for herself.... I remember crying with happiness on the way to the hospital at 4:00 a.m. saying we made it through to the end of the semester, and being relieved. That is so sad to me.

IT IS ALL IN THE TIMING

The second theme that emerged out of the interviews was that one cannot fit a pregnancy or a delivery into a one-size-fits-all kind of policy. The timing just cannot be predicted. Every woman described something that did not go as planned—whether it was an order for bed rest, an early delivery, an emergency cesarean, or in the worst-case scenario the death of the newborn. Despite good communication throughout the pregnancy with both immediate supervisors and human resources, there are some life events that cannot be reduced to a written policy or built into a prearranged or negotiated "deal."

Interviewee 10, a pharmaceutical representative, went into labor 6 weeks early. Her boss did all of her work that was left undone. She said, "There

FIGURE 7.3
Baby at door.

wasn't anything I felt guilty about not doing, or that I had dropped the ball on because of the way our industry is set up to work ... we do a team-effort approach, so they picked up the slack." Conversely, in higher education, even during labor and immediately thereafter, some of these women continued to work. Interviewee 12 said, "I was working after they gave me the epidural." One interviewee said, "I know I shouldn't have drug in the laptop to the hospital, but I thought if I waited I would have all those student e-mails to deal with when I got home."

In another example, Interviewee 3, who was ready to return to work 9 weeks after giving birth, ran into a problem with the day-care provider she had chosen. The facility did not have an opening for a newborn at the time she was ready. She had applied to this provider immediately upon finding out she was pregnant, but rules regarding the ratio of staff to newborns interfered with her placing her baby at the time she needed care. She had to wait until other babies were old enough to "age out" and be ready to move out of the "newborn" category. She resolved her problem by having family and friends fill in while she waited for an opening, but had to deal with the stress this added on her as a first-time mom returning to work.

Tied to the theme of "timing" is the timing of childbirth in relation to the academic year. In the literature and in the academic world, this is referred to as having a "May baby" or a "summer baby." Interviewee 8 said she was told by other women in her department that "it is easier if you try to give birth during the summer." She was successful in doing this, and

FIGURE 7.4
Mom with baby in stroller and dog.

was glad that she didn't have to feel guilty about "pushing my teaching off on someone else."

Interviewee 4's experience involved adoption of two children. Her first was not a newborn, but she still needed the summer to bond with the child. Her second child was a newborn when her family adopted the baby, and she was able to take a semester off as well as "cash-out" some of her accrued leave. "I was happy to have the time off … No one asked me to do anything while I was out." Interviewee 4 said she knew of one woman who led a class via Skype during the semester in which she gave birth rather than take maternity leave. As noted earlier, Interviewee 2 took on a course overload before her baby was born, so she could have more time to work from home after the baby arrived. Interviewee 5 said she was able to deliver in July, so she had six weeks before the new semester started, but it was not maternity leave. "I was worried about not coming in … and I didn't want people to think I wasn't doing my job…. If I had been in a tenure-track position, then I would have been terrified."

Also tied to the theme of "timing" is the biological clock issue faced by some of the interviewees. Whether we are talking about women in academics or in the private sector, the clock keeps ticking. While only a couple of these women reported experiencing infertility issues, they knew of women who were concerned that they had waited too long to try to have a baby. As previous research has shown, if women working in higher education delay childbirth until after they attain tenure, they may have waited

FIGURE 7.5
Baby eating.

too long to become pregnant. Some also reported that fertility treatments were covered by their insurance company but only until a certain age—further limiting the opportunity to have a baby. Interviewee 9 said, "I know second-hand about people having trouble conceiving, and they are only assisted through age 40 at our company."

Others reported that their insurance only covered office visits to fertility specialists, but not the treatments. Interviewee 13 said, "When we really started to try I was 35, so it took a long time and actually we didn't think we could have children." Interviewee 4 said, "I had a notion we could have a summer baby, but the more desperate I became to become a mother, the less the timing became important. I was still reluctant to ask for time off." As women delay having children until later in life—which can affect fertility—the convenience of timing a birth to the "summer" months may not be a realistic option, although it seems to still be a "norm" in terms of expectations in the academic setting with regard to time off for maternity leave.

TRANSITION BACK TO WORK

Interviewee 3 describes her return to work at nine weeks as "very draining" as she had no opportunity to ease back into her professional routine as a staff member at a university. It appears new mothers may not be prepared

FIGURE 7.6
Baby playing with books.

for the difficulties they may experience as they transition back to work. This theme is explained by Interviewee 6 who describes feeling "very sad to leave my child each and every time … as there was no bridge back to work," supporting the idea that a more gradual transition period would have been helpful to her return. Interviewee 13 said "I coveted every day I was home…. I knew, I squeezed it, every second I could get…. I thought I knew how difficult it was going to be to go back to work…. I underestimated the emotional difficulty of it."

Interviewee 12, whose youngest child was 6 months old at the time of the interview, expressed the difficulties she was experiencing with returning to work. She said:

> I've been in a couple of times to the office during the summer, but going back now in September, I've just been hit. I am still barely standing; I don't know how I'm still standing. It has been a juggling act. I'm behind on paperwork. I'm behind on deadlines. I'm behind and I have limited time. It takes me longer to get things done. I've changed so much in that regard; I don't check my phone messages. I don't check my e-mails.

FIGURE 7.7
Baby and dog at window.

Interviewee 13, who was always available before the birth of her child to come in early and stay late said, "Now, I feel bad when I am late for work, so I don't take lunch … because I want to make sure that I am giving more than I am taking." These comments from these two interviewees show the great expectations that women have of themselves and what they think others are expecting out of them in the workplace.

Interviewee 8 said, "It was hard to come home and have enough energy to meet the energy level of my daughter." She also recounted stories later on of cooking and processing vegetables in the middle of the night, so her child could have organic baby food the next day at the day care. Interviewee 7 recounted stories of having to prepare a lot in advance in order to "juggle" all the demands. Interviewee 6 said, "I have a great, supportive husband, too. Finding that routine where everything fits in … it is a new routine."

Another issue that arose within this theme of transitioning back to work involved the physical aspect of motherhood and how to manage all the competing demands. Interviewee 13 said:

> I did struggle with thinking of how I was going to manage being a mother, being an employee, but also being me. I still haven't figured that out. I've been a runner since I was seventeen…. Part of being a runner is experiencing the outside, it is touching the pavement, it's the wind, it's the rain, it's the sun, it's changing seasons … so much of it is your senses…. I would feel guilty because I was not with him, I can't justify running right now. This is such a huge shift in personality, my personality, because running was like

FIGURE 7.8
Dad and baby.

> brushing my teeth. I kept saying, oh, I can run at midnight, but I can't run at midnight, I am tired.

Interviewee 19 said her return to work was

> overwhelming at first.... I would say it took a good 3 to 4 months to get into a good routine.... Certain things went by the wayside, like cleaning, cooking, even responding to e-mails or phone calls. I think all of that was pretty much put on hold.

Interviewee 2 also faced multiple challenges initially upon returning to work. During the last stages of one pregnancy, she was extremely tired, but she had block classes on Mondays from 9:00 a.m. to noon and then from 6:00 p.m. to 9:00 p.m. On these days, she admits she had to take a nap in her office—luckily she had a couch! When she returned to work, she found she was scheduled for evening classes again. This presented problems with day care, as the facility closed before her husband got off work. With her last child, she had no maternity leave. She said, "I literally came home from the hospital and answered e-mails from students.... I like to think I have some flexibility with my job, but more work got brought home. I told my older kids I had homework just like they did."

Interviewee 10 had lots of support at home, but appreciated the opportunity to return to work part time, initially utilizing "flextime"—in part because she felt a little rusty returning to "sales" but especially because she only had to leave her baby for 2 days a week. She said:

> I was one of the first people in my district to take flextime and people were very supportive of it. Those Tuesdays and Thursdays were long days because I wanted to focus on the baby the rest of the week. I remember being nervous to ask my boss about flextime. I had the impression that he had to approve my use of the benefit, but he said it was mine to take.

An experienced mother, Interviewee 9, has learned to "work" differently. Where in the past she would do a lot of work in the evenings, saying she "almost let it consume me," she now does all work during the daytime, and even leaves her cell phone in the car at night so she won't hear it beeping. Her time at home is reserved for her family. Interviewee 10 says that the introduction of Blackberries has been difficult, as one hears every alert. "Fortunately I have a supportive spouse, so while he is bathing the baby or reading to her, I can check e-mails. It is a real challenge because I can't leave work at five o'clock. My work comes home with me." Interviewee 1 made the decision to return to work in a three-quarter-time position—and she took a pay cut to do so. Despite the continued pressures from her supervisors to work full time, to teach more, to be in the office 5 days a week, and in the face of financial challenges, she does not regret this decision to remain at less than full time.

CHILD CARE

Surprisingly, the theme of child care did not result in a lot of "horror" stories. For the most part, the interviewees were happy with their available child-care choices.

One problematic issue, however, with day care is the requirement (which is true of most day-care providers) that one must pay the full rate whether one's child attends every day or not. As discussed in Chapter 2, child care in the United States costs thousands of dollars per year for working families. Interviewee 1 works three-quarter time but pays the full rate even though her child is at home part of the week. She also has to pay year round, or she will "lose" her spot in day care. There is no concession or reduction in charges for family vacation time or for families that do not need year-round day care.

Some interviewees reported utilizing family members for child care, which greatly alleviated some of the worry and financial burden.

FIGURE 7.9
Dad with guitar and baby.

Interviewee 18, who commuted to work 1 hour each way, recounted that her child was born with some serious health issues. Her parents came from another country to help and stayed the entire semester. She said, "I just called my parents and said, you just have to come here, there is no other way.... I mean there is no other person you can trust other than your parents, or brothers, or sisters, or other family members." Her child did enter day care at one year of age.

Interviewee 12 reported that her husband's job allows him some flexibility, so they were initially able to alternate days that they each went to the office so one of them was home all the time. Now, they have a sitter who comes to their home, which is a preferred arrangement reported by several of the interviewees.

There are restrictions at most day care centers as to the age at which a newborn can enter day care; additionally, most providers charge a premium for newborns because they require greater one-on-one attention. Interviewee 6 reported that she and her husband received the letter of acceptance to the day care of their choice before the baby was born. She and her husband were extremely excited because they did not know what they would have done if the baby had not been accepted, as their families lived very far away. Interviewee 8 and her husband shared child-care responsibilities for the first six months. She worked two 12-hour days per week, and he stayed at home on those days. Later, when the baby went to day care, Interviewee 8 said the baby loved it, but she called every hour to check on the baby for quite a while.

Interviewee 19 also reported researching child-care arrangements, and then registering her child for day care when she was about four months pregnant. Even with all that early preparation, Interviewee 19 said the most stressful part about returning to work was

> because of the anxiety of bringing him to day care. Of course, as time goes on, I learned to get over that. He goes to a phenomenal day care that he loves, but the anxiety was definitely with me during the day while I was out working.

Interviewee 15 reported discussing the first time her child went to day care with a friend who reassured her when she commented that the baby "smelled like them." She said, "He didn't smell like food or cleaning supplies, he smelled like laundry, different fabric softener. I just sort of said that to my friend in Colorado who adopted her daughter … and she said 'that's good, that means that he's held enough.'" This statement reassured the new mother.

BREAST-FEEDING, PUMPING, AND THE WORKPLACE

The theme of breast-feeding and pumping was quite an enlightening and unexpected surprise that came out of the interviews. Initially, no interview questions were included on this topic. Most of these interviewees did breast-feed, and some were committed to breast-feeding their infants past one year of age. This, of course, meant that they needed to pump at work.

Two important issues surfaced. The first was about the physical demands on the body—which was perhaps enhanced by the mental and emotional stress placed on these young women. In an effort to be "good" moms and provide the best start for their babies' health, they committed to breast-feeding, and for some that meant they would feed their baby nothing but breast milk for the first six months of life. The commitment these young mothers showed was nothing less than amazing.

Interviewee 3 experienced a production problem that at the time of the interview she was still trying to work through with her physician. She reported pumping at 2 a.m., in addition to pumping at least twice a day at

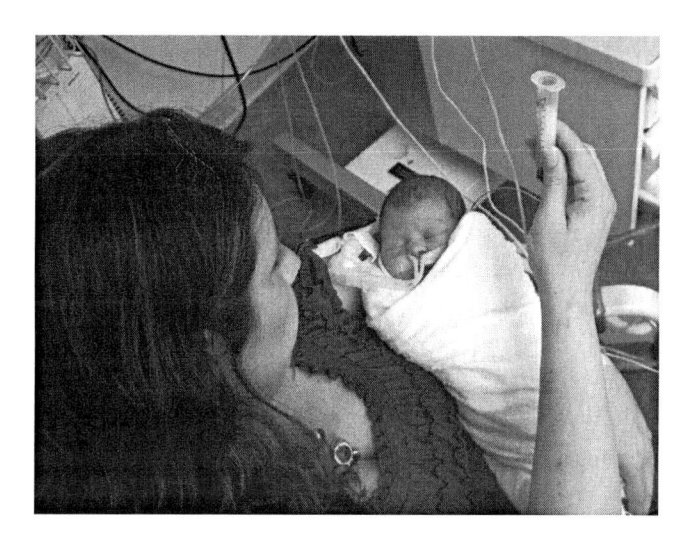

FIGURE 7.10
Mom with breast milk for baby in hospital.

work, so she could have milk to send to day care the next day. Interviewee 8 had problems with her child latching on, because the infant was born premature, but she continued to pump and give the baby breast milk from a bottle.

Some interviewees felt pressured by their families to try to breastfeed. Interviewee 18 said:

> My child couldn't nurse because of health issues. I was just so stupid! This is how I feel now…. My mom and my husband pressured me to pump. So, I ended up pumping for nine months…. I had so much milk, and you feel horrible because the child is not doing well, and when you put him on formula he is getting worse…. So, I tried to pump at work but it was so difficult, I just gave up.

Another interviewee did not choose to breast feed either of her two children. Interviewee 16 said:

> I thought about it with my first child, but I started thinking about the logistics of being there to feed her or being able to pump and deal with all of that. I had heard all the horror stories, so I thought just time-wise this is just not going to work. So, when my second child came along, I thought I know it's supposed to be healthy and everybody tells me that's what you're supposed to be doing. But again I thought about the time commitment, and I was already tired and I was already committed at work with all of these projects.

The second issue that surfaced among mothers that chose to breast-feed was about pumping—where, when, and how often—and what about the need for privacy? Just to review, you must keep pumping in order to produce. You must pump when necessary, or you will leak. These are just the realities of breast-feeding. You must also get plenty of fluids, eat well, and get a lot of rest—all a challenge for anyone with a newborn. Some of these interviewees were still breast-feeding at the time of the interviews, so their experiences were fresh.

The pharmaceutical representatives interviewed spend most of their working time in their company-provided automobiles. For these interviewees, finding privacy to pump presents unique challenges. Interviewee 10 would drive around looking for a "quiet" street on which to park and pump. Interviewee 19 said:

> I breast-fed for the first four and one-half months of my child's life. When I returned to work, it wasn't very easy to keep up with pumping. Obviously, I don't work in an office environment, so you know I had to pump in a parking lot somewhere. It affected my supply.

Multiple interviewees reported using the new, and much-improved "hands-free" pump. For the pharmaceutical reps, this meant they could drive and pump at the same time—thereby keeping on schedule to get to the next doctor's office within their sales territory. Clearly, this is a safety concern for these women, but it also suggests that corporate support is lacking or these women would not feel pressured to drive in an unsafe manner.

Interviewee 9 said, "I wanted to breast-feed. So a lot of it was trying to figure out how to breast-feed on the road, in between what I'm supposed to do, and when to do it if I'm riding in the field with my boss, or at meetings. I never felt like I shouldn't do it or couldn't do it." Interviewee 10 reported that when her direct supervisor was in the car with her, he would tell her to drop him off at a coffee shop while she stayed in the car to pump at the necessary time. When she was done she would text him "all clear" and he would return to the car. Even though he was personally supportive of her breast-feeding, he never acknowledged that she still had to do all her work within the same time-frame as she did before she was breast-feeding. There was no allowance made for this extra time she needed. In her words, she wanted to be "not penalized, and have it acknowledged that I might be a little less productive" in terms of sales. She wanted to "feel less guilty, less pressured, less stressed." She said, "I felt like the clock was ticking as I was pumping, and you need to be relaxed to breast-feed or pump."

Many faculty and staff offices at universities do not have locks, or they have too many windows for the space to feel private. Interviewee 1 reported having a private office and she did not have a problem, but one of the staff members in her department, who did not have a private office, had to find an empty room or office every day for pumping. Interviewee 8 could lock her door, but she reported people knocking, and then "jiggling" the handle. She said she held her breath every time even though she knew the door was locked. Again, this was not the most relaxing way in which to pump. She also reported that her university did have a room for nursing mothers, but it was not convenient to use due to the distance from her building. Interviewee 2 said, "I found it impossible to pump at work—due to privacy. I could close the door, but people were walking by all the time. I was just very uncomfortable. I was concerned, and I didn't think families were valued here."

Another interviewee had more success in finding privacy, although she describes the time period of pumping as horrible. Interviewee 17 said:

> I breast-fed both of my children for a year, and when I returned back to work full time, I would pump. You are taking me back to a horrible time. I would pump in my office, and I would hang a sign on the door that read, please do not disturb. It was a very large sign. I remember I was pleasantly surprised with the fact that while no one had given birth recently, people were really supportive and very understanding.

Further complicating the commitment to breastfeeding is the issue of storage. Milk must be kept cold. Most interviewees reported bringing cold packs or ice packs to keep the milk cold in the car or office. Some academic departments had refrigerators, some did not. Further, remember this has to be done at a minimum every four hours or so, and sometimes more frequently.

Interviewee 7, a pharmaceutical representative, reported that she was told by another rep that when she was traveling overnight, she pumped, and then went to the Federal Express office to pack the milk on dry ice, and ship the milk home to her baby. Interviewee 6 recounted an overnight stay at a hotel where she had to request a mini fridge, and she reported feeling that the hotel was very accommodating.

Interviewee 15 made the decision not to pump at work and went back and forth from home to her campus office when she needed to breast-feed the baby. She did not want to introduce a bottle to the baby. She said, "My husband was at home, and I fed the baby, ran to class. I was gone two hours, and I ran back." This is just another example of true commitment.

UNMET NEEDS AND PROFESSIONAL CONCERNS

Many women expressed having unmet needs during maternity leave and upon their return to work. The kinds of stories that interviewees told demonstrated a willingness to make things better for other women that are having children now. This is evident in the following examples. All the interviewees expressed the thought that there needed to be more consistency in the communication between them and their human resources staff, and between them and their direct supervisor.

Some interviewees described the need for an official, written maternity leave policy. The inconsistencies in interpretation of leave policy across departments in universities are troublesome. Interviewee 4 said her advice to new mothers is "prepare to be penalized … whether overtly or covertly; there is not much hope for improvement." Interviewee 5 said pregnant women "need to stop the tenure clock, negotiate time off, ask for a reduction in course load, or a semester off, or teach online, but get it in writing." It may be this need to negotiate and the lack of consistency in policy administration that further perpetuates the reluctance of young, untenured faculty members to even ask for time off or modified duties.

Interviewee 16 said:

> With my first job, I was a little naïve … I was in a male-dominated department, and it was embarrassing to say, "this is my due date, I have these doctor appointments scheduled, and this is what I need." I don't think that is a good position to be in for a faculty member, especially one that is untenured.

This same interviewee was in the job market during her last pregnancy. She chose to not reveal her pregnancy until she was offered the job. At that point, she asked for an additional year for tenure, but ultimately did not choose to use it. She said:

> I wasn't sure what the climate around here would be for pregnancy and maternity.... I realized about a year ago that there was no reason to add another year, it would not have accomplished anything.... Had I gone to another place, I certainly would have needed the extra time to meet the tenure requirements.

One interviewee who negotiated a reduced teaching load for the semester immediately following the birth of her child ran into a problem because her "workload" on paper was redistributed to decrease her teaching load but increase her research effort. She taught one evening class that semester. Interviewee 17 said:

> It became a big bone of contention at the time of my annual evaluation.... I protested a little bit because I thought it was unjust.... They greatly increased my research effort to accommodate my lack of service and teaching, which didn't penalize me to be honest because you know how long it takes to get things published. So on paper it looks like I had a great year, but I clearly wasn't at home that semester doing incredibly in-depth research.

With her second child, she negotiated the same reduction but worked more at home during this semester on her research. She said, "I worked more on research just because of where I was at in my professional trajectory. I had a lot of projects in the pipeline, revise and resubmit, or copyediting, for things that were due to come out in press."

This interviewee also negotiated to stop the tenure clock but did not use the extra time and went up for tenure on schedule. Interviewee 17 said that she went up for tenure on schedule partly because she had heard that in other departments and colleges at her university, some tenure review committees had

> started to increase expectations about research productivity, based on the fact that a woman had taken an additional year or two for a child. I realized I was ready, but I did not want to chance that.... I heard that there were people who would say well she had seven years, why does she only have X number of articles? ... My concern was then not about having had two children, but would they find that I had a worthwhile tenure file?

One interviewee, who relied on a male colleague to cover a couple of classes for her immediately after she gave birth, said he forgot to go to one of the classes. He realized his mistake, and e-mailed her. She said the sub-

FIGURE 7.11
Mom and baby with bubbles.

ject line read, "only a man can screw up this bad," and he was apologetic, but she felt she should not have had to deal with the situation a week after the birth. Upon her return, he said the moral of the story is not to teach bi-term courses. She replied, "The moral of the story is to negotiate my maternity leave better than I did."

An unanticipated need described by two women involved the death of a child. One interviewee told of a friend who worked in another work setting, in a very large organization, who took all accrued and unpaid leave available to be at home after the birth of her child, and then some time later the baby died. At that point, this woman had no more leave available to take. "She had three days to grieve, and then had to return to work." Similarly, another interviewee was pregnant with twins, but she had one child who did not survive birth. This first-time mother similarly expressed how difficult it was to experience the joy of having a baby, while making funeral arrangements for the surviving baby's twin. Clearly, given the FMLA's limitations, we need to think through what happens when our policies fail to address every situation. Even when organizations and individuals acknowledge that these are extreme cases, supervisors still have a responsibility to think through the unthinkable "what if's."

As unfortunate as it is, I did find some examples of "horror" stories related to utilization of maternity leave benefits. First, interviews with the pharmaceutical representatives did not result in the private sector looking

FIGURE 7.12
Mom and baby at orchard.

much better than the institutions of higher learning. Yes, the pharmaceutical industry typically has consistent policies and administers them fairly and equitably, but the reaction of colleagues to absent mothers is no better there than anywhere else. However, for these women interviewed management seems to be more supportive. For example, Interviewee 9 reported that her male colleagues made inappropriate remarks about the absence of another female colleague gone on maternity leave longer than expected due to health complications. At the time of this conversation, the offending male colleagues clearly knew that the interviewee had also returned from maternity leave only a short time before, and one of the men present had even taken six weeks paid paternity leave. One of the men said in reference to the woman not in attendance that she was *"milking the system."* Interviewee 9 said her male colleagues never would have said this in the presence of their boss. In stark contrast, the same "boss" supported Interviewee 9's decision to take an additional six weeks of maternity leave when company policy changed while she was out on an initial six weeks paid maternity leave. Interviewee 9 said:

> Our boss is very strict, by the book, so I reached out to him about this change in policy…. I felt a little guilty…. At six weeks you are just getting the hang of things, so when offered the additional six weeks due to the change in policy, I wanted to take it. My boss said, "this only happens once in your life. What if you come back from maternity leave now, and you regret it a few years from now. You can't have that time back, so I have no problem with you taking this time."

Conversely, Interviewee 7 reported having to fight with her superiors for permission to take her new baby on a week long trip for training after she returned to work so that she could continue to breast-feed. Typically, pharmaceutical representatives have to share a room at conferences. Taking a baby meant that she needed a room to herself, so it cost the company more money for her attendance at the conference.

Interviewee 6 has struggled to move up the corporate ladder in her organization where she says upper managers are still primarily male. The presence of a glass ceiling is apparent in the leadership training groups that she has been a part of in the recent past. She is furthering her education as a step in the direction toward working for a promotion. While tuition costs are reimbursed, taking classes at nights and on the weekends keeps her from her family but she is determined to continue her education.

In another example, one interviewee, who did not want to be identified even by number, when asked about advancement opportunities, she said:

> I am sure any supervisor, whether it is appropriate or not, thinks in the back of their minds when considering promoting someone about the fact that the person has a small child or is in their childbearing years like me. Having a baby has not negatively impacted me, but work takes a back-seat priority to my family now.

Second in the list of "horror" stories with regard to the utilization of maternity leave benefits comes from the academic arena. At one school where a committee was appointed to address the "consistency" in maternity leave policy, one suggestion was that maternity leave be limited to "three" times maximum. After the third child, there would be no maternity leave available. In reference to a discussion of this proposed policy, Interviewee 1 said she heard a woman say, "I heard this person got paid for her maternity leave, I haven't had a baby in 20 years. How is that fair?"

Interviewee 2 recounted a new colleague looking at a bulletin board in a faculty/staff copy room where the newly arrived baby pictures were displayed, under which one said "baby #4," indicating that this was the fourth baby born in the department. The new colleague said, "Thank God, I couldn't imagine who the idiot would be who would have four children!" It happened that she made this remark to the person for whom this was her third baby—Interviewee 2. It was also made clear that children were not welcomed at faculty/staff picnics. Interviewee 2 said, "I disengaged, I didn't want to share anything about kids, my family." Since her last

FIGURE 7.13
Mom and baby smiling.

pregnancy, Interviewee 2, who was not eligible for paid leave under FMLA for her maternity leaves, has tried to be supportive of all persons needing maternity leave. She recounted the story of a tenure-track faculty member who was told by the department head that she could have 12 weeks paid leave under FMLA, but after that she would need to return to work for the remainder of the semester or take off the remaining four weeks of the semester unpaid. At this school, tenure-track faculty are ranked, and therefore have paid leave under FMLA, nonranked faculty do not; staff, however, earn and accumulate sick, vacation, and personal leave. Thus, there is three-tiered system. Interviewee 2 said:

> I think she could have appealed this. The department head could have let her have that additional time off without impacting the budget, without hiring additional help. We need rank equity here, too.

Interviewee 18 recounted her experience with trying to cope with the stress of the last month of pregnancy. She said:

> That period was extremely stressful ... we were not ready mentally or financially ... and there was no maternity leave at this school. I was going to deliver in September right after the semester started. I was told I would have to start teaching, and I was commuting an hour to the school at nine months pregnant. Then after six weeks, I was to come back and teach the same class.... My chair gave me the two most experienced teaching assistants—graduate students—so they could take over while I was out. In the

end it worked out, but I did not know until the end of those six weeks.... On the Friday before I was to start teaching on the next Tuesday, my chair wrote to me and said the dean gave additional money to the department, and the faculty met and said this is ridiculous, take the money and pay the teaching assistants, and let her off for the rest of the semester. So, I didn't have to go back. It was wonderful, but I had been stressed out for almost a year. I am not complaining, but the fact that there was no official maternity leave meant I had experienced all that stress.... My chair said later that he didn't want to tell me earlier or give me hope, because he didn't know how the faculty would react.

Interviewee 8 works in a department of 25 men and 5 women. Work expectations are high. She reported working many 12-hour days before she had a baby. She initially sought advice from outside her university when considering starting a family. One woman said she should have a child in the summer. Another said to treat making the decision like you worked anywhere else—that there was no need to talk to her department head in advance. Interviewee 8 did talk to her female colleagues about having a baby before she decided to start a family, and she was told "they can't punish you for having children, set your own path." One colleague, a single mother, told her that even with significant help at home to provide child care, there are times when she still spends 14 hours at work per day. This is okay with this particular individual, but that was not what Interviewee 8 envisioned for her family. In retrospect, Interviewee 8 says she would advise young women to

> do what you are comfortable with. Planning to have a baby in the summer was best for me.... I imposed a lot of how I thought they (her colleagues) would react on myself, and that did not turn out to be true.

Interviewee 4 experienced a significant career challenge due to her maternity leave. After being told that she could apply for promotion from assistant to associate professor (tenure is handled separately, but a promotion delay will also delay the tenure consideration) by her department head, her dean told her to withdraw her application because the semester she had taken off for maternity leave had left her a semester "short" of required years of teaching experience at their university (she had several years experience as an adjunct prior to taking this position). The dean told her to submit a request asking for another three-year contract. There were other complications involved, which are not recounted here to protect her privacy, but in short, consideration of her promotion may be delayed a full year even though she took only a semester off despite the fact she was told one thing by her department head and then given contradictory information by the dean. She appealed this decision to the personnel committee of the university, asking for an exception to the number of years teaching requirement. (This particular example has nothing to do with the stopping of the tenure clock to allow a person enough time to meet publishing requirements, etc.) The situation has left her feeling unappreciated, undervalued, taken advantage of, and helpless—in effect professionally harmed, all because she took maternity leave. Regardless of the final outcome, her commitment to the university and her trust in her supervisors is irreparably harmed. Further, she is fearful of losing her job. She says it is "taking a lot of effort to come to peace with this."

Even as they recounted stories of disrespect and of facing challenges that were in some cases abhorrent, each of these women exemplified "professionalism" and commitment to their organizations and to their respective professions. Thankfully, none of the women let their professional concerns interfere with their decision to start a family. As Interviewee 6 said:

> what my colleagues would think about me never crossed my mind—I had seen other people start families, and I knew the company was very supportive.... I don't want to say I held my career in a spot, but now I am moving it along. It was the choice I made for my family.... Sometimes the question comes up as to why *now* do I want to go into management after being in sales for 13 years.... I respond that *now* is the time.

She acknowledges that she absolutely does not think she would have been asked this particular question if she was a man.

Interviewee 9 said she wants to advance in her profession, but only to a certain level as she knows if she did go further up the career ladder, "I would feel like it could consume me. I don't want that." Interviewee 10 said:

> I've never wanted to be a district manager, but I know it would be a challenge as a mother. There is a lot of responsibility outside the 8 to 5 time. If I were the district manager, I would have to choose the position or motherhood, or not be good at either.

Interviewee 8 recounts two interrelated stories that exemplify what it means to be a dedicated, academic professional. Upon returning to work she told her department head she was worried about her student evaluations of her teaching. She was worried that with a reduced teaching load that her students would rate her as less available or less willing to meet with them. He said not to worry that he expected the evaluation ratings to fall. Several months later, when her evaluation results arrived, her ratings had gone up. In a second story, she recounts that during her first semester back to work she had to bring the baby to an evening test review session at 7:00 p.m. due to an ill husband. She expected the evening to be a disaster, but everything went fine. She lectured for an hour. Some of those same evaluations mentioned this study session in the written comment sections—and conveyed how impressed the students were that she was able to lecture with a baby on her hip.

Interviewee 1 says she has been offered promotions, but she is not sure she will be interested even when her children are older. She said:

> I am not sure if this is because of the decision I made to have a family or the boundaries that I have placed on myself. I am not interested in promotion. I want to protect my time and the balance I have created.

Similarly, Interviewee 3 said:

> I don't worry about the decision to have a baby holding me back, I worry about psyching myself out and potentially holding myself back, and that is a whole other thing about motherhood that I did not expect—putting someone else's needs before mine.

Clearly, work and family balance is not a realistic "expectation" at the top of the corporate ladder or in higher education, but any one of these exceptional young women could rise in their organization and be successful at achieving a balance. Each woman has managed to cope with the myths and realities of maternity leave despite the price she paid, and eventually each has created her own balance that works for her family.

8

The Other Voices

In this chapter we consider the other voices that are important to this project, but not a part of the interviews of women that are central to our study. To better inform and to add meaning to the interview findings, here we examine the views of other parents, colleagues, and administrators. Each of their stories is important and adds value to this study. We listen to these other voices to compare and contrast their perceptions and stories with the interviews and themes reported and discussed in Chapters 6 and 7, and we listen to make sure that we are getting a complete picture of what maternity leave means, both in policy and in practice.

STUDENTS WHO ARE MOTHERS: IS IT BETTER TO HAVE CHILDREN AT A YOUNGER AGE?

When I had my third child, I was an undergraduate student in my late twenties. I was lucky enough to have one professor who let me bring my baby to his class when she was a newborn. She would sleep in the corner in her stroller as my professor would lecture on the given topic of the day. Although he was near retirement age, in his younger years he had sole care for his young daughter as a single father, because his wife had died at an early age. I think his level of consciousness about the demands of balancing school and family were finely honed by his experience as a single parent. His example and his understanding meant a lot to me, and contributed to my success as a student, a parent, and eventually, as a teacher.

Twenty or so years later, I sat in my office on campus and overheard a young female student asking someone if there was a room available in which she could pump. My ears perked up, as I heard someone say, "no."

So, I got up, left my office, and followed her. I offered to let her use my office any time she needed to, and I told her about my study on maternity leave, and to contact me if I could help further with her pumping issues. As someone who had been treated with kindness when I was a student with a newborn, I thought it was the least I could do.

My conversation with her got me to thinking about whether it was better to have children when one is younger. As presented in Chapters 6 and 7, there are several examples in which fertility issues may surface if a woman chooses to wait to have children until after her career is established. But what about on the other end of the spectrum? What do young women think about having children at a younger age, especially while still in college? What support is there from universities if students make that choice?

A few weeks later, Interviewee 14 agreed to answer some questions about her decision to have children early. Her first child was born when she was 17, and her second was born before she was 20. At the time of the interview she had a 3-year-old child and a 6-month-old child. She said:

> I knew I would always want to have kids, but I actually got pregnant when I was 17. I had enough credits to graduate at the time, so I graduated early from high school. I took a semester off, and then started taking college classes. When I was younger, my sister and I fought all of the time. She was four years younger. We always said to my mom, why did you have us so far apart? We were always at different stages, never having anything in common. I said I'm going to have my kids close together because that is the best way to do it. So even though I was young and I was still trying to get through school, I wanted to have a second child so they would be close in age. However, it was a big decision for me. Usually I am really quick to decide what I want, but I talked to my mom a lot, she is like my best friend, and I always go to her for advice. I was worried that people were going to say, "she is just out there making babies and not doing anything productive." I was worried about that because I like to feel like I have accomplished something, so having a second child was going to set me back some with my goals, and I didn't like that.

In response to questions about being a student, a new mother, and breastfeeding, Interviewee 14 said that eventually she found a place for pumping that she was comfortable with when she was on campus. She said:

> In the office I use now, they have supplies and files, a microwave, and a sink, and they let me sit in there. I put a "do not disturb" sign on the door

and do my thing. I can leave my pump there, so I'm not carrying it around campus all day. That was another fear I had that I would be carrying this pump around plus my backpack. The first two days of school I was almost in tears, thinking I cannot carry this thing around all day. Now, I go back at the end of the day and get everything.

Interviewee 14 did recount the story of being turned away from using a room in my hallway for pumping. I apologized again profusely on behalf of the "unhelpful" person she had asked permission from. She said:

After that happened that day, I did actually think about giving up breastfeeding. I was thinking, okay people aren't very accommodating and it is hard carrying this equipment around. It was stressing me out, and I went home and thought I am going to quit. I am going to dry up. For a few days I didn't feed as often, but that was good because I was actually pumping too much. I was pumping so I would have two extra feedings a day stored as backup so I would have a supply when I was away. I am glad I didn't give up, because now that I have a place to go it is not a problem at all. However, I would say the university needs to provide a place to pump, because it is needed in almost every building. If you just have one place, but your classes are too far away from there, then that doesn't make sense. I'm not going to walk all the way across campus to pump. I wouldn't have time. And a place is needed to store the milk because I'm really suspicious of people. What if someone knew you had milk stored? What if some sick person just wanted to put something poisonous in the milk? I would worry if I didn't trust the ladies where I pump.

When asked about balancing the demands of being a mother and student, Interviewee 14 said:

My house isn't as clean as I want it to be. I feel like the quality, the time I spend with my kids isn't always quality time. I feel like it's a lot of me sitting on the computer studying with my kids playing on the floor, and I don't like that, but I mean that's what happens when you have kids and you are trying to go through school.... I guess the average college student takes 15 hours of credit and thinks nothing of it because that is the norm, and for me, I am stressing over it.

While Interviewee 14's story is perhaps not typical of students considering whether to have children while in school, it highlights some of the issues faced by all students who may start a family prior to graduation.

While Interviewee 14 did not need or take maternity leave, this issue of students—particularly graduate students—having children, has become of interest to some universities. For example, at Western Kentucky University, a director of a graduate program in one department reported that a graduate student had asked her what she should do to take a semester off for maternity leave, and not enroll in any classes. The office of graduate studies referred her to the graduate handbook, which says a student can decide not to enroll for two semesters without doing anything. When ready, one can simply enroll again. It only becomes an issue if he or she opts out for more than two semesters, at which point he or she would need to reapply for admission to the program.

A related thread in the literature indicates that some universities are taking this issue a step further and proactively adopting policies that cover leave for graduate students and graduate assistants. Even paid graduate assistants or doctoral students are probably not going to meet FMLA requirements for a university—because they will not have worked long enough or worked enough hours to satisfy FMLA requirements, and they certainly will not accrue any paid leave due to the nature of these positions (Goulden, Mason, and Frasch 2011, 154). However, some of these students are trying to avoid the "pitfalls" of pregnancy and the utilization of maternity leave during the early tenure-track years by making the decision to have children during graduate school.

Mendoza (2006) describes the approach of MIT and Stanford to accommodate this life decision. Both schools offer pregnant graduate students a period of time before and after childbirth to postpone meeting academic requirements. Funding, insurance, and housing benefits continue (12). The policy does not allow for accommodations for males that become parents (13). Princeton University followed this example adopting a policy for graduate students "that provides a three-month suspension of academic work for birth" of a child (Cliatt 2007, 1). As reported by Jaschik (2007), Yale University also adopted policies to "let students suspend academic responsibilities in the semester in which a birth or adoption occurs, yet remain registered as students." There appears to be sufficient research on the impact of having a child on the individual's career to question whether early childbirth timing will really help in the long run in terms of attaining promotion and tenure. Wyatt-Nichol (2011, 49) reports that studies have found that "women who had children after 5 years of receiving the Ph.D. or who did not have children at all achieved higher tenure rates than women with early babies." So, while these schools may have good intentions of helping their graduate students, these policies may not help women reach their ultimate career goals.

FATHERS WHO UTILIZED PATERNITY LEAVE

To understand the male perspective, an interview was conducted with a young father of two children. The youngest of his children was six weeks old, and his oldest child was 2½ years old at the time of the interview. Interviewee 20 has a bachelor's degree in marketing, and he worked for 7 years for a pharmaceutical company, where he took paid paternity leave with his first child. He has worked for his current employer for a year now, where they do not offer paid paternity leave as an employee benefit.

As with some of the stories about "timing" told by mothers interviewed for this project, nothing ever goes as planned. Both of Interviewee 20's babies arrived early. With his first child, the baby came two weeks early, so he and his wife were, as he describes it, a little unprepared. He said:

> You are young and you are inexperienced, and when your doctor gives you a due date, you think that is when the baby will come. I was lucky enough at the time to have a really nice manager that I reported to, and he said take a week at home on your own, and then we will talk about what you want to do, and you can call human resources and begin your six weeks leave.

Interviewee 20 did ultimately decide to take a full six weeks of paid paternity leave as allowed per company policy. Interviewee 20 recalled contacting the human resources department early on in his wife's pregnancy. He said:

> My company, much to my surprise, had a very generous paid paternity leave policy. They granted six weeks of paternity leave, which was pretty amazing. It was a big surprise. I had heard of my friends working at other companies that didn't offer any paternity leave. The company I am with now offers no paternity leave, so I look back at my time there, and just say those six weeks were a blessing. I did fill out FMLA paperwork, too.

Interviewee 20 says that he and his wife had dated since college, and they always discussed having a family, and knew that one of them would stay at home with their children. He said:

A year after we married, we decided to try to start having kids. We were blessed to get pregnant quickly.... My mother stayed home and her mother was a homemaker, so we both thought there was a lot of value in one of us staying home. At the time, I was making more money with my job, and she was a teacher, and we felt as though if she left the teaching world, and wanted to come back, it would be easier than in corporate America. We weighed the pros and cons and decided that she would use up her FMLA leave, and then she would stay home.... She was on my health insurance, so there was no impact in terms of that for her to leave her job, as she did not have to switch insurance.

Interviewee 20 described his wife and her experience, saying:

She was a fifth-grade schoolteacher and worked until eight months pregnant. She was granted six weeks leave with her job, and then took FMLA for another six weeks, which then carried her into the summer and the end of the school year. In late summer, when she told her school that she was not going to return...there was a lot of commotion and emotion about leaving her career behind because she had just received "teacher of the year award" and she is an excellent teacher. She loves teaching and she is very talented. When our children go to school she will be back in the classroom.

When Interviewee 20's six weeks of paternity leave were up, he returned to work. Prior to this, he and his wife had divided up the nightly feedings. He said:

It was a team effort between my wife and me. Our daughter wasn't very good at nursing so my wife was pumping breast milk which allowed me to get up to give our little one bottles at night. That lasted for six weeks. After that, my wife assumed all responsibility at night, because I had to have some semblance of sleep and be able to function in the morning.

With the new baby, Interviewee 20 took one week of paid vacation to be home, and then had to return to work. He said, "Things are more demanding, I have to wake up at 4:00 a.m. often to travel to places 2 and 3 hours away from home. This time around things are more stressful with a newborn and a toddler." He further elaborated:

We rely heavily on my mother and my wife's mother to do some overnight stays at the house just to give my wife a break. It is a different dynamic the second time around. I don't know how we would have gotten through these first six weeks without the baby's grandmothers this time.

Similar to what we heard from the female pharmaceutical representatives in Chapters 6 and 7, when he returned to work, he had to hit the ground running. In sales there are high performance expectations. Interviewee 20 said:

> Day one, you are expected to perform as you did on the day you left. I remember being very anxious, and the sales team I was part of was very male dominated. To take 6 weeks off in a male-dominated type of atmosphere, I won't say it was frowned upon, but maybe they thought I could have come back a little sooner. That was never expressed directly, but you kind of got the sense that 6 weeks away, maybe you are missing too much. And then you really feel like you have to catch up when you get back.

When asked how the decision to have children has impacted his career goals, Interviewee 20 said, "This is a subject that is very sensitive to me. It has impacted my career trajectory, but by my choice." He knows he could have advanced within his previous company, but it would have meant physically moving his family two or three times—away from his current location. Living close to his extended family is important to his family. He says, "I don't have any regrets." He said the company he is with is more geographically stable, and he will be able to advance without moving. This is something that his former employer could not provide. Interviewee 20 said:

> The new company is a growing company, and there was a lot of opportunity for career advancement on a local level. That was a major deciding factor for us. This company is more transparent and candid. The discussions about my potential career trajectory are more direct, and there are opportunities for financial incentives with this company that do not require moving.

Interviewee 20 raised some interesting points when asked what advice he would give fathers and employers about paternity leave. He said:

> After having stayed at home for the six weeks with my first child, during that time I had apprehension about doing it. I felt like I was maybe missing out at work, but now that I look back on it, I was able to be with my wife and my newborn child. It was a very small, but very important piece of my new life and I have zero regrets about taking those six weeks off. So my advice is

new fathers should take the leave if offered and don't feel bad about doing it. It is time you can never get back in life. At the end of the day, it is a very small portion of your life.

To supervisors and administrators, he has an interesting message too. Interviewee 20 said,

> Corporations are so worried about productivity and efficiency ... and if you have a young man who is expected to perform and contribute on a daily basis during those first six weeks ... it is a really chaotic time at home, and to be honest you are in survival mode, and not a lot of sleep is taking place. I question how much productivity you are really offering to your company at that point. In my opinion, offering six weeks to allow someone to spend time at home, establish their family life, it is going to allow for more productivity in the future. Ultimately, if your family is content and happy and settled that will lead to better productivity in the field.

The company he previously worked for has eliminated the paternity leave benefit formerly offered, although unpaid FMLA leave is still available. Interviewee 20 said:

> The company always prided themselves as being a top company for women and men to work for. I had several male colleagues there, some who only took 2 weeks paternity leave and some who were in a position to take the full 6 weeks. I think at the end of the day, a lot of the pressure about whether to take leave and how much to take came from the person that you directly reported to, he would steer and navigate your decision-making process on taking paternity leave. That played a part in my decision to take the leave. My boss, who was supportive, said, "take the leave and don't think twice about it." Other guys didn't have that support from their managers. I believe women bear the pressure about how much leave to take far more than men do in that same situation.

The importance of the father–child bond cannot be overstated (Barnett 1999). Unfortunately, fathers who utilize paternity leave apparently are not immune to judgment and negativity from unsupportive colleagues and supervisors. However, if fathers begin to utilize paternity leave and FMLA on a regular basis, it will only strengthen a woman's choice to do the same. Paternity leave not only strengthens the bond between father and child, it makes the transition back to work easier on the working mother in the family, and sends the message that "raising a child is a two-parent job"

(Brill 2007, 540), which is an important reminder for all of us. Further, as these young men become supervisors in their organizations, they may be more supportive and understanding of fathers and mothers who need their approval to utilize these leave benefits at an important time in their lives.

CHALLENGES FACED BY SAME-SEX COUPLES WHO DECIDE TO BECOME PARENTS

Interviewee 21 is a newly tenured associate professor, and is the mother of one child who was 2½ years of age at the time of the interview. Her family's story is unique, not because she is in a same-sex relationship, but because of the Herculean effort it took for these two young women to become parents, and the obstacles they faced and continue to face to be able to raise their young child together. Interviewee 21's partner is pregnant with their second child, and she is currently a stay-at-home mom.

Interviewee 21 did not give birth to her first child, but she did donate the frozen embryo that her partner carried after in vitro. Interviewee 21 initially tried to carry their baby, and had three miscarriages. She said, "It was my desire to have a baby, but physically, it did not work." She describes the 18 months that she and her partner went through fertility treatments as a stressful and horrible time. It was a financial hardship too. Medication was covered under health insurance, but the procedures were not. For her partner, there were health problems during the pregnancy, and she had to be placed on bed rest at 24 weeks. She was in the hospital for another 7 weeks, and then gave birth to a premature baby via emergency cesarean section.

I approached this interview, just as I did all of the others, utilizing the interview questions as presented in Chapter 5 to guide the interview. It soon became quite apparent as the story unfolded that this story may present the most compelling arguments for paid leave that I have heard. In response to the question about starting a family, Interviewee 21 said she had concerns about starting a family before she was done with her dissertation, but felt okay to do so once she was in a tenure-track position. She said, "I was a little concerned, but not a lot … about my own ability to be productive, not how others would perceive it." Interviewee 21 said her department head was supportive, but she was not aware of the details of the process during the time that she, and then subsequently her partner were trying to get pregnant. Interviewee 21 said, "I was concerned with the fact that this is really hard, and how am I going to keep doing my job?"

As far as researching what her benefits would be from her employer, Interviewee 21 said:

> I knew we would have no paid maternity leave, but I knew the baby would go on my health insurance. The year before she was born the university had adopted domestic partner benefits. My partner was working at that time, but she did not have paid maternity leave available either.

The baby was in the hospital for a month after the birth. Once the baby was born, Interviewee 21 would go to work every day, and drop her partner off at the hospital on her way, and then return there every evening.

In response to questions about her partner's employment at the time of the birth, Interviewee 21 says she was "forced out of her career." As she explains it:

> She first used up all her vacation and sick days when she was on bed rest. She had only been in her job a year, so she did not have a lot of leave. Then, she was on unpaid FMLA for as long as she could, but that expired and she had to either go back to work full time or quit. The clock had started ticking when she went on bed rest, not when the baby was born. So, at that point when it expired, it was when the baby was just out of the hospital and was not developmentally ready to be left in any one else's care. She worked for the state, and there was a lot of overtime associated with her position, and no part-time option available.

Interviewee 21 said she was only eligible for unpaid FMLA at that point too, and felt she needed to keep working for her family's economic stability. She said, "If I had paid leave, I would have taken it." During this period she continued to work full time. No modified duties or reduced teaching load were offered to her for her four-four teaching course load. Interviewee 21 said:

> Informally, I did not do any research or service, and my department chair encouraged me in that way. I was not tenured then, but I just viewed it as I can only manage to teach this semester. The next summer I taught too, because we had lost a lot of income because my partner had quit working.

When asked about stopping the tenure clock, Interviewee 21 said:

> A lot of people suggested it, but I didn't feel that I needed it because I knew the baby was coming, so I had the semester before made sure I had some research out there, and had done kind of double what I would normally have done. I thought delaying tenure would only delay me getting the salary raise that we needed to support the family.

In terms of balancing home and work responsibilities after the baby came home from the hospital, Interviewee 21 laughingly said:

> I got lost driving on the way to work one day. It was tough! I had no idea where I was. After that, we changed our nighttime routine. With a preemie there is a lot of stress and extra care, and feeding was incredibly difficult. She was not a good sleeper. It felt like we were at the infancy stage forever. Breast-feeding was a struggle too. The baby needed a bottle from the very beginning because she needed extra iron and nutrients. It was hard to get her to nurse, so there was a lot of pumping. My partner pumped for a whole year, but it was really hard.

In response to the question about the impact having a baby has had on their careers, Interviewee 21 said:

> For my partner, she had to quit, and she was a female scientist, those are rare to begin with. She was forced out of her career, which she was okay with. For me, it has lowered my research productivity because I have to take on as much extra teaching as I can, so I teach summer term, winter term, take on extra advising, supervising internships. I just have to keep working harder, so I can go up for full professor. I need to financially do that on time. I am discouraged with my salary, because I am under more financial pressure.

When asked about a sabbatical possibility to give her more time for research, Interviewee 21 said, "I am not eligible for two more years, and it is only paid in full if it is for one semester." When asked if her employer might give her a reduced teaching load when the new baby comes, she said, "I think they are restricted by our union agreement here. Any concessions would have to be informal arrangements and I don't see a reduced teaching load happening."

In a follow-up question, I asked if her partner had been eligible as a state employee for any "sick leave bank" benefits. Several states including Connecticut, Georgia, Mississippi, Oklahoma, and Washington have provisions for the creation of this type of leave pool for state employees to draw upon when all paid leave options have been exhausted (Sloan Work and Family Research Network 2006, 5). This is leave donated by other employees to fill in the gaps when there are catastrophic illnesses, such as those described by Interviewee 21. She said:

> Yes, she applied to her employer, and she was denied. She was told that she was determined ineligible because it was determined that her condition was not life threatening to her when she went on bed rest. We thought she would get it because the baby's life was at risk. She had to relearn how to walk she was in bed so long. She was flat on her back for seven weeks. She could not roll over or sit up.

This young woman's experience with starting a family demonstrates and validates the reasons why organizations need to adopt paid maternity leave and/or some type of paid parental leave when a child is ill. It also speaks to the issue that a family cannot afford to lose the income when one parent is ill or is needed at home to care for a sick child. Even when one person does quit his or her job, the other person's income is needed to keep the family afloat. Single-parent families are even more at risk for financial difficulties in these circumstances.

As an afterthought, one other procedural issue about leave and benefits came up at the end of the interview that was not a consideration in the interviews of women in heterosexual couples. Interviewee 21 said, "Others don't have to file a form to say they are in a domestic partnership arrangement. We have to do that every year. I don't understand why we have to do this every year on an annual form." This form, with identifying information removed regarding which state it comes from, is included in the Appendix. It would appear that perhaps the filing of this form is an outdated requirement by organizations.

There is strong public support for offering same-sex domestic partner benefits. For example, in one study, 60% of heterosexual respondents agreed that most employee benefits should be offered to employees in same-sex domestic partnerships, and 73% of the same respondents agreed that FMLA benefits should be extended to domestic partners (Astray-Caneda 2011, 94). However, the U.S. Department of Labor (2010) does state that the employer may require a statement that an employee stands *in loco parentis* to a child. The DOL statement reads: "A person who will co-parent a same-sex partner's biological child may take leave for the birth of the child and for bonding" (2). In Interviewee 21's situation, the child is actually her biological child, and so for her it seems redundant to be required to reassert or reaffirm this familial relationship every year.

WOMEN WHO DECIDED NOT TO HAVE CHILDREN

For a variety of reasons, some women decide not to have children, so taking maternity leave does not become a professional issue they have to address. However, the personal decision-making process about having children and when to have them does involve professional considerations. The first time I had a real conversation with Interviewee 22 she said something to me about not having children. As she told me about herself she said she was reaching a milestone birthday soon, and it was almost as if she felt compelled to explain to me who she was within the context of this missing part of her life. My perception of her was that she was a smart, talented, vibrant, and funny person that I would have loved to get to know in any circumstance. Her status of "mother" or "parent" would not have been a conversation that I would have ever initiated with her. However, because of this conversation, 2 years later, I approached her about talking to me about her decision to not have children. I particularly wanted to understand her perspective within the context of her experience of teaching in higher education. Further, I wanted to understand maternity leave from the context of an employee who had not utilized that employee leave, and I wanted to understand her perceptions about others who did utilize this benefit.

When asked about her perception of maternity leave, in her role as an employee at a public institution of higher learning, Interviewee 22 said:

> A lot of my friends have had babies lately, and none of them have been given real maternity leave. Not real "maternity leave." I mean every university technically follows FMLA, but the semester is longer than that. They all felt like they had to work with their department chair to come up with a different solution, and they all felt cheated. For instance, someone at my school who has a four-three teaching load got to reduce that teaching load down to either two-two or two-three, and she said she thought, "this is ridiculous, I'm not getting any time off." I guess I don't know anyone who has been directly discriminated against in academia for taking maternity leave, but I

don't feel like it's treated fairly. I'll add one more thing, that's the reason why we don't have kids. We decided that if we had kids my career would suffer. I guess I'm not that worried about tenure and promotion, but I'm worried about publishing because that's my goal. I don't think I am going to get a tenure-track job, but I did decide that I could not have a baby and achieve my career goals. I had to choose. I felt that way, and I often think I should have had a baby when my husband and I were twenty-two or twenty-three because we had the time, and our careers were not the center of our lives.... But I think it makes sense that if you want to have a career, then have a kid young and get that over with, because when you are our age you cannot have children and have a serious career, that's how I feel. I hate to say that.

Interviewee 22 further elaborated about her observations of colleagues and their attempts to balance both a career in higher education and parenthood. She said:

I think that in my department there are almost no women with children, it's really strange. The men who are retirement age, they all had families. But even so, there aren't very many men in our department who have children. I think it is because you are working seven days a week, 10 to 12 hours a day when school is in session, and I could have a kid over the summer, no problem, but what would I do the other 9 months of the year? I think it's not just academia, but it is high-pressure jobs that don't allow women to have children. That's how I feel, that it is very difficult unless you have a stay-at-home husband. And that's what we thought, that one of our careers would suffer, and we knew because we know our personalities that it would be mine. I'm more maternal, which isn't to say that men can't do it, they can, and we didn't want that to happen. It was a really tough decision. I did think that it might be hard to have kids in the first place, but I also feel like that a lot of exceptions are made for people who have kids, male or female, in the workplace. I feel like they get the best schedules or get excused from meetings or committees. We've noticed that since graduate school, and that was always our complaint. One of our best friends was a mom and she was married, but she would never get 8:00 a.m. classes and she always got a Tuesday/Thursday class schedule. I feel like a jerk for saying it, but it was really frustrating for me because I had gone to the trouble of not getting pregnant, which is not easy. It's not. It's very difficult to be married and in a relationship for years and not get pregnant. You have to work at it, it's a chore, and so it felt like you get penalized if you don't get pregnant. If you're responsible and choose whether or not to have your child, then you get penalized by having a tougher schedule and people expect more from you.

When asked about examples that Interviewee 22 had observed about whether the decision to have children had hurt the careers of women in higher education, she replied:

> What I have witnessed is one example where it did hurt someone. One of my friends has her PhD in Psychology, and she is widely published. She's huge in her field, she is one of the top names in her field, but she chose to stay home with her children, and not have a tenure-track job. When her children were in school, she decided to then get a tenure-track job and she can't get one…. She says she should get credit coming in towards tenure, but no one will give it to her…. She can't get anyone to recognize her years of research while she was at home with her children as counting toward tenure. Her big point is that the academy has no room for someone who decides to do research while they raise their children, and only teach one class a year…. I don't know if that would happen if she were a man. Both she and her husband feel like she is discriminated against because she made the choice to stay home with her kids.

When Interviewee 22 was asked if looking back if she had any regrets about her decision to not have a child, she explained it as follows:

> When I told one of my friends, who is an academic, that we're not going to have kids because I realized you can't have everything, she said that is ridiculous. She said of course you can have everything and she started naming people, but I guess that from my point of view I wanted something different. I wanted something that is truly extraordinary, so I felt like you want to have this extraordinary career, you want your husband to have the extraordinary career, and if you are going to have children and a healthy marriage, it is too much. We did consider adopting, and we had started the adoption process, and then some things happened and we did not…. I did feel like once that happened, that we made a decision, then I was free to just focus on writing…. It does feel to me that we do push intelligent women, who do have careers, away from having children. I don't think it is just academia, but there is certainly not the sense in my world that you should go out and have a baby. It is definitely like, you're having a baby? It seems that it doesn't feel like people are thinking that you can really have a career and have a baby. It feels like they may say one thing, but mean another.

The perspective of Interviewee 22 raises a lot of interesting points. First, she recognizes that maybe having children at a younger age could potentially be helpful to women who want to focus on their careers later. It is a time in their lives when moving in and out of the workforce is not frowned upon as much. Second, she is honest enough to acknowledge some resentment toward those colleagues both male and female who she perceives as getting special treatment because they have children. Most interesting, she articulates that there is almost a double standard in her opinion, in that you are penalized if you have children and you are penalized if you do not. She recognizes that there are messages being sent to women, that starting a family is not necessarily valued by some persons in some organizations, which is illustrated in the examples she gives. Finally, despite all this, she still acknowledges and gives validity to the feelings of her female colleagues who felt cheated by the amount of maternity leave they were granted by their organization and for the way they were treated after starting families.

UNSUPPORTIVE VERSUS SUPPORTIVE COLLEAGUES—THE STEREOTYPES AND BIASES

Most distressing to me as a researcher is the duty to report the stories of women begrudging women help in balancing their careers and family, and offering little or no support as young women make the decision to take maternity leave. Charles and Brunn (2011) in a discussion of work–family conflicts, recount one woman's conversation with another female faculty member—"[she] expressed concern that the women on the faculty were all having more than one child. She did not think they understood how detrimental it could be to their career. That was coming from a woman" (245). If this type of "professional concern" is meant to be helpful, we have a long way to go before the conversation about maternity leave is resolved.

Perhaps the previous statement is more understandable placed in the context of the following sobering statistics. The reality in higher education is that women faculty members "account for about 50% of assistant professors, 38% of associate professors, and 24% of full professors," and these percentages are up significantly over the same figures in 1975 (Madsen 2012, 132), which is a positive step toward correcting gender inequities in higher education. However, women make only 82% of the salary that male faculty members earn, which is down from 83% in 1972 (133).

Further, Wyatt-Nichol (2011) suggests that both the absence and presence of family-friendly policies result in gender inequities in organizations.

Women may be overlooked for promotion because it is assumed they will not work long hours, and women may face having to make choices regarding their roles in work and family. While academicians have some autonomy and flexibility, they may lose productive time for conducting research and publishing because of their home responsibilities. Women in academics are less likely than their male counterparts to be tenured, less likely to be employed at tier 1 research universities, more likely to be in part-time positions, less likely to be promoted as quickly, and more likely to be in non-tenure-track positions to begin with. The organizational culture may reinforce the bias that exists—and women may then overcompensate for this bias by not utilizing family-friendly policies available to them (45–65).

Finkel, Olswang, and She (1994) reported that faculty supported both paid and unpaid leave, but only a small percentage took all available leave—citing that they feared they would be hurt professionally if they took the leave. This applied to both tenured and untenured persons in their study. Within the research area of family-friendly benefits (McCurdy, Newman, and Lovrich 2002, 47), there is also some discussion of whether the use of family-friendly benefits actually resulted in women "being perceived as less committed, less willing to make the necessary sacrifices for career advancement."

Faced with these professional and economic realities, maybe some women are made a little bitter by the treatment they received from their organizations. Often the stories that are recounted by young women today clearly reflect that some senior women are articulating to young colleagues the message that if they, the senior faculty member, had no support or help, then those women who follow must go through the same difficult and trying times with regard to starting a family and utilizing maternity leave. I find it difficult to understand this line of reasoning, as it would seem we should all want things easier for our daughters and our organizational successors, but these messages are being sent and biases are being reinforced.

It is also important that we acknowledge that men and women may view the need for effective and equitable maternity or paternity leave policies differently. For example, among 181 students surveyed, of which 91% did not have children, women ranked the importance of maternity and paternity leave higher in importance than their male counterparts (Waner, Winter, and Mansfield 2007). Also, employees at different life stages in both their personal and professional lives may view maternity and paternity leave policies differently. These views may be affected by whether they have experienced having children while working. Newman and Mathews have argued since 1999 that we must encourage the use of family-friendly policies if women are to ever succeed professionally.

At one university, a group of women wrote a reflection piece to describe their experiences in starting families in the same academic year in one department where no one had had a baby in years. Aubrey, Click, Dougherty, Fine, Kramer, Meisenbach, Olson, and Smythe (2008) described the most difficult challenge was trying to make sense of the unclear university policies that seemed to be in place, but were hard to locate, and then reconcile those policies with the department precedents that were set years before. Their department head had to be informed by the young women of the university policies in place that provided for stopping the tenure clock and reducing teaching loads. He was not aware of even where to look for information. In addition to the procedural difficulties of using maternity leave and other options available to them, these women described feeling guilty and anxious about how to balance research, teaching, and parenthood responsibilities (192).

In a separate reflection piece (Kramer 2008), the department head of these young women described his honest assessment of his feelings of not being prepared in an administrative sense to deal with multiple women having children in the same academic year. He clearly was supportive of these young women, and recounted how he had tried to treat each of them fairly and equitably, and how he had described the options available to each one of them. Unfortunately, almost as if he could not stop himself—he actually writes, "I could probably stop here … and perhaps I should" (199). However, he goes on to recount how other members of his department might have been adversely impacted in order to accommodate the women on maternity leave. He suggests that allowing maternity leave might not be fair to employees who would never be "eligible" to take that benefit. He states, "I have to wonder about the equity of policies that favor faculty parents of newborns" (200). He goes on to compare granting maternity leave to granting "accommodations so I can oversee the construction of my new house" (200). He had a wonderful opportunity to show his support for women and their families and to encourage other administrators to do so in similar circumstances, and then he backtracked and, in my opinion, undid all the good he had accomplished with those few sentences.

In an effort to get another perspective of the experience of women in higher education, I interviewed a semiretired professor about her experiences decades ago with utilizing maternity leave, and how she views these issues now. Interviewee 23 did receive paid maternity leave 35 years ago, twice in fact. When asked about her experiences with maternity leave, Interviewee 23 said:

> As of 1977, there had never before been at my university a woman faculty member, full-time, tenure-track (not a part-time person who did not get benefits) that asked for maternity leave. I was astonished at the time about that, but then as I met more people, and of course I knew there were not a lot of female faculty at that time, but as I had more of a chance to interact with people, I found that of the women who were tenure-track, many of them had been part time when they had children and paid maternity leave was not an option for them. In 1977, I was told we don't have a maternity leave policy for faculty, and my department head was told there is not a policy. The reaction was, "we will have to figure something out." The department head could not have been more supportive. The dean at the time could not have been more supportive. They treated me like a valuable employee that they wanted to help. They demonstrated that having children was a valuable thing. Primarily because of the attitude of my department head, I never had the sense that this was a controversial thing. In subsequent years, as I got to know other women around campus, it was quite clear to me that other department heads were not as supportive. I was very fortunate, in that my department head was wonderful.

When asked about institutional support for women being promoted to full professor, Interviewee 23 said:

> I like being a woman, a wife, and a mother. Being a professor is what I do, it is not who I am. My family is more important, so it was okay with me to take a little longer to be promoted to full professor. We need to have a system that recognizes that there are different timelines for different people to advance on different developmental tracks. For example, if you are an associate professor for a certain amount of time, and if you haven't gone up for promotion, then that means to some people that you cannot, that you never will be promoted. I think it would help if we had some sort of formal recognition of the fact that there is going to be a period of time when our energies are going to be directed at other things—like starting a family. I think this should be available for men and women, and apply for other life events too like caring for elderly parents. So, if you get to the point when you are ready to go back at your research again, then you do…. And perhaps your colleagues could help you return to your research agenda and maybe do some joint publications. This would refresh your skills. Why wouldn't we

want to help this person if this is someone we want to see stick around? To me this is family friendly.

When asked about what her reaction would be if she heard a senior female faculty member being less than supportive to a junior female faculty member, Interviewee 23 replied:

> It is not just about maternity leave. There are a lot of women's issues—older women sometimes have been accused of wanting to be queen bees, and have the attitude that I had it tough so you shouldn't have it easy. I don't know how you change those attitudes. But maybe you acknowledge that for them and say, "yes, it was tough, I don't mean to underestimate how difficult it was for you, but I hope that you would like to keep that from happening to other people." I think some people are just more bitter than others. I was very fortunate, and I know it. I don't have anything to be bitter about, maybe that helps, but it goes back to the leadership. If you have an attitude among the leadership that it is not me against you, but we are all working together, and we will do what is best for our students and our program, our university, then the other things will fall into place. I am in the developmental stage of my life where I want to help the people that follow me. That means helping them work through the system, and who does it help by making life more difficult? If you have a faculty member who is a good teacher and scholar, don't you want to do what you have to do to keep her?

ADMINISTRATIVE VIEWS—RULES VERSUS DISCRETION

These comments in the previous section are important, as they reaffirm the need for universities to address the potential loss of talented women who may leave higher education as a trade-off to being mothers. For example, Goulden, Mason, and Frasch (2011) state that women in the sciences who are married with children are 35% less likely to enter a tenure-track position than married men with children, and are 27% less likely than men to achieve tenure if they do enter a tenure-track position (147). The implication here is that if you are in a tenure-track position, and you are not approved for tenure, you will be out of a job a year later. The lack of supportive policies that would help women in any field or discipline succeed and stay in their positions is sometimes the very reason women leave (Dow 2008).

According to Yoest (2004), who surveyed both individuals and 168 schools of higher learning (done in two samples drawn of 84 schools each), private institutions of higher learning do a much better job of offering maternity or paternity leave than do their public sector counterparts (6). In terms of the "policies" utilized at the birth of a child, Yoest found among survey respondents a reported use of FMLA to be most prevalent (35%), followed by use of sick leave (25%), then a full semester off (18%). The least used types of leave were the following: 8 to 12 weeks of paid leave, then paid short-term maternity leave, then a reduction in pay or course relief, and lastly, a 2-week maternity leave or postponed duties (combined 22%) (7–8). When Yoest asked on the survey a question about whether the "respondent had heard praise and/or criticism for their university's policies" 58% of respondents reported that they had heard praise and 39% had heard criticism (14). Respondents were also asked if the policy users encountered any bias or fear of stigma and the respondents denied any bias existing, but then went on to provide written comments that clearly showed bias existed toward women who used the policies (15).

As reported in Aubrey et al. (2008) when the employees have to "dig" to find information about maternity leave—via calls to human resources or via intensive website searches, or must "inform" their supervisor of what the university policy actually is, it does not help or encourage women to ask for or to make the decision to take maternity leave or any other benefit available to them. Further, if women do not see others successfully using these policies, and without penalty, they may be reluctant to use them. Jackson (2008, 231) reminds us that the presence of a policy does not mean it will be used, and if coworkers are not supportive of those persons that do use the policies, they send the message via peer pressure to not use those policies or risk being penalized. If they do use the policies available, women may feel guilty about it (Gilbert 2008, 205), and that guilt coupled with the message that they are not in effect "good" enough or not committed enough to manage both job and motherhood without extra help, may exacerbate the problem.

McGovern, Dowd, Gjerdingen, Moscovice, Kochevar, and Murphy (2000) suggest that time taken off after childbirth is in reality a function of the organizations' or employers' maternity/paternity policy and the other leave policies that may apply—short-term disability, sick leave, vacation leave, personal leave—and the constraints of family income. In higher education, there are some other factors to consider. Some examples of related policies available to women to manage time off during maternity leave (Shoenfelt and Schirmer 2005, 6, 14) include these options:

- Have the employee teach extra classes in a semester before or after the birth
- Hire a temporary instructor
- Have other faculty cover classes without pay
- Pay other faculty to cover the classes
- Have the employee teach an online course
- Have the employee teach a bi-term that best works for delivery and recovery time
- Grant the employee a sabbatical for research
- Hire a graduate student to assist with faculty responsibilities
- Have the employee team teach with another faculty member who covers class during her absence
- Have the employee not teach, but cover student supervision of independent studies, internships, and theses
- Have the employee not teach, but conduct research
- Reduce the workload and the pay of the employee

If universities do have formal policies for maternity leave, it reduces the uncertainty and inequitable treatment. However, the absence of formal policies gives the administrator the possibility to offer to the employee an arrangement that works best for both employer and employee. The above list shows that workable options are available. Wyatt-Nichol (2011) reports inconsistencies across universities in terms of formal maternity leave policies, including a tendency for many faculty to have to negotiate time off after childbirth (54). This indicates that deans and department heads hold a lot of the power in terms of what leave is taken, no matter what the written, formal policy is at the institution. Armenti (2004) supports that even good policies "are flawed because department chairs (mostly privileged white males) have the discretion to interpret, implement, and enforce them" (225).

It is when the administrator fails to look at the employee's perspective that this ad hoc or negotiated arrangement becomes problematic. Exercising administrative discretion in favor of the employee and her family will only result in good things for the organization. Further, if administrators who refuse to negotiate think that silence from the employee means acquiescence, they may be mistaken. Silence may "hide disappointment and resentment" (Dow 2008, 160), which may lead to a woman ultimately leaving her job. It would be so much better for employer and employee if all stood united to demand the organizational changes to maternity leave policies that would make things easier for the next woman who announces she is pregnant.

In Chapter 9, we examine the maternity leave policies offered by other countries to their workers. This chapter explores some of the reasons the United States is still lagging behind.

APPENDIX

State System of Higher Education
Annual Declaration of Tax Status for Tax-Qualified Same-Sex Domestic Partner or Domestic Partner's Child(ren) for Faculty, Non-Faculty Coaches and Managers

Instructions: This form is to designate the tax status of a Same-Sex Domestic Partner (hereinafter referred to as Domestic Partner) and/or Domestic Partner's children covered under the state's active health care program. This form must be completed on an annual basis by the employee and filed with the university human resources office if the Domestic Partner/and or Domestic Partner's child(ren) is/are to be considered as a tax-qualified dependent(s) by the employee under the Internal Revenue Code (IRC) Section 152.

Calendar Year __2012_____

Employee's Name	Personnel Number

It is understood that if the Domestic Partner or their children do not qualify as the dependents of the employee under the applicable requirements of Section 152 of the Internal Revenue Code, the cost of providing health benefits for them will be considered taxable income and subject to income and payroll tax withholding for the employee. The state must rely completely upon the information from and representations of the employee on this form in determining whether all or any portion of benefits provided to the employee and their dependents is taxable. Any under-reporting of income or under-withholding of tax by the state which is caused, directly or indirectly, by the employee having provided inaccurate or incomplete information or having failed to notify the state of any change in circumstances which affects the taxability of all or any portion of the employee's benefits is the responsibility of the employee and the state will have no liability for such under-reporting or under-withholding.

The state recommends that each employee who has enrolled a Domestic Partner or children of the Domestic Partner under any state benefit program consult with a qualified tax professional for guidance as to the tax issues involved and their application to the employee's specific situation. A summary of applicable definitions of "dependent" in the Internal Revenue Code is attached for information purposes only and is not intended as tax advice.

(The following must be completed by the employee.)

The following Domestic Partner is a qualified dependent of the employee for federal income tax purposes.		
Domestic Partner Name	❏ yes	❏ no
The following child/children is/are qualified dependent(s) of the employee for federal income tax purposes.		
Child's Name	❏ yes	❏ no
Child's Name	❏ yes	❏ no
Child's Name	❏ yes	❏ no
Child's Name	❏ yes	❏ no

I agree to provide the state a notarized state *Termination of Same-Sex Domestic Partnership form* within 30 days of the date of termination of our Domestic Partnership.

_____   _____
Signature of Employee   Date

Received as of _____ by _____
              Date   University Human Resource Office

REFERENCES

Armenti, C. 2004. May babies and posttenure babies: Maternal decisions of women professors. *The Review of Higher Education* 27 (2): 211–231.

Astray-Caneda, E., III. 2011. Offering same-sex domestic partner benefits to government employees: Reasons, examples, and methods. *Public Personnel Management* 40 (2): 89–100.

Aubrey, J., M. Click, D. Doughterty, M. Fine, M. Kramer, R. Meisenbach, L. Olson, and M. Smythe. 2008. We do babies! The trials, tribulations and triumphs of pregnancy and parenting in the academy. *Women's Studies in Communication* 31 (2): 186–195.

Barnett, R. 1999. A new work-life model for the twenty-first century. *Annals of the American Academy of Political and Social Science* 562: 143–158.

Brill, S. 2007. Strengthen paternity leave by encouraging voluntary standards for businesses. *Policy Studies Journal* 35 (3): 540–541.

Charles, C., and R. Brunn. 2011. Beating the odds: Female faculty, students and administrators in schools of public affairs. In *Women in Public Administration: Theory and practice*, ed. M. D'Agostino and H. Levine, 239–250. Sudbury, MA: Jones and Bartlett.

Cliatt, C. 2007. University expands family friendly policies for graduate students. http://www.princeton.edu/main/news/archives (accessed February 2, 2011).

Dow, B. 2008. Does it take a department to raise a child? *Women's Studies in Communication* 31 (2): 158–165.

Finkel, S., S. Olswang, and N. She. 1994. Child rearing as a career impediment to women assistant professors. *Review of Higher Education* 17: 259–270.

Gilbert, J. 2008. Why I feel guilty all the time: Performing academic motherhood. *Women's Studies in Communication* 31 (2): 203–208.

Goulden, M., M. A. Mason, and K. Frasch. 2011. Keeping women in the science pipeline. *The Annals of the American Academy* 638: 141–162.

Jackson, L. 2008. Reflections on obstacles and opportunities: Suggestions for improving the retention of female faculty. *Women's Studies in Communication* 31 (2): 226–232.

Jaschik, S. 2007. The "family friendly" competition. http://www.insidehighered.com/news/2007/04/25/(accessed February 2, 2011).

Kramer, M. 2008. The year of the newborns: A department chair's reflections. *Women's Studies in Communication* 31 (2): 196–202.

Madsen, S. 2012. Women and leadership in higher education: Current realities, challenges, and future directions. *Advances in Developing Human Resources* 14 (2): 131–139.

McCurdy, A., M. Newman, and N. Lovich. 2002. Family-friendly workplace policy adoption in general and special purpose local governments: Learning from the Washington state experience. *Review of Public Personnel Administration* 22 (1): 27–51.

McGovern, P., B. Dowd, D. Gjerdingen, I. Moscovice, L. Kochevar, and S. Murphy. 2000. The determinants of time off work after childbirth. *Journal of Health Politics* 25 (3): 527–564.

Mendoza, V. 2006. Wanted: The retention of female graduates. *Diverse* 23 (3): 12–13. http://www.diverseeducation.com (accessed February 2, 2011).

Newman, M., and K. Mathews. 1999. Federal family-friendly workplace policies: Barriers to effective implementation. *Review of Public Personnel Administration* 19 (3): 34–48.

Shoenfelt, E., and A. Schirmer. 2005. Western Kentucky University faculty pregnancy leave practices 2005: A report on current practices and a comparison to practices in 1995. Unpublished technical report.

Sloan Work and Family Research Network. 2006. 2005–2006 Legislative summary sheet: Survey of family leave bills introduced into state legislators. https://workfamily.sas.upenn.edu/sites/workfamily.sas.upenn.edu/files/imported/pdfs/familyleavebills.pdf (accessed October 22, 2012).

U.S. Department of Labor, Wage and Hour Division. 2010. Fact Sheet #28B: FMLA leave for birth, bonding, or to care for a child with a serious health condition on the basis of an "*in loco parentis*" relationship. http://www.wagehour.dol.gov.

Waner, K., J. Winter, and J. Mansfield. 2007. Family benefits—What are students' attitudes and expectations by gender? *Journal of Education for Business* 82 (5): 291–294.

Wyatt-Nichol, H. 2011. Case study: Female-friendly policies in the academe. In *Women in Public Administration: Theory and Practice,* ed. M. D'Agostino and H. Levine, 45–65. Sudbury, MA: Jones and Bartlett.

Yoest, C. 2004. Parental leave in academia. http://www.faculty.virginia.edu/familyandtenure (accessed February 2, 2011).

9

An International Comparison— The Other Kingdoms

In this chapter, we take a very brief look at what the "other kingdoms" offer in terms of maternity leave, paternity leave, and parental leave benefits. The employee benefits offered in other countries are in some cases just as complicated and difficult to interpret as those offered in the United States. In other countries, the conditions under which an employee may qualify and utilize the benefits are much easier to understand. Many countries seem to be much more consistent in the provision and administration of these benefits. This chapter is not meant to provide an extensive or exhaustive list of countries and benefits or an in-depth analysis of why these benefits are offered. We hope that, throughout the other chapters included in this book, we have made the case for why paid maternity leave is beneficial to mother, child, family, and society. This chapter serves to reinforce those reasons but primarily serves as a reference point for those interested in conducting further comparisons of benefits between the United States and other countries.

WHAT MATERNITY LEAVE, PATERNITY LEAVE, AND PARENTAL LEAVE BENEFITS ARE OFFERED IN OTHER COUNTRIES?

Within the body of literature on work–family balance from an international comparative basis, there is a focus by some researchers on understanding whether the intent of related policies emphasizes the rights of citizens and workers (Sweden, Norway, Finland); emphasizes gender equality (Germany, the Netherlands, France); or emphasizes no intervention (United States). For some researchers, the focus is on finding balance between work and family; for others, the focus is on whether women are allowed to give priority to either family or work at different times in their lives. So, in the latter case, the employer is encouraged to allow women to reduce the hours they work, or move in and out of the workforce until their children go to school, and there is no formal support for child care because it is assumed the mother will fill this caregiver role (Tremblay 2010).

Maternity and paternity leave policies generally differ in four ways: who is eligible, length of leave, whether the leave is paid or unpaid leave, and presence or absence of flexibility of when the leave is used. Member countries of the European Union provide for paid leave for at least 3 months to care for a newborn. In comparison, the United States only provides for 12 weeks of unpaid leave for eligible employees. Most countries provide for some level of job protection, so the employee can return to his or her job when leave is exhausted. Some countries provide for the costs of paid leave through national insurance, others through payroll taxes, and some through income taxes. Some countries provide for 100% of wage replacement, others replace wages up to 80%, and still others provide no wage replacement. In some countries, the level of wage replacement is based on the length of leave, so a shorter leave means a higher level of wage replacement, and a longer leave means a lower level of wage replacement.

In terms of flexibility of when the leave may be used, generally maternity and paternity leave is provided just for those employees with newborns, but in the "Netherlands, Sweden, Denmark and the United Kingdom, parents have the option of using their leave flexibly by dividing it," with some countries allowing use of leave up until the child reaches the age of 8 (U.S. Government Accountability Office 2007a, 8–9). Other countries refer to this type of leave as "parental leave," and, for this reason, it is important to note that the use of the term *parental leave* is differentiated from maternity and paternity leave. This term may also have a different connotation in other countries than in does it the United States, and so direct comparisons may be difficult. In other countries, the terms *paternity leave* and *parental leave* are used interchangeably, which further complicates the comparisons (O'Brien 2009, 193). Specific provisions of maternity leave, paternity leave, and parental leave are presented by country in Tables 9.1, 9.2, and 9.3, respectively (U.S. Government Accountability Office 2007b, 34–40). It is important to note that some of these provisions may have been amended since the GAO collected this information in 2007.

TABLE 9.1
Maternity Leave in Selected Countries

Country	Length of Leave	Eligibility	Payment	Conditions
Canada	Length of leave for private employers governed by the provinces, which generally allow 17 weeks of unpaid leave.	Must generally have worked for the same employer for a continuous period that ranges from 13 weeks to 12 months. However, three provinces do not have this requirement.	Payment of 55% of average insured earnings, up to yearly maximum earnings of $40,000, is available for a maximum of 15 weeks for women who have worked for at least 600 insured hours in the last year. Payment can begin up to 8 weeks prior to the expected birth.	2-week waiting period prior to receiving payment.
Denmark	18 weeks	Must have been employed for at least 120 hours in the 13 weeks prior to the leave. Women who are self-employed, have completed vocational training for a period of at least 18 months, are doing paid work placement as part of a vocational training course, or are unemployed are also entitled to cash benefits.	Based on the hourly wage of the employee, up to a maximum. In 2003, on average, the compensation rate was 60%–70% of former earnings.	Leave includes 4 weeks before the expected date of confinement and 14 weeks following confinement.

Continued

TABLE 9.1 (Continued)
Maternity Leave in Selected Countries

Country	Length of Leave	Eligibility	Payment	Conditions
France	16 weeks of maternity leave for a woman's first child, and 26 weeks for subsequent children.		Generally paid at full earnings for women with a minimum level of social insurance contributions or hours worked.	
Ireland	26 weeks of maternity leave, and 16 weeks of unpaid maternity leave.		Generally paid at 80% of earnings, subject to a minimum and maximum payment, for women with a minimum level of social insurance contributions.	
The Netherlands	16 weeks		100% of the daily wage, up to a maximum, which is paid by the general unemployment fund.	Leave generally begins 6 weeks prior to the expected date of birth.
New Zealand	14 weeks	Unpaid leave for 14 continuous weeks is available to women who do not meet minimum work eligibility requirements.	100% of weekly pay, up to a maximum, is available to women who have worked at least 10 hours per week in the 6 or 12 months preceding baby's expected date of birth.	Paid leave by women must be taken at the same time as unpaid leave for which they are eligible. If a woman's spouse or partner meets the eligibility criteria, the mother can transfer all or a part of this leave to them.

An International Comparison—The Other Kingdoms • 273

Sweden	12 weeks	80% of earnings.	Leave is for 6 weeks before and 6 weeks following the birth of a child.
United Kingdom	52 weeks	90% or less of weekly average earnings is available for 39 weeks to women whose earnings qualify for the national insurance program and who have worked for the same employer continuously for 26 weeks prior to the 15th week before the child is due. Women who do not meet these requirements may receive payment of 90% or less of earnings for 39 weeks through a maternity allowance.	Payment period for statutory maternity pay/allowance is 39 weeks.

Continued

TABLE 9.1 (Continued)
Maternity Leave in Selected Countries

Country	Length of Leave	Eligibility	Payment	Conditions
United States	12 weeks	Must have worked for employer for at least 1 year, and for more than 1,250 hours during the last year.	Unpaid	Allows eligible employees to take up to 12 weeks of job-protected leave in a 12-month period for qualifying reasons, including the birth or placement of a child for adoption or foster care, the employee's own serious health condition, or to care for a qualifying family member with a serious health condition. Leave for the birth or placement of a child must conclude within 12 months of the birth or placement.

Source: U.S. Government Accountability Office. 2007b. Women and low-skilled workers: Other countries' policies and practices that may help these workers enter and remain in the labor force. Report #GAO-07-817. Washington, D.C. http://www.gao.gov/cgi-bin/getrpt?GAO-07-817 (accessed October 28, 2012).

TABLE 9.2

Paternity Leave in Selected Countries

Country	Length of Leave	Eligibility	Payment	Conditions
Canada		See table on parental leave as paternity leave was largely replaced by this leave in the 1990s.		
Denmark	2 weeks	Employed or self-employed.	In 2003, on average, the compensation rate was 60%–70% of former earnings.	Must be taken continuously within 14 weeks following the birth.
France	11 days, or 18 days, in the case of a multiple birth		Generally paid at full earnings for fathers with a minimum level of social insurance contributions or hours worked.	Must be taken continuously.
Ireland	No legal entitlement to paternity leave			
The Netherlands	2 days		Employer pays 100% of wages.	
New Zealand	1 or 2 weeks	1 week unpaid leave is available to partners with 6 months of eligible service, and 2 weeks unpaid is available to those with 12 months of eligible service.	Unpaid	

Continued

TABLE 9.2 (*Continued*)

Paternity Leave in Selected Countries

Country	Length of Leave	Eligibility	Payment	Conditions
Sweden	10 working days.		Paid at 80% of earnings.	
United Kingdom	1 or 2 weeks.	Must have worked for the same employer continuously for 26 weeks prior to the 15th week before the child is due.	90% or less of average weekly earnings for those who qualify for the national insurance program. Those who do not qualify based on earnings may be eligible for other income support.	Leave must be completed within 56 days after the child's birth.
United States	As with maternity leave, the Family and Medical Leave Act (FMLA) provides 12 weeks.	Must have worked for employer for at least 1 year, and for more than 1,250 hours during the last year.	Unpaid	Allows eligible employees to take up to 12 weeks of job-protected leave in a 12-month period for qualifying reasons, including the birth or placement of a child for adoption or foster care, the employee's own serious health condition, or to care for a qualifying family member with a serious health condition. Leave for the birth or placement of a child must conclude within 12 months of the birth or placement.

Source: U.S. Government Accountability Office. 2007b. Women and low-skilled workers: Other countries' policies and practices that may help these workers enter and remain in the labor force. Report #GAO-07-817. Washington, D.C. http://www.gao.gov/cgi-bin/getrpt?GAO-07-817 (accessed October 28, 2012).

TABLE 9.3
Parental Leave in Selected Countries

Country	Length of Leave	Eligibility	Payment	Conditions
Canada	Duration of leave ranges from 35 to 52 weeks, and is determined by the province.	Must generally have worked for the same employer for a continuous period that ranges from 13 weeks to 12 months. However, some provinces do not have this requirement.	Payment of 55% of average insured earnings, up to yearly maximum earnings of $40,000, is available for a maximum of 35 weeks for parents with at least 600 insured hours in the last year.	2-week waiting period prior to receiving payment. Benefits can be claimed by one parent or shared between the two, but cannot exceed a combined maximum of 35 weeks. When combined with maternity benefits, payment is available for up to 50 weeks.
Denmark	32, 40, or 46 weeks.		60% of a worker's unemployment benefit, as reported in 2003.	After the 14th week following the birth of a child, parents share this leave, which can be split or postponed, until the child turns 9. If parents choose the 40- or 46-week leave, their benefits are frozen to the amount paid for the 32-week leave.

Continued

TABLE 9.3 (Continued)
Parental Leave in Selected Countries

Country	Length of Leave	Eligibility	Payment	Conditions
France	Family entitlement to leave until a child reaches 36 months.	Eligible for payment with two children if parents have worked for at least 2 of 5 years preceding birth; eligible for payment for three or more children if parents have worked for 2 years at any time in the 10 preceding birth.	Flat-rate benefit payment within 6 months of maternity leave for one child, or immediately for 2 or more children.	Leave can be taken by the mother or father, or can be shared following one another.
Ireland	14 weeks.	Generally must have been working for employer for 1 year.	Unpaid	Both parents have a separate entitlement to 14 weeks of leave, which may be used until the child turns 8, and can be taken continuously or in separate blocks. If the child has a disability, the 14 weeks of leave can be used until the child has reached age 16.

An International Comparison—The Other Kingdoms • 279

The Netherlands	Amount of leave is based on working hours and is calculated on a part-time basis over 13 weeks.	Must have worked for the same employer for at least 1 year.	Unpaid	Must be used before a child turns 8. With agreement from an employer, the leave can be split into a maximum of three parts.
New Zealand	52 weeks, less any maternity leave (maximum of 14 weeks).	Must have worked for the same employer for a minimum of 12 months.	Unpaid, less any paid maternity leave (maximum of 14 weeks).	Leave can be taken simultaneously or consecutively and can be shared between parents where they are both eligible.
Sweden	480 days per family.		For 390 days, 80% of previous income, up to a maximum, and a fixed daily rate for the remaining 90 days. Parents who were not employed before the birth of a child receive a flat daily rate for 390 days followed by a lesser amount for the remaining 90.	Of the 480 days, 60 days are set aside exclusively for each parent, and cannot be transferred while the remaining days can be shared. Paid leave must be taken before a child turns 8 and can be taken continuously or in blocks.
United Kingdom	13 weeks, or 18 weeks for parents of children with disabilities.	Must have completed a year of continuous service with current employer.	Unpaid	Leave can be taken until the child turns 5 and in short or long blocks, with the consent of an employer.

Continued

TABLE 9.3 (*Continued*)

Parental Leave in Selected Countries

Country	Length of Leave	Eligibility	Payment	Conditions
United States	As with maternity leave, the Family and Medical Leave Act (FMLA) provides 12 weeks.	Must have worked for employer for at least 1 year, and for over 1,250 hours during the last year.	Unpaid	Allows eligible employees to take up to 12 weeks of job-protected leave in a 12-month period for qualifying reasons, including the birth or placement of a child for adoption or foster care, the employee's own serious health condition, or to care for a qualifying family member with a serious health condition. Leave for the birth or placement of a child must conclude within 12 months of the birth or placement.

Source: U.S. Government Accountability Office. 2007b. Women and low-skilled workers: Other countries' policies and practices that may help these workers enter and remain in the labor force. Report #GAO-07-817. Washington, D.C. http://www.gao.gov/cgi-bin/getrpt?GAO-07-817 (accessed October 28, 2012).

One example that highlights some of the difficulties of making direct comparisons between types of leave policies is Norway. In Norway, fathers are offered the option to take 6 weeks of parental leave for care of a child. Norway has one of the most generous paid-leave policies for fathers. The idea is that fathers should share in the care of children, and the mother and father should be able to combine the leave time taken from work to care for small children. There are some fathers who would prefer to transfer this leave time to their spouses, because their wives would prefer to stay home longer, but that is not allowed. That type of flexibility would be welcome by some and, for others, this seems to defeat the purpose of allowing fathers the time off to bond with the child (Brandth and Kvande 2009). In some countries, there is a prohibition of this type of leave transfer, or it may be referred to as a "use it or lose it" benefit and is based on the idea that to allow the father to transfer the leave to the mother would only serve to keep women out of the workforce longer, and thus contribute to a further reduction in female lifetime earnings (Ray, Gornick, and Schmitt 2009, 10). Regardless of the individual preference about how to use the leave, the policy as it is seems to be accepted as a standard employee right in Norway, and as such has been accepted within the workplace culture (Brandth and Kvande 2009).

The acceptance of paid leave for fathers is not found everywhere. There is some indication that, in some traditionally male-dominant occupations or sectors such as police departments, the use of parental or paternity leave is met with resistance and may have a negative effect on a man's career. The only way to move toward acceptance is to change the organizational culture and for supervisors to formally support these policies (Tremblay 2010, 98). Further, if men are required to take leave during the same time period as the mother—usually immediately after the birth of the child, then the family loses the option to extend the time that one parent can be at home, and this requires the family to find other child-care arrangements and drives up the cost to the family for child care (Tremblay and Genin 2011, 251). Parental leave at the time of birth seems to be perceived as more legitimate than taking leave later as newborns require a lot of care and attention (263). Perceptions about the obstacles to taking parental leave within police departments in Québec included staffing concerns in small departments, lack of supervisor support, lack of colleague support, and negative impact on careers. Those who had taken parental leave were more likely to agree that these obstacles were of concern more so than employees who had not taken the leave (257–259).

Consistent with research on use of maternity leave, paternity leave is much more likely to be taken by fathers and for longer periods of time when the leave is paid. Further, in countries in which the income replacement is higher (more than 50%), there is greater use of the leave. This perpetuates a two-tier system, with those who can afford to take leave utilizing it, and those with lower family incomes not utilizing it (O'Brien 2009). Fathers who take leave report that it contributes to their ability to bond with the child, and it also offers them the opportunity to be a positive role model for their older children who observe them in the caregiver role with the infant (Doucet 2009, 94).

WHY IS THE UNITED STATES LAGGING BEHIND OTHER COUNTRIES IN PROVIDING MATERNITY LEAVE BENEFITS?

As noted in Chapter 2, the reason maternity leave remains unsupported are manifold, but to answer the question of why the United States is lagging behind other countries is simply and precisely because the leave is unpaid. Until there is support to make maternity leave paid, we will not be on par with other countries. To accomplish this, paid maternity leave also has to be supported by employers. At demonstrated in Chapters 6 and 7, women are reluctant to use maternity leave even when it is available, which means the organizational culture has to change if women are going to utilize the leave available to them.

In a study of 21 countries and their maternity and paternity leave policies, Ray, Gornick, and Schmitt (2009) state that the countries that offer the best benefits are those that (1) offer paid leave; (2) do not allow parental leave to be transferable between parents (so that women's lifetime earnings are not substantially reduced, and so women are not kept out of the workforce longer than men); (3) have universal policies that apply to all workers in all settings, industries, and locations, and if there are conditions of length of employment, earnings, etc., that there is a minimal threshold; (4) have a funding mechanism so that costs are shared across all employers; and (5) allow some scheduling flexibility, including a return to work part time (20). In their analysis, Ray et al. (2009, 21) found that the United States "has the least generous policies among the 21 high-income countries … studied."

An International Comparison—The Other Kingdoms • 283

Anthony (2008) concurs. She acknowledges that there are differences in duration of leave among countries, differences in funding mechanisms, and differences in who is responsible for paying for leaves for the workers, but she points out that most leaves are longer than what is provided in the United States. Anthony suggests that the United States could learn "some valuable lessons" by looking toward the leave policies in other countries. The United States could investigate what works best and learn from the experience of others (483).

Even Australia, which until recently had no mandatory paid leave, adopted a policy of paid leave effective January 1, 2011. See Figure 9.1 on maternity leave. Australia has a long history of providing paid maternity leave in the public sector, but not so in the private sector. This new paid parental leave policy allows for 18 weeks of leave for eligible employees, at the national minimum wage of $543 per week. There is an upper income limit for eligibility, but the primary purpose is to see that these benefits are extended to many employees who previously had no access to paid leave, many of whom are part-time workers or workers employed by very small companies. The hope is that the paid leave will encourage more women to stay in the workforce and solidify the commitment of Australia to issues

FIGURE 9.1
Maternity leave. (Source: © Copyright Judy Horacek 1996. First published in the Alternative Law Journal in October 1996.)

important to working women and their families, and that new mothers will be allowed to stay at home longer with their infants (Commonwealth of Australia 2009, 1). A review conducted a year after the paid parental leave was enacted showed that many new mothers, who previously had not been eligible for any paid maternity leave, had applied for assistance under this government-provided program so that they could take more time off during the early months of their child's life. Further, a majority of the private sector employers interviewed during the review process, and which had previously provided paid maternity leave for employees, had not reduced or changed that employee benefit. Rather, the government provided benefit was seen as an added benefit for eligible employees (Commonwealth of Australia 2012, 116).

Mechanisms utilized to pay for maternity leave in other countries include general government revenue, contributory taxes for family leave benefits, health and sickness funds, unemployment compensation funds, and social insurance funds. Social insurance funds that are collected and distributed across society minimize the burden on individual employers and may also serve to reduce an employer's tendency to discriminate against women of childbearing age (Ray, Gornick, and Schmitt 2009, 17).

This chapter has presented some comparisons of maternity leave benefits between the United States and policies found in other countries. The experiences of other countries do not support the idea that offering paternity leave will necessarily open the way for the acceptance of paid maternity leave. If men and women have more choices about how to handle their family responsibilities, and if they are able to have paid leave available to support those choices, they may be more inclined to use leave that is available. Use of leave will not happen if organizations and supervisors do not support that use (Tremblay 2010, 98).

At a minimum, the example set by other countries of funding maternity leave is one the United States should follow. There are several mechanisms available that could be used to fund this leave, and none are out of our reach. The findings of other studies highlight the importance that other countries place on women in the workforce and on children. These countries show this support through the policies they have adopted and the way in which these policies are administered. Offering paid maternity and paternity leave provides families with economic security and the ability to return to their respective jobs after the leave, and most important, it offers parents the opportunity to be with their child during the first months of the child's life (O'Brien 2009, 192). Primarily, this brief international comparison supports the idea that the United States falls short in showing appropriate commitment to women in the workforce and more so falls short on the value we place on children. It is time to join the rest of the world in recognizing and correcting our shortcomings.

Next, in the concluding chapter, we offer some final thoughts about the long and winding journey toward understanding maternity leave and suggest some practical recommendations for policy and organizational change.

REFERENCES

Anthony, D. 2008. The hidden harms of the Family and Medical Leave Act: Gender-neutral versus gender equal. *American University Journal of Gender, Social Policy and the Law* 16 (4): 459–501.

Brandth, B., and E. Kvande. 2009. Gendered or gender neutral care politics for fathers? *The Annals of the American Academy* 624: 177–189.

Commonwealth of Australia. 2009. Australia's paid parental leave scheme: Supporting working Australian families. *Pamphlet.* http://www.fahcsia.gov.au (accessed September 24, 2012).

Commonwealth of Australia. 2012. Occasional paper #44: Paid parental leave evaluation, phase 1. http://www.fahcsia.gov.au (accessed October 30, 2012).

Doucet, A. 2009. Dad and baby in the first year: Gendered responsibilities and embodiment. *The Annals of the American Academy* 624: 78–98.

O'Brien, M. 2009. Fathers, parental leave policies, and infant quality of life: International perspectives and policy impact. *The Annals of the American Academy* 624: 190–213.

Ray, R., J. Gornick, and J. Schmitt. 2009. Parental leave policies in 21 countries: Assessing generosity and gender equality. Washington, D.C.: Center for Economic and Policy Research. http://www.cepr.net (accessed October 10, 2012).

Tremblay, D. G. 2010. Paid parental leave: An employee right or still an ideal? An analysis of the situation in Québec in comparison with North America. *Employee Responsibilities and Rights Journal* 22: 83–100.

Tremblay, D. G., and F. Genin. 2011. Parental leave: An important employee right, but an organizational challenge. *Employee Responsibilities and Rights Journal* 23: 249–268.

U.S. Government Accountability Office. 2007a. Women and low-skilled workers. Efforts in other countries to help these workers enter and remain in the workforce. Report #GAO-07-898T. Washington, D.C. http://www.gao.gov/cgi-bin/getrpt?GAO-07-989T (accessed October 28, 2012).

U.S. Government Accountability Office. 2007b. Women and low-skilled workers: Other countries' policies and practices that may help these workers enter and remain in the labor force. Report #GAO-07-817. Washington, D.C. http://www.gao.gov/cgi-bin/getrpt?GAO-07-817 (accessed October 28, 2012).

10

Conclusion: Can the Fairy Tale Be Realized or Should It Be Rewritten?

WHAT ARE THE OBSTACLES TO A HAPPY ENDING FOR OUR DAUGHTERS?

This project was started with the goal of "understanding" maternity leave, in both policy and practice, in the United States. It is a subject that is both complicated and complex. We have come to understand, through listening to young mothers about their personal and professional experiences and perceptions of using maternity leave, why it is that they deserve access to a reasonable length of paid maternity leave. The two conversations recounted in Chapter 1 were not anomalies. Both overt and covert discrimination does exist against women who utilize the benefits provided and allowed by their organizations.

As a society, we are doing a dreadful disservice to parents and to their children. Will these young mothers (and fathers) survive it if nothing changes? Of course, they will. They are strong, talented, and resilient. But why should these young families have to struggle so? With the exception of the monetary cost, there are nothing but positive outcomes if we amend our maternity leave policies in the United States. Meaningful change can start immediately if we disavow discriminatory and unfair practices.

The obstacles identified that get in the way of improving maternity leave policies for our daughters are manifold, and some would say insurmountable. In Chapter 2, we retraced our steps to understand the related legislation that has led us to where we are today with maternity leave policies. We identified problems and issues with FMLA and other legislation. While FMLA ensures job protection, its weakness is that it only provides for unpaid leave, and most working women cannot financially afford to take 12 weeks of unpaid leave. One of the purposes of FMLA was to structure leave to make it gender neutral. This was done deliberately in an effort to prevent potential employment discrimination against female employees and job applicants. However, one of the unintended consequences of FMLA is that organizations have in many instances done away with formal maternity leave policies. When this occurs, there is no consideration of the mother's physical need to recover from childbirth, or the need for the child to bond with the parents. This is a policy area in which gender neutrality is not helpful to employees. We must "acknowledge that women and men are affected differently by organizations" (Acker 1990, 142). We must embrace these differences in attitudes and behaviors, rather than ignore them.

Further, if only some of our employees can afford to use benefits provided under FMLA, then FMLA presents its own set of obstacles to reasonable and responsible maternity leave policies. We found that low-income families are further disadvantaged in their use of FMLA, because they either do not qualify due to working part time or because they work for small companies that are not subject to FMLA provisions. The result is that the use of FMLA is oftentimes counter to the legislative intent, and maternity leave benefit policy is intertwined with so many other policies that it complicates an already complicated issue.

In Chapter 3, our journey led us to an examination of specific maternity leave policies, and we found policies to be onerous and confusing at best, both in the public and private sectors. The level of benefits allowed first evolved and then subsequently devolved over the past decades to a point where some organizations only allow unpaid maternity leave as provided by FMLA. Organizations stay true to the letter of the law, but not the intent. Detailed policies seem to be most helpful but are often hard to develop, interpret, and administer (Untener 2008). Consistency in the administration of FMLA and maternity leave policies is imperative to prevent legal challenges (Untener 2008), but responsible administrative discretion is needed too. Still, the reality is that inconsistencies abound.

In Chapter 4, we examined the health issues faced by young women as they begin their families and utilize maternity leave. There are many mental, emotional, physiological, physical, and societal reasons to provide a longer maternity leave for the benefit of the mother, and these reasons are often discounted in the policies set by organizations. Further, babies benefit physically, developmentally, and socially from longer maternity leaves, in part because breast-feeding can continue longer without the mother facing obstacles in the workplace which make breast-feeding more difficult when she returns to work.

In the fifth, sixth, and seventh chapters, we heard directly from young women who utilized maternity leave policies. Through their voices, we learned of the constraints and obstacles they faced both personally and professionally when they used these benefits, and as they balanced the return to work with caring for a newborn. We learned the administration of maternity leave benefits was inconsistent, and there was great uncertainty about the leave available. A lack of communication from human resources departments and immediate supervisors served to compound these issues. We heard of examples of young women working while in the hospital and immediately upon returning home with a newborn. We heard of examples of the pressure these young women are under, although some of it is self-imposed. We heard stories about their reluctance to ask for accommodations, and the perceived bias and stigma they feel when asking for maternity leave. We also learned of the amazing lengths that women will go to in order to provide the best start for their babies, and at the same time to advance within their careers.

In Chapter 8, our journey took a winding path as we heard from the voices of people who were not central to this study, but who each had unique stories that needed to be told. We also heard about the obstacles that unsupportive colleagues and supervisors can and do impose on young women in the workplace. We heard examples of how the informal culture in an organization can have a negative impact on the decisions women and men make about whether to take leave or how much leave to take, even when good organizational policies are in place. We also heard examples of the possible negative financial and professional consequences for women who stop the tenure clock to spend more time with their newborn. Finally, in Chapter 9, our journey led us to far-off lands, as we examined examples from other countries that help us understand why we should implement paid maternity leave, and how we can overcome the financial obstacles to a paid maternity leave in the United States. We examined concrete examples of how the United States could realistically pay for maternity leave.

WHAT CAN WE REASONABLY EXPECT TO CHANGE WITHIN OUR ORGANIZATIONS?

Women in higher education face a unique set of professional challenges. Institutions of higher learning are going to have to take specific actions to ensure that all understand that adopting family-friendly employee leave policies is not enough. Institutions must have both formal and written policies, and informal support networks in place to ensure that policies are carried out equitably. Granting leave on a case-by-case basis does not ensure each woman will be treated fairly. Women may not use policies if they fear they will be unfavorably compared to their male counterparts "for having 'indulged' in time off" (Stockdell-Giesler and Ingalls 2007, 38). Untener (2008, 1) says "settling for a policy that lacks any real substance and essentially says, 'maternity leave will be accommodated within departments working through deans' is unacceptable, but, regrettably, all too common." As recounted by Interviewee 23, we heard an example in Chapter 8 where leave was negotiated. While the subject had a good outcome—the allowance and support for two paid maternity leaves, at a time 35 years ago when there was no formal organizational policy in place—other women were not and still are not so fortunate. Stockdell-Giesler and Ingalls (2007, 40) succinctly summarize how the maternity leave accommodation issue should be viewed in higher education: "when we put pregnancy and childbirth into the context of the typical faculty career, a semester-long maternity leave is a mere blip on the screen of a commitment to an institution that often spans decades."

Short of this enlightened view, there are also improvements that individuals can make within any organization to improve maternity leave policies. Women must recognize that they must work within the confines of their organizational culture. The culture must be understood before we try to change it. Policy change will need to be slow and gradual, but the presence of women in the workplace will ensure its inevitability (Short-Thompson 2008, 257). We must all commit to participate in working for positive change.

According to Madsen (2012, 135), "we need to help prepare and support (e.g., increase aspirations, obtain mentors and coaches, provide flexible work environments) more women for leadership roles." At the individual level, the presence of a meaningful relationship with a mentor can be critical to the success of a woman's professional and personal life. As described by O'Meara and Campbell (2011), often mentors are "bad, few, or nonexistent" (456). Yes, a mentor is often going to be struggling to balance his or her own professional and personal lives, but the mentor and the mentee can help each other along. Give someone a chance to become a mentor. If you need assistance, ask for advice and open the lines of communication. At the same time, be cautious. Take the benefit of learning from a mentor's experience, but do not make it your own. Do not let the negative experience a senior colleague had in the past with regard to maternity leave influence the decisions you make about your family today.

At the individual level, women must learn to say no! Supervisors and colleagues will always ask more than an employee can reasonably be expected to give. It is hard for young women to make the distinction sometimes between a request and an order. Women must learn the subtle nuance between those two, in order to make the workload more manageable and to balance work and family demands. This is especially important during pregnancy and after returning to work from maternity leave.

Also, at the individual level, women must not be afraid professionally to share that there may be a need for workplace accommodations at some point throughout the pregnancy. Plans to take maternity leave should be articulated. Women must set expectations high, and expect others to rise up to meet them. The best way to ensure that your high expectations will be met by an organization is to always deliver on your promises. Show your employer that they can count on you (Short-Thompson 2008, 257) before it is time to discuss maternity leave.

Every creative and innovative way we learn to accommodate maternity and paternity leave within an organization will make it easier for the next woman or man. Buzzanell and Liu (2005) argue that maternity leave will not change unless the organizational structure changes. This change will only happen if we recognize the importance of the values of caring and nurturing (20). While I am not advocating that we must transform every "family friendly" policy, such as maternity leave into "care" leave, as would be suggested by some, there is merit in considering care as a common good.

> The proper care ... of human beings has an effect on a number of people in addition to the individual parents who brought that person into the world. Care and nurturing should be treated ... as one more facet of corporate/institutional social responsibility ... well-cared-for individuals are fundamental to creating a developed and ethical society. (Tracy 2008, 171)

Within the pharmaceutical industry, we have learned that some companies are reducing benefits for maternity and paternity leave. Even in these difficult financial times, it is counterproductive to reduce benefits that are so important to employees and their families. Such actions have a negative effect on morale, productivity, and job satisfaction of employees. Attractive employee benefit packages do both attract and retain the best and brightest employees. The pharmaceutical industry's provision of generous maternity and paternity leave benefits needs to continue to be the gold standard against which we measure and hold all private and public employers.

Ultimately, we need to have organizational and institutional policies that do not make women choose between devotion to work or devotion to family (Tower and Alkadry 2008; Armenti 2004). The women interviewed for this research project are balancing that tenuous divide, but our workplace policies often do nothing to assist them. There are many institutional policies and informal cultural norms that might reduce this incompatibility of roles. In addition to extending the length of paid maternity leave, offering options of a slower transition back to work, shorter work days, fewer work days per week, flexible work hours, scheduling flexibility to care for a sick child, or the ability to work at home—any or all of these might help to balance work and family demands (Tower and Alkadry 2008, 161). Support for paternity leave could also send a positive message to all employees about the value placed on women and families by the organization (162).

Human resources departments may need to serve as a conduit between organizations and employees, focusing on establishing and strengthening trust between the organization and the employees. Buzzanell and Liu (2005) suggest that every human resources department have an employee assigned to serve as a woman's advocate. The advocate would serve as a resource to help all women, but particularly women who are having problems negotiating for specific accommodations or time off. This would be helpful to women "who feel discouraged about their employment or career opportunities and those who feel as though they lack legitimate forms of power" (20). Prior to conducting this research project, I would not have thought this drastic step was necessary, but upon reflection it could actually be helpful.

Buzzanell and Liu (2005) also call for periodic reviews of maternity leave policies and suggest that women, pregnant women, and women with children be invited to share information and suggestions for improvements to all policies that affect employees with children (20). In the area of higher education, Untener (2008, 1–3) suggests appointing a committee to review policies periodically and that the committee be charged with making recommendations for change. He suggests that the committee ask the following questions: (1) Do the terms of our policies match our institution? What are the financial implications? (2) Is the policy legal? (3) Does it open us up to legal challenges? (4) Are faculty and staff served well under this policy? Are students served well under this policy? (5) Have we considered all related issues? Have we considered adopted children, paternity leave, stopping the tenure clock, and modified duties?

Change will be much easier in an environment that encourages open dialogue. Communication on maternity leave must be initiated, and sustained. Each of us must join this important and timely conversation, and we must make sure that the voices of young women are not silenced.

WHAT IS BEST FOR SOCIETY?

This book does not provide the answer about what a fair and equitable maternity leave policy is or should be. I am absolutely sure it needs to be more than the 12 weeks of unpaid leave promised under FMLA. The National Center for Children in Poverty, a nonpartisan public interest research organization, issued a press release on April 17, 2012, calling for the establishment of a national policy of 14 weeks of universal paid leave for new mothers. The specific recommendations called for extending coverage to both full- and part-time employees and to include small businesses. Further, in an effort to present a reasonable proposal that would include small employers, the center recommended wage replacement at two-thirds of the employee's normal wages to ensure that the employer could afford the cost and that the employee would be paid enough to be able to afford to take the leave.

Beyond following the laws and policies in place, now or in the future, we must encourage both the public and private sectors to be concerned about the spirit of the law—for justice that varies by situation (Frederickson 1997, 104). The reality is that to change policy we may have to make small and incremental movements toward the optimum duration of paid maternity leave, by "satisficing." We do not have perfect information, unlimited time, or other resources necessary to make the best decision or to find the best solution. We must settle for an alternative that suffices, that satisfies some, and requires sacrifice from still others (Simon 1957). We will have to consider policy changes that are moderate, that can be adapted to meet organizational needs, and that are full of compromises, aiming for policies that are acceptable as long as we are moving toward a goal that provides for some paid maternity leave for all families. As a society, we must understand that the economic and financial cost is a consequence of this goal, but we have a higher moral duty and responsibility to consider "that certain actions whose costs outweigh their benefits are morally right and therefore should be taken nevertheless" (Stone 2002, 234). We now have a better understanding of maternity leave—both policy and practice, but we still face the greatest obstacle on our journey—finding the political will and the political strength to take action. We are at a crossroads, and we may have to use our imaginations and think creatively in order to decide which path to follow.

RESTORING THE FAIRY TALE

A fairy tale is a story that is retold generation after generation (Maggiore 2003). Its purpose may be to give hope, or it may serve as a cautionary tale. Fairy tales also serve to establish and reinforce roles and rules in society. Some fairy tales recount stories of the princess being rescued by the prince. While the princess, in her subordinate role, is waiting, she must be passive and patient. She must endure her hardships in silence.

Maternity leave in the 21st century may be the last fairy tale told to and believed by young women in the United States. This is the story about having both personal and professional fulfillment. This is the story about having a baby, taking a little time off to recover, to enjoy the experience of being a new mom, to take it all in, even if just for a little while. Yes, young women understand that the "wolf" will come knocking at the door, reality will return. The new mom will need to and actually even want to return to work, but just for a little while … she believes in the hopeful maternity leave fairy tale that she has been told.

Unfortunately, this tale of hope has become a cautionary tale—one where women are penalized professionally for using employee benefits due to them, and one where there is not enough time off work to be with their new baby. In 1914, Alexandra Kollontai wrote about the roles of a working woman and mother, and she described the differing experiences of those who had no economic need to work, compared to those women who worked for a living—ladies and laundresses, as she called them. Kollontai (2005) contrasted the experiences of these women through pregnancy, childbirth, recovery, and breast-feeding and then to a return to their respective "normal" activities.

Kollontai (2005) also writes of a society in which she imagines that these economic differences and hardships are erased. She calls for women to unite and to work for change so that all can enjoy motherhood. She writes:

> When the mother wants to be with her children, she only has to say the word … when she has no time, she knows they are in good hands. Maternity is no longer a cross. Only its joyful aspects remain…. But such a society, surely, is only … found in fairy tales? (130)

One hundred years later, through the narratives of the young women in this study, we have learned that maternity leave in policy and practice is not what young women expected or what they were promised it would be. Reality is much different than the fairy tale, but Kollontai's words convey hope. Hope, because a century later, I understand the injustices she described and her words invoke in me the same feelings she had about the need to change things. Most important, I share her feelings that change can occur. I have just as much confidence now, as she did then, in the abilities of women to enact meaningful and substantive change.

The maternity leave fairy tale, as it stands today, is a cautionary tale. It is my hope that this fairy tale can be restored to include if not a happy ending, then at a minimum a happier interlude. It is my hope that young families will take a stand to assist in rewriting this fairy tale, so that when their daughters decide to have a family, those young women will not be suffering in silence through an unpaid maternity leave that is inadequate and antiquated. It is my hope that all men and women join together to fight for the retelling of this fairy tale into a story of hope once again, one in which promises are realized. Apparently, our journey and our work have only just begun.

REFERENCES

Acker, J. 1990. Hierarchies, jobs, bodies: A theory of gendered organizations. *Gender and Society* 4 (2): 139–158.

Armenti, C. 2004. May babies and posttenure babies: Maternal decisions of women professors. *The Review of Higher Education* 27 (2): 211–231.

Buzzanell, P., and M. Liu. 2005. Struggling with maternity leave policies and practices: A poststructuralist feminist analysis of gendered organizing. *Journal of Applied Communication Research* 33 (1): 1–25.

Frederickson, H. G. 1997. *The Spirit of Public Administration.* San Francisco, CA: Jossey-Bass.

Kollontai, A. 2005. Working woman and mother. In *Feminist Theory: A Reader*, ed. W. Kolman and F. Bartkowski, 126–130. New York: McGraw Hill.

Madsen, S. 2012. Women and leadership in higher education: Current realities, challenges, and future directions. *Advances in Developing Human Resources* 14 (2): 131–139.

Maggiore, B. 2003. Female discrimination in fairy tales: A feminist critique. Unpublished paper.

National Center for Children in Poverty. April 17, 2012. Researchers: Moms need more than 6 weeks maternity leave: Urging national paid family leave policies. Press Release.

O'Meara, K., and C. Campbell. 2011. Faculty sense of agency in decisions about work and family. *The Review of Higher Education* 34 (3): 447–476.

Short-Thompson, C. 2008. A parenting odyssey: Shouldering grief, welcoming joy. *Women's Studies in Communication* 31 (2): 249–257.

Simon, H. 1957. *Administrative Behavior: A Study of Decision-Making Processes in Administrative Organizations*. New York: Macmillan.

Stockdell-Giesler, A., and R. Ingalls. 2007. Faculty mothers. *Academe* 93 (4): 38–40.

Stone, D. 2002. *Policy Paradox: The Art of Political Decision Making*. New York: W. W. Norton and Company.

Tower, L., and M. Alkadry. 2008. The social costs of career success for women. *Review of Public Personnel Administration* 28 (2): 144–165.

Tracy, S. 2008. Care as a common good. *Women's Studies in Communication* 31 (2): 166–174.

Untener, J. 2008. Giving birth to a good policy. *The Chronicle of Higher Education* 54 (45): 1–3.

Index

A

Abruption of placenta, 121
Abuse of children, 131
Administrative practices, 262–265
　inconsistencies in, 219–221
Adoption process, 183–184, 257
Affordable Care Act, 21, 112–113, 223
AFL-CIO. *See* American Federation of Labor and Congress of Industrial Organizations
AFSCME. *See* American Federation of State, County and Municipal Employees
AIDS Foundation of Chicago, 43
Alabama, birth, fertility rates, 87
Alaska, birth, fertility rates, 87
Alertness, decreased, 132
Alliance for Early Care and Education, 43
American Academy of Nursing, 44
American Academy of Pediatrics, 122
American Association of University Women, 44
American Civil Liberties Union, 43
American Federation of Labor and Congress of Industrial Organizations, 44
　Department for Professional Employees, 44
American Federation of State, County and Municipal Employees, 44
American Federation of Teachers, 44
American Nurses Association, 44
American with Disabilities Act, 18
Antenatal leave, 104–105
Anxiety levels, 121, 128, 201, 211, 230
ARHP. *See* Association of Reproductive Health Professionals
Arizona, birth, fertility rates, 87
Arkansas, birth, fertility rates, 87, 122
ART. *See* Assisted reproductive technology
Asian Pacific American Women's Forum, National, 45
Assisted reproductive technology, outcomes of, 115
Association Employees Union, 44
Association of Reproductive Health Professionals, 44
Association of Women's Health, Obstetric and Neonatal Nurses, 44

B

Baby blues, 125
Balancing work/home responsibilities, 152, 158, 174, 179, 202, 209
Bay Area, Nine-to-Five, 43
Benefits protection, FMLA, 53–55
Biological clock issue, 223
Birth rates, 85–93
Black Women's Health Imperative, 44
Bonding of mother, child, 127
Brain structure, 129
Breast-feeding, 23, 121–123, 153, 190, 206, 214, 230–234
　difficulty in, 132
　equipment, 23
　privacy issues with, 232
Breast pumping equipment, 23
Business and Professional Women's Foundation, 44

C

California
　birth, fertility rates, 87, 104–106, 120
　Nine-to-Five, 43
California Women's Law Center, 43
Canada, leave policies in, 271, 275, 277
Career goals, 153, 159, 161, 164, 169–170, 179, 182, 190, 203–204, 209, 261. *See also* Professional concerns, Tenure

297

CBO. *See* Congressional Budget Office
Census Bureau, 14, 85–86, 89, 93, 95–96, 112, 114–115
Center for Law and Social Policy, 44
Certification, FMLA, 52–54
Certification of Health Condition, Family and Medical Leave Act, 73–80
Cesarean section, 120–121, 125, 130, 177, 221, 251
Change within organizations, 289–293
Chicago AIDS Foundation, 43
Child abuse/neglect, 131
Child care, 128–129, 135, 156, 158–159, 170, 173, 181, 205–206, 226–231
   family characteristics, 13–14
   need for, 13–14
   patterns, 13–14
   supply, 13–14
   tax credits, 11–14
Childbearing in United States, 86
Childbirth Connection, 44
Childlessness, decision for, 255–258
Civil action by employees, FMLA, 56
Civil Rights Act of 1964, 6, 32–33, 38–39
Civil service employees, FMLA, 60–65
   benefits protection, 64
   coercion prohibition, 64–65
   employment protection, 64
   health insurance, 65, 89, 106, 111–114, 118, 146, 188, 213, 248, 251–252
   leave requirement, 60
   nonappropriated funds, payment from, 65
Civilian noninstitutional women, employment status, 90
CLASP. *See* Center for Law and Social Policy
Coalition of Labor Union Women, 44
COBRA. *See* Consolidated Omnibus Budget Reconciliation Act
Cognitive development, 128
Colorado
   birth, fertility rates, 87, 102, 144, 230
   Nine-to-Five, 43
Commerce, defined, FMLA, 48
Commission on leave, FMLA, 65–67
   sec. 304. compensation, 67
   termination, 67
   voluntary service, 67

Commissions for Women, National Association, 45
Commitment to employer/institution, 153, 159, 161, 164, 169–170, 179, 182, 190, 203–204, 209
Communications Workers of America, 44
Community Service Society, 44
Complications of pregnancy, 121, 127, 130
Conceiving child, 156, 195, 216
Concentration, decreased, 132
Congressional Accountability Act of 1995, 33–35
Congressional Budget Office, 112–113
Congressional employees, FMLA, 69–71
Connecticut, birth, fertility rates, 87, 144, 253
Consolidated Omnibus Budget Reconciliation Act, 111
Contribution of wives' earnings to family income, 92
Course overload, 220, 223
Credits, tax, child care, 11–14

D

Decision not to have children, 255–258
Decision to have children, 150, 155, 160, 163–164, 171, 175, 180, 182–183, 186, 191, 193, 198–199, 205, 208, 212, 215
Definitions, FMLA, 48–50
Delaware, birth, fertility rates, 87
Delivery process, 119–121
Demands of family, 291–292
Demographics, research interviewees, 145
Denmark, 270–271, 275, 277
Department for Professional Employees, American Federation of Labor and Congress of Industrial Organizations, 44
Department of Labor, 15–20, 23, 89–92, 254
   clarification, 186
   Final Rule on Family and Medical Leave, fact sheet, 19
Depression, 125, 128, 132, 135
Developmental needs of child, 127–128
Direct Care Alliance, 44

Disability, 6, 16, 18, 94–96, 101, 103–105, 118, 156, 163, 177–178, 187–188, 190, 208, 211–212, 263, 278
Disability leave, 94–96, 104–105, 177–178, 190, 208, 211
Disciples Justice Action Network, 44
Disciples of Christ, 44
Disciples Women, Christian Church, 44
DOL. *See* U.S. Department of Labor
Domestic Workers Alliance, National, 45
Duties of employee, FMLA, 52

E

Eastern New York, Occupational and Environmental Health Center of Eastern, 45
Economic Growth and Tax Relief Reconciliation Act, 11
Economic Opportunity Institute, 44
EEOC. *See* U.S. Equal Employment Opportunity Commission
Eligible employee, defined, FMLA, 48
Emotional needs of children, 127–128
Employees of pharmaceutical industry, 98, 103, 144, 199–217. *See also* Pfizer
Employer, defined, FMLA, 49
Employment benefits, defined, FMLA, 49
Employment history, women, before first birth, 93
Employment Justice Center, 44
Employment Law Project, National, 45
Employment Lawyers Association NY, National, 45
Employment patterns, and use of maternity leave benefits, 85–93
Employment protection, FMLA, 53–55
Enforcement, FMLA, 56–58
Enterprise bargaining, 283
Equal Employment Opportunity Commission, 8
  pregnancy discrimination charges received by, 9
Equal Opportunity Act, 8
Equal Rights Advocates, 43
Equipment for breast pumping, 23
Equivalent employment position, restoration to, FMLA, 59
Every Child Matters Education Fund, 44

Evolution maternity leave, 85–110
Examples of maternity leave policies, 98–104
Exit from workplace, 105–108
Expectations, maternity leave, 2–3

F

Fact sheet, Final Rule on Family and Medical Leave, Department of Labor, 19
Failure to return from leave, FMLA, 54
Fair Housing Alliance, National, 45
Fair Labor Standards Act, 20, 22
Family and Children's Ministries, Disciples Home Missions, 44
Family and Medical Leave Act, 15–21, 26, 47–76, 185–189, 293
  certification, 52–53, 77–80
  civil action by employees, 56
  civil service employees, 60–65
    benefits protection, 64
    coercion prohibition, 64–65
    employment protection, 64
    health insurance, 65, 89, 106, 111–114, 118, 146, 188, 213, 248, 251–252
    leave requirement, 60
    nonappropriated funds, payment from, 65
  commerce, defined, 48
  commission on leave, 65–67
    sec. 304. compensation, 67
    termination, 67
    voluntary service, 67
  congressional employees, 69–71
  definitions, 48–50
  eligible employee, defined, 48
  employer, defined, 49
  employment benefits, defined, 49
  employment protection, 53–55
  enforcement, 56–58
  failure to return from leave, 54
  general requirements for leave, 48–59
  health benefits maintenance, 54
  health care provider, defined, 49
  highly compensated employees, exemption concerning, 54
  instructional employees, 58
  investigative authority, 56

leave requirement, 50–52
   duties of employee, 52
   entitlement to leave, 50
   foreseeable leave, 51
   intermittently-taken leave, 50
   notice, 51
   reduced leave schedule, 50
   same employer, spouses employed by, 52
   substitution of paid leave, 51
   local educational agencies, employees of, 58
   loss of benefits, 53
   notice, 60
   problems of, 14–21
   prohibited acts, 55–56
   promises of, 14–21
   protection of benefits, 53–55
   reduced leave schedule, defined, 50
   restoration denial, 54
   restoration to position, 53, 59
   sense of congress, 71–72
   serious health condition, defined, 50
Family demands, 291–292
Family Equality Council, 44
Family Forward Oregon, 44
Family income, contribution of wives' earnings, 92
Family support, 125
Family Values Work Consortium, 44
Feminist Majority, 44
Fertility, 113–114
Fertility rates, 85–88
   employment patterns and, 85–93
Final Rule on Family and Medical Leave, fact sheet, Department of Labor, 19
Florida
   birth, fertility rates, 87
   Federation of Business and Professional Women's Club, Inc., 44
FLSA. *See* Fair Labor Standards Act
Foreseeable leave, FMLA, 51
France, 270, 272, 275, 278

G

GAO. *See* Government Accountability Office
Geduldig v. Aiello, 6
General Accounting Office, 131
General Electric v. Gilbert, 6
General requirements for leave, FMLA, 48–59
Georgia, birth, fertility rates, 87, 191, 253
Goals, career, 153, 159, 161, 164, 169–170, 179, 182, 190, 203–204, 209. *See also* Professional concerns, Tenure
Government Accountability Office, 131, 270, 274, 276, 280
Government Employee Rights Act of 1991, 36–38
Guilty about, 196–197, 219, 222–223, 263

H

Hadassah, Women's Zionist Organization of America, Inc., 44
Hawaii, birth, fertility rates, 87, 105
Health benefits maintenance, FMLA, 54
Health care, 111–138
   American Academy of Pediatrics, 122
   anxiety, 121
   assisted reproductive technology, 115
   baby blues, 125
   brain structure, 129
   breast-feeding, 122–123, 132
   child abuse, 131
   cognitive development, 128
   complications of pregnancy, 121, 127, 130
   Consolidated Omnibus Budget Reconciliation Act, 111
   delivery, 119–121
   developmental needs of child, 127–128
   emotional needs of children, 127–128
   family support, 125
   fertility issues, 113–114
   health insurance, 111–113
   holistic approach, 132–136
      alertness, decreased, 132
      concentration, decreased, 132
      physical distress, 132
      sleep disorders, 132
   immunizations, 121
   infant mortality, 118–119, 121
   infection, 121, 128

intended pregnancies, 114–116
learning potential, 129
length of maternity leave, 127–128
    bonding of mother, child, 127
    mental health, 128, 132
    physical needs of children, 127–128
    physical recovery, 127
    social support systems, 128
long-term development, 129
milk production (*See* Breast-feeding)
mortality, infant, 118–119
neglect, 131
nurses, 125, 129–131, 151
otitis media infection, 129
pediatricians, 130, 132
placenta previa, 121
placental abruption, 121
postnatal health care, 121
postpartum depression, 124–127
psychiatrist intervention, 125
quality of care, 129
rhythms of newborns, 129
sanitation, 121
school failure, 131
stress, 121
support, lack of, 123, 170
unintended pregnancies, 114–116
upper respiratory tract infection, 129
U.S. General Accounting Office, 131
welfare dependency, 131
well-baby doctor visits, 123–124
Women, Infants and Children Nutrition Program, 122
World Health Organization, 122
Health care provider, defined, FMLA, 49
Health condition, defined, FMLA, 50
Health insurance, 111–113
Health Statistics, National Center for, 86, 88, 116, 118–119
Healthy Teen Network, 44
Highly compensated employees, exemption concerning, FMLA, 54
HIV PJA. *See* HIV Prevention Justice Alliance
HIV Prevention Justice Alliance, 44
Holistic approach, 132–136
Home, working from, 152, 154, 189

Home responsibilities, balancing, 152, 158, 174, 179, 202, 209
Home/work responsibilities, balancing, 152, 158, 174, 179, 202, 209
H.R. 5647, 30–45
Human resource policies investigation, 155, 165, 167–168, 172, 177, 180, 186, 195, 200, 207, 210, 212
Human Rights Project for Girls, 44

I

Idaho, birth, fertility rates, 87
Illinois, birth, fertility rates, 87
Immunizations, 121
In loco parentis status requirements, 254
Income of family, contribution of wives' earnings, 92
Inconsistencies in maternity leave administration, 219–221
Indiana, birth, fertility rates, 87, 144
Indiana Toxics Action Project, 44
Infant mortality, 118–119, 121
Infection, 121
Infectious, 128
Institute of Child Health and Human Development, National, 14
Institution, commitment to, 153, 159, 161, 164, 169–170, 179, 182, 190, 203–204, 209
Instructional employees, FMLA, 58
Intended pregnancies, 114–116
Intent of legislature, symbolism of public policies, 5–83
Intermittently-taken leave, FMLA, 50
International approaches, 269–285
International Union, United Automobile, Aerospace & Agricultural Implement Workers of America, 44
Interview analysis, research, 141–143
Interview questions, 146–147
Interviewee demographics, research, 145
Interviews, 149–218
Investigation of HR policies, 155, 165, 167–168, 172, 177, 180, 186, 195, 200, 207, 210, 212
Investigative authority, FMLA, 56

Iowa, birth, fertility rates, 87
Ireland, leave policies in, 272, 275, 278

J

Jewish Women, National Council of, 45
Jewish Women International, 44
Job Opportunities Task Force, 44

K

Kansas, birth, fertility rates, 87
Kentucky, 14, 87, 91–92, 99–101, 104, 144, 246

L

La Raza, National Council of, 45
Labor Project for Working Families, 44
Leadership Conference on Civil and Human Rights, 44
Learning potential, 129
Leave requirement, FMLA, 50–52
   duties of employee, 52
   entitlement to leave, 50
   foreseeable leave, 51
   intermittently-taken leave, 50
   notice, 51
   reduced leave schedule, 50
   same employer, spouses employed by, 52
   substitution of paid leave, 51
Legal advice, seeking, 186
Legal Aid Society-Employment Law Center, 43
Legal Momentum, 43
Legal Voice, 44
Legislative intent, symbolism of public policies, 5–83
Length of maternity leave, 127–128
   bonding of mother, child, 127
   mental health, 128, 132
   physical needs of children, 127–128
   physical recovery, 127
   social support systems, 128
Local educational agencies, employees of, FMLA, 58
Long Island Women's Fund, 46
Long-term development, 129

Los Angeles, Nine-to-Five, 43
Loss of benefits, FMLA, 53
Louisiana, birth, fertility rates, 87
Low birth weight, 119, 131
Loyalty, 24, 122, 179, 204–205

M

Main Street Alliance, 44
Maine, birth, fertility rates, 87
Maryland, birth, fertility rates, 87
Maryland Women's Coalition for Health Care Reform, 44
Massachusetts, birth, fertility rates, 87, 106
Maternity leave
   administrative policies, 262–265
   benefits protection, 53–55
   biases, 258–262
   certification, 52–54
   civil action by employees, 56
   civil service employees, 60–65
      benefits protection, 64
      coercion prohibition, 64–65
      employment protection, 64
      health insurance, 65, 89, 106, 111–114, 118, 146, 188, 213, 248, 251–252
      leave requirement, 60
      nonappropriated funds, payment from, 65
   colleagues, unsupportive *vs.* supportive, 258–262
   commerce, defined, 48
   commission on leave, 65–67
      sec. 304. compensation, 67
      termination, 67
      voluntary service, 67
   congressional employees, 69–71
   decision to not have children, 255–258
   definitions, 48–50
   economic policies, social, 24–27
   eligible employee, defined, 48
   employer, defined, 49
   employment benefits, defined, 49
   employment protection, 53–55
   enforcement, 56–58
   equivalent employment position, restoration to, 59

evaluative perspective, 287–296
evolution, 85–110
expectations, 2–3
failure to return from leave, 54
general requirements for leave, 48–59
health benefits maintenance, 54
health care, women's, 111–138
health care provider, defined, 49
highly compensated employees, exemption concerning, 54
inconsistencies in administration, 219–221
individuals' experiences, 149–218
infant mortality, 118–119
instructional employees, 58
intended pregnancies, 114–116
international approaches, 269–285
interviews, 149–218
investigative authority, 56
leave requirement, 50–52
    duties of employee, 52
    entitlement to leave, 50
    foreseeable leave, 51
    intermittently-taken leave, 50
    notice, 51
    reduced leave schedule, 50
    same employer, spouses employed by, 52
    substitution of paid leave, 51
legislative intent, 5–83
length of, 127–128
local educational agencies, employees of, 58
loss of benefits, 53
notice, 60
outside U.S., 269–282
paid, 93–96
paternity leave, 247–251
perceptions, 149–218
policies of, 24–27
policy examples, 98–104
Pregnancy Discrimination Act, 5–11
problems of, 14–21
profiles, research, 149–218
prohibited acts, 55–56
promises of, 14–21
public policy, 5–83
realities of, 2–3
reduced leave schedule, defined, 50

research, 139–147
    themes, 219–242
restoration denial, 54
restoration to position, 53
same-sex couples, 251–255
sense of congress, 71–72
serious health condition, defined, 50
social implications, 24–27
social policies, 24–27
societal benefit, 293–294
stereotypes, 258–262
student mothers, 243–247
types of, paid and unpaid, 93–96
unintended pregnancies, 114–116
unpaid, 93–96
USC Ch. 5 Title 3 coverage, 35–36
use of, 85–93
Mental health, 128, 132
Methodology, research, 139–141
Mexican American Legal Defense and Educational Fund, 44
Miami Restaurant Opportunities Center, 45
Michigan, birth, fertility rates, 87
Military Family Association, National, 45
Milk production. See Breast-feeding
Milwaukee, Nine-to-Five, 43
Minnesota, birth, fertility rates, 87, 127
Mississippi, birth, fertility rates, 87, 253
Missouri, birth, fertility rates, 87, 144
MomsRising, 44
Montana, birth, fertility rates, 87, 98
Morale, 17–18, 107, 122, 164, 291
Mortality, infant, 118–119
Mothering Justice, 44
Mothers' Centers, National Association of, 45

N

NAACP. See National Association for Advancement of Colored People
NACCRRA. See National Association of Child Care Resources and Referral Agencies
NACW. See Commissions for Women, National Association
National Association for Advancement of Colored People, 45

National Association of Child Care Resources and Referral Agencies, 12, 14
National Crittenton Foundation, 45
National Education Association, 45
National Gay and Lesbian Task Force Action Fund, 45
National Infertility Association, 45
National Organization for Women, 45
NCHS. *See* Health Statistics, National Center for
NCLR. *See* La Raza, National Council of
Nebraska, birth, fertility rates, 87
Neglect of child, 131
Negotiations, 168, 172, 192, 235
Negro Women, National Council of, 45
Neighborhood Funders Group, 45
Netherlands, 270, 272, 275, 279
NETWORK, A National Catholic Social Justice Lobby, 45
Nevada, birth, fertility rates, 87
New Hampshire, birth, fertility rates, 87
New Jersey, birth, fertility rates, 87
New Jersey Citizen Action, 45
New Mexico, birth, fertility rates, 87
New York
 birth, fertility rates, 87, 105, 144
 National Employment Lawyers Association, 45
New Zealand, leave policies in, 272, 275, 279
NICHD. *See* Institute of Child Health and Human Development, National
Nine-to-Five Bay Area, 43
North Carolina, birth, fertility rates, 87
North Carolina Justice Center, 45
North Dakota, birth, fertility rates, 87
Not having children, decision regarding, 255–258
Notice, FMLA, 51, 60
Nurses, 125, 129–131, 151
Nutrition, 113, 121–122, 125, 135

O

Occupational and Environmental Health Center of Eastern NY, 45
Ohio, birth, fertility rates, 87
Oklahoma, birth, fertility rates, 87, 253
Online courses, 2, 264
Oregon, birth, fertility rates, 88
Otitis media infection, 129

P

Paid leave, 2, 19–21, 93–97, 100–101, 103, 105–107, 121, 124, 127, 162, 177, 246, 251–252, 254, 263, 270, 272, 279, 281–283, 293
Parental leave, outside U.S., 277–280
Part time employment, 2, 20, 128, 146, 194, 197, 201, 207, 209, 212, 214, 219, 227, 261, 282, 288
Participants in research, 144–146
Partnership for Women and Families, National, 43
Partnership for Working Families, 45
Paternity leave, 18, 96–98, 102–103, 125, 146, 159, 170, 197, 201, 211, 247–251, 259, 263, 269–270, 275–276, 281–282, 291–293
 outside U.S., 269–282
Patient Protection and Affordable Care Act, 21–23, 112
PDA. *See* Pregnancy Discrimination Act
Pediatric AIDS Chicago Prevention Initiative, 45
Pediatricians, 130, 132
Pennsylvania, birth, fertility rates, 88
Permanent exit from workplace, 105–108
Personal leave, 19, 219, 239
Pfizer, 103, 105
Pharmaceutical industry, 98, 144, 199–217. *See also* Pfizer
Physical distress, 132
Physical needs of children, 127–128
Physicians for Reproductive Choice and Health, 45
Placenta previa, 121
Planned Parenthood, 45
Postnatal health care, 121
Postpartum depression, 124–127
PPACA. *See* Patient Protection and Affordable Care Act
Praxis Project, 45
Pregnancy
 administrative policies, 262–265
 biases, 258–262

certification, 52–54
civil action by employees, 56
civil service employees, 60–65
    coercion prohibition, 64–65
    employment protection, 64
    health insurance, 65, 89, 106, 111–114, 118, 146, 188, 213, 248, 251–252
    leave requirement, 60
    nonappropriated funds, payment from, 65
colleagues, unsupportive *vs.* supportive, 258–262
commerce, defined, 48
commission on leave, 65–67
    Sec. 304. compensation, 67
    termination, 67
    voluntary service, 67
complications of, 121, 127, 130
congressional employees, 69–71
decision to not have children, 255–258
definitions, 48–50
eligible employee, defined, 48
employer, defined, 49
employment benefits, defined, 49
employment protection, 53–55
enforcement, 56–58
equivalent employment position, restoration to, 59
evaluative perspective, 287–296
evolution of maternity leave, 85–110
failure to return from leave, 54
general requirements for leave, 48–59
health benefits maintenance, 54
health care, women's, 111–138
health care provider, defined, 49
highly compensated employees, exemption concerning, 54
individuals' experiences, 149–218
infant mortality, 118–119
instructional employees, 58
intended pregnancies, 114–116
international approaches, 269–285
interviews, 149–218
investigative authority, 56
leave requirement, 50–52
    duties of employee, 52
    entitlement to leave, 50
    foreseeable leave, 51
    intermittently-taken leave, 50
    notice, 51
    same employer, spouses employed by, 52
    substitution of paid leave, 51
legislative intent, 5–83
local educational agencies, employees of, 58
loss of benefits, 53
notice, 60
paternity leave, 247–251
perceptions, 149–218
Pregnancy Discrimination Act, 5–11
profiles, research, 149–218
prohibited acts, 55–56
public policy, 5–83
realities of, 2–3
reduced leave schedule, defined, 50
research, 139–147
    themes, 219–242
restoration denial, 54
restoration to position, 53
same-sex couples, 251–255
sense of congress, 71–72
serious health condition, defined, 50
stereotypes, 258–262
student mothers, 243–247
unintended pregnancies, 114–116
USC Ch. 5 Title 3, employees covered by, 35–36
Pregnancy Discrimination Act, 5–11, 16, 21, 42
Pregnant Workers Fairness Act, 7, 42–43
Pride at Work, 45
Privacy issues with breast-feeding, 232
Private universities, employees of, 183–199
Process of adoption, 183–184, 257
Productivity, 15, 122, 250, 253, 291
Professional concerns, 3, 146, 150–151, 155, 160, 162, 164, 171, 176, 178, 180, 182, 185, 188, 191–192, 197, 199–200, 207, 212–213, 219, 234–242, 258. *See also* Tenure track
Professor Mommy: Finding Work-Family Balance in Academia, 10
Progressive Maryland, 45
Prohibited acts, FMLA, 55–56

306 • Index

Psychiatrist intervention with depression, 125
Public Health Institute of Metropolitan Chicago, 45
Public Justice Center, 45
Public Law 95-555, 29–30
Public policy symbolism, 5–83
Public universities, employees of, 150–183
Pumping, breast-feeding, 10, 22–23, 126, 128, 158, 190, 202, 206, 210, 214–215, 230–234, 243, 245

Q

Qualitative research, rationale, 139–141
Quality of care, 129
Questions, interview, 146–147

R

Ragsdale v. Wolverine World Wide, 17
RAND Report, 14
Rates of birth, 85–93
Recovery time, 151, 196, 211, 213, 264
Reduced leave schedule, FMLA, 50
Religious Coalition for Reproductive Choice, 45
Requirements for leave, FMLA, 48–59
Research, 139–147
    interview analysis, 141–143
    interview questions, 146–147
    interviewee demographics, 145
    limitations, 143–144
    methodology, 139–141
    participants, 144–146
    study limitations, 143–144
    themes, 219–242
        administration of maternity leave, 219–221
        biological clock issue, 223
        breast-feeding, 230–234
        child care, 228–230
        privacy issues, 232
        timing, 221–224
        transition back to work, 224–228
RESOLVE: National Infertility Association, 45
Restaurant Opportunities Centers United, 45

Restoration denial, FMLA, 54
Restoration to position, FMLA, 53
Retail Action Project, 45
Retaliation, prohibition against, 39
Rhode Island, birth, fertility rates, 88, 144
Rhythms of newborns, 129
Ritz Clark & Ben-Asher LLP, 45

S

Sabbaticals, 264
Same-sex couples, 251–255
Sanitation, 121
School failure, 131
Second child, leave for, 208
SEIU. *See* Service Employees International Union
Sense of congress, FMLA, 71–72
Serious health condition, defined, FMLA, 50
Service Employees International Union, 45
Sexuality Information and Education Council of U.S., 45
Short-term disability leave, 104–105, 163
Sick leave, 19, 96, 98–100, 102, 162, 167, 177–178, 180, 187, 189, 192, 195, 206, 219, 239, 253, 263
SIECUS. *See* Sexuality Information and Education Council of U.S.
Sleep disorders, 132
Social support systems, 128
Societal benefit of maternity leave, 293–294
Society for Women's Health Research, 45
South Carolina, birth, fertility rates, 88
South Dakota, birth, fertility rates, 88
Spouse taking leave, 157, 173, 181, 189, 197, 201, 208, 211
Spouses employed by same employer, FMLA, 52
Stress levels, 104–106, 121, 128, 135, 153, 159, 182, 201, 211, 222, 230, 239, 253
Structure of brain, 129
Student mothers, 243–247
Substitution of paid leave, FMLA, 51
Sugar Law Center for Economic and Social Justice, 45

Support
    from family, 125
    lack of, 123, 170
Supreme Court, 112
Sweden, 269–270, 273, 276, 279
Symbolism, public policies, 5–83

T

Tax credits, 11–14
Tennessee, birth, fertility rates, 88
Tenure track, 150–151, 162–165, 171–176, 178, 185, 234–242, 261. *See also* Professional concerns
Texas, birth, fertility rates, 88
Timing, 221–224
Transgender Equality, National Center for, 45
Transition back to work, 224–228
Types of maternity leave, 93–96

U

UAW. *See* International Union, United Automobile, Aerospace & Agricultural Implement Workers of America
UN Women - Greater L.A. Chapter, 45
Unintended pregnancies, 114–116
Unitarian Universalist Association of Congregations, 45
Unitarian Universalist Women's Federation, 45
United Food and Commercial Workers International Union, 46
United Kingdom, 270, 273, 276, 279
Universities, private, employees of, 183–199
Unpaid leave, 5, 19, 21, 51, 93–98, 106, 162, 177, 181–182, 259, 270, 272, 275, 279, 287, 293
Upper respiratory tract infection, 129
U.S. Census Bureau, 14, 85–86, 89, 93, 95–96, 112, 114–115
U.S. Code, Ch. 5 Title 3, 35–36
U.S. Department of Labor, 15–20, 23, 89–92, 254
U.S. Equal Employment Opportunity Commission, 8
    pregnancy discrimination charges received by, 9
U.S. General Accounting Office, 131
Utah, birth, fertility rates, 88

V

Vacation time, 19, 96, 98–99, 102–103, 124, 127, 156, 160, 162, 167, 187, 189, 192, 197, 201, 203–205, 208–209, 211, 220, 228, 239, 248, 252, 263
Vermont, birth, fertility rates, 88
Virginia, birth, fertility rates, 88
Vital records, 86

W

Washington, birth, fertility rates, 88, 93, 95–96, 115, 253, 274, 276, 280
Washington Area Women's Foundation, 46
Washington Work and Family Coalition, 46
Welfare dependency, 131
Well-baby doctor visits, 123–124
West Virginia, birth, fertility rates, 88
Western New York, Planned Parenthood of, 45
What To Expect Foundation, 46
WHO. *See* World Health Organization
WIC. *See* Women, Infants and Children Nutrition Program
Wider Opportunities for Women, 46
Wisconsin, birth, fertility rates, 88
Wives' earnings, contribution to family income, 92
Women, Infants and Children Nutrition Program, 122
Women Donors Network, 46
Women Employed, 46
Women's Conference Committee, National, 45
Women's Employment Rights Clinic, Golden Gate University School of Law, 46
Women's Fund of Long Island, 46
Women's Law Center, National, 43
Women's Law Project, 46

Women's Organizations, National Council of, 45
Work and Family Legal Center, 43
Work/home responsibilities, balancing, 152, 158, 174, 179, 202, 209
Working from home, 152, 154, 189
Working Mothers Network, 103
Working Women, National Association of, 43
  Nine-to-Five, 43

World Health Organization, 122
Wyoming, birth, fertility rates, 88

Y

Young Workers United, 46